At Your Own Risk!

How the Risk-Conscious Culture Meets the Challenge of Business Change

At Your Own Risk!

How the Risk-Conscious Culture Meets the Challenge of Business Change

Gary S. Lynch

WILEY

John Wiley & Sons, Inc.

Published by John Wiley & Sons, Inc., Hoboken, New Jersey.

Published simultaneously in Canada.

For general information on our other products and services, or technical support, please contact our Customer Care Department within the United States at 800-762-2974, outside the United States at 317-572-3993 or fax 317-572-4002.

Wiley also publishes its books in a variety of electronic formats. Some content that appears in print may not be available in electronic books.

For more information about Wiley products, visit our Web site at *http://www.wiley.com*.

Library of Congress Cataloging-in-Publication Data:

Lynch, Gary S. (Gary Scott), 1958-
    At your own risk!: How the risk-conscious culture meets the challenge of business change/Gary S. Lynch.
        p. cm.
    Includes index.
    ISBN 978-0-470-25941-2 (cloth: acid-free paper)
 1.   Organizational change. 2.   Risk management.   I. Title.
    HD58.8.L96 2008
    658.4'06–dc22

                                                                              2008008488

Printed in the United States of America

10   9   8   7   6   5   4   3   2   1

To Kenneth Lynch—my Dad

Fifty-five years of service as a Fireman.
Risk is his job.
Risk is his life.

Table of Contents

About the Author

Gary S. Lynch, CISSP, is the Global Leader of Marsh's Supply Chain Risk and Intelligence Solutions practice. During his 30-year career, he has held a number of senior positions in operational risk, business resiliency, and IT security at Chase Manhattan Bank and The Prudential. Before joining Marsh, he was a partner at Booz Allen Hamilton and, prior to that, at Ernst & Young. He was also global research director and market analyst for the Gartner Group. A graduate of New York Institute of Technology with a BS degree in Finance, Gary has been a guest lecturer on operational risk at the NYU Stern School of Management, has contributed to the World Economic Forum (WEF) 2007 and 2008 Global Risk Report, and been a panel member at the 2008 World Customs Organization (WCO); 2007 Asia Pacific Economic Region (APEC), and 2006/7/8 Risk and Insurance Management Society forums.

Gary has appeared on CNBC *Asia Squawk Box*, the Discovery/Equinox Channel, *NBC Nightly News*, and the ABC broadcast network. He has been published in *CEO Magazine*, the *Wall Street Journal, Knowledge@Wharton, CIO Insights, Financial IT Decisions, The Asset, Business Review Weekly*, and *Business Insurance Magazine*, as well as a number of other publications.

Gary received a commendation from the U.S. Secret Service for his contribution during the 9/11 crisis and was awarded the Silver Medal of Valor by the Nassau County Fire Service, New York.

Gary has four children and lives in Mendham, New Jersey.

Acknowledgements

As I sat down to compile the list of people that I wanted to acknowledge, I could not help but be distracted by two breaking news stories. By the time you have picked up (and hopefully read) this book, these stories will have been analyzed from every angle. I reflect for a moment because I cannot help but be concerned at these real examples of rapidly escalating risk; Societe Generale's $7.2 billion alleged trading fraud (exposure estimated at one point to be in excess of $70 billion[1]) and, General Electric's Money unit misplacing a computer tape that contained the personal records of 650,000 J.C. Penney customers.[2] I think back to the days of working as an operational and IT risk manager. One of the first people I'd call for advice was Craig Goldman. I would like to acknowledge Craig as the ultimate risk advocate in his role as the first CIO of the Chase Manhattan Bank (now JPMorganChase) and a board member of a number of companies. Retired now, Craig is still committed to raising awareness. He not only sacrificed countless hours providing valuable insight for this book, but he was the first executive that I encountered who backed the talk with action. I consider Craig a mentor and visionary, but most of all I consider him a friend. This book would *not* have been possible without Craig's help and support.

I would also like to thank Karen Avery, who inspired me to write this book. She is a dear friend, and together Karen and I have been "breaking a lot of glass" over the years, trying to get executives to heed the warning and embrace the issues

---

[1] *Wall Street Journal,* January 27, 2008.
[2] *CNN Money,* http://money.cnn.com/2008/01/17/news/companies/penney_data .ap/ index.htm?postversion=2008011722.

I'd also like to acknowledge my consulting clients, and members of my private network. There are a few that stand out; Lou Belsito at DRS Technologies, thanks for your incredible commitment to execution and believing in the message (and me), long before all others; Gary Mucha and Diane Foley at BAE Systems for your insight, vision, and willingness to execute; Dave Carpenter at PepsiCo for your broad perspective based on reality; John Barbano at Johnson & Johnson, thanks for the initial stakeholder hierarchy; Roger Lyster formerly at Chase, who inspired me to pursue all negative information; Jim O'Brien at the Albright Group for valuable insight and a public-sector context (I enjoyed traveling the globe with you and the entire Albright team in our quest to advance pandemic prepared- ness); Jim Woolsey for sharing his incredible insight and experience; Lenny Goldstein, thanks for being committed to the cause and making risk a priority; Michael Liebowitz at NYU and former president of RIMS, thanks for the great debates and valuable insight—I really enjoyed working with you over the past three years, trying to raise awareness of the need to be better prepared for a health emergency such as a pandemic (let's keep wearing them down!); Harry Leff at Marsh, thanks for the introduction and the "going beyond" support; John DeRemigis, executive editor at Wiley, for your patience; Michael C. Thomsett for your writing and support; John Merkovsky at Marsh, thank you for your support in getting this project moving; my brother/sister firefighters in the Floral Park and Mendham Township Fire Departments, 30 years of endless friendship and preparation, I will never forget the lessons learned and life experiences; and of course, my children; thanks for the constant reminder of why I stay committed to the cause. Finally, in memory of Ashley Carlton and Robert Newton, you will serve as a constant reminder of how painful and everlasting risk can be when it becomes a reality.

Introduction:
Cause and Effect in the Brave
New World

O brave new world, that hath such people in it.

—WILLIAM SHAKESPEARE, 1612–13

When Huxley wrote *Brave New World*, taking his title from one of Shakespeare's later works, he aptly described some aspects of the society we live in today. In *Brave New World,* a Utopian future society has created a culture of complete dependence in exchange for specific benefits, but at the cost of lost personal freedom and responsibility.

The equivalent in today's organizations is that with amazing technological development, instantaneous communications, globally distributed customer base and workforce, and lean/modularized supply chains, it has become difficult to manage—that is, identify, assess, prioritize, mitigate, and monitor—*potential* risk. The reality of this brave new world is that risk is on the rise; threats have become more pervasive and vulnerabilities more relevant.

These issues should concern every organization and individual since the lack of consciousness, priority, resources, and action jeopardize our social and economic infrastructures. Unlike the catastrophic or "low-probability/high-impact" event, these everyday risks, when aggregated or repeated, can become a "flash point" for an undesirable outcome. Beware: the vulnerability gap is widening at an exponential pace. Change to our new and constantly evolving global economy is outpacing many organizations' ability to systematically manage the risk. I provide a graphic that describes this widening gap or chasm in Chapter 2.

One of the principles of capitalism is the idea of control. Small businesses desire less oversight and more autonomy. As a result, corporations can quickly and easily find themselves in a conflicting position. By over-stratifying supply chains, incorporating numerous tertiary parties, businesses create quite the opposite result of autonomy. In reality, they have created a long line of interdependency, leaving each link in the chain contingent on the previous link. Control has been relinquished to so-called "partners," but in reality, many organizations know very little about all those that they depend on to create value. Worse yet, blind assumptions are being made about their partners' ability to understand, assess, and manage risk in a way that is consistent with their own risk expectations. Many of these partners, and their partners' partners, are operating in environments prone to hazard, political, environmental, societal, health, and criminal risks. Many of these partners share their capabilities and resources with your organization's competitors. And many of these competitors operate in locations without labor, environmental, privacy, intellectual property, and product regulation or oversight. All of these threats and vulnerabilities are real and relevant. In the past six months many organizations have witnessed—or worse, fallen victim to—many of these risks. Here are just a few examples:

- The supply of the lifesaving blood-thinning drug heparin was halted in February 2008. A Chinese facility responsible for the production of the active product ingredient has been suspected of being contaminated, resulting in the deaths of four people and hundreds of others with allergic reactions.[1]
- The financial viability of a major financial institution was brought into question when a rogue derivatives trader was able to bypass

controls and defraud the institution of $7.2 billion. At one point, the bank had open positions of approximately $73 billion. The fraud has raised comparisons to the 1995 Barings fraud of $1.38 billion that wiped out the bank's cash reserves.[2]

- The backbone of many organizations' e-mail and voice communications services came to a screeching halt when the BlackBerry smart phone environment was halted throughout the majority of the United States and Canada. Although short lived, the outage was felt by most AT&T and Verizon customers and raised some eyebrows about just how much organizations rely on these services to run their business.[3]

- Food supply chains were severely disrupted when a primary supplier of beef to school districts, big-box distributors, and restaurant chains recalled 143 million pounds of raw and frozen beef because of animal cruelty and the concern that the downer cattle (cattle requiring veterinarian confirmation that they were injured, not diseased) were entering the food supply, in violation of federal regulations. Unfortunately, it is believed that the approximately 37 million pounds that went to schools has already been eaten The story broke when the Humane Society of the United States released a video. The supplier, Hallmark/Westland Meat Packing Company, is now potentially facing serious brand and financial risk.[4]

- The sugar supply chain became at risk when a major sugar refinery (operated by Imperial Sugar) that accounts for approximately 9% of U.S. capacity was destroyed by an explosion and fire. Shares of the company tumbled immediately after the blast.[5]

- The toy manufacturing industry, after being severely impacted by the lead paint and magnet recalls, is now being challenged again as they are being significantly influenced by consumer and environmental groups to get rid of polyvinyl chloride (PVC) in toys.[6]

- The U.S. energy supply chain was at risk when Venezuela threatened to suspend Exxon oil shipments.[7]

- Johnson & Johnson issued a recall of a pain patch because of manufacturing issues that could lead to accidental overdoses.[8]

- Personal data is at significant risk from covert Internet attacks. At-tackers are using the massive cyber infrastructure to launch an in-creasingly complex and varied set of attacks against corporate, government, and home-user machines, all with the goal of corralling as much personally identifiable information as possible. According to Jerry Dixon, former executive director of the National Cyber Security Division at the Department of Homeland Security, while speaking at the Black Hat conference stated: "We need more trained law enforcement personnel at the state and local level. The feds are swamped." He also went on to say that current research shows more than 3.5 million active (botnet) command and control servers.[9]

This is not just an academic exercise; there are serious consequences for not considering risk or complying with requirements. In litigious societies, executives and directors who fail to demonstrate due care could lose their reputation, job, and personal freedom. In other societies, negligence and "bad behavior" are also viewed negatively, and the penalty is much more severe and seldom financial in nature.

Of course, taking risk is an essential element for innovation, expansion, and change. But does taking on risk always translate into reward when looking at the long view? When measured over a longer period of time, the risk–adjusted value can actually be a net negative effect such as experi-enced in the Enron and subprime mortgage crises. However, few seldom take the long view when measuring risk and the associate reward. Quite frankly there is little incentive to do so and those usually involved with creating the "quick hit" opportunity and thus the risk, are seldom held accountable (or still employed by the organization) when the brass begins to tarnish and the risk is realized.

This book presents a practical view of today's most neglected areas of risk and a game plan to identify and manage a range of risks faced in this "brave new globalized world" of changing market dynamics and complex high-tech value networks. Working as a practitioner, consultant, and advisor to numerous CEOs and executive managers, throughout the world and in many different industries, I have, over my three decades in the risk manage-ment business, gained a broad perspective and a long-term view of the kinds of risk experienced through eyes of all participants in the many overlapping and sometimes intersecting value chains. I felt the urgency to present many of my observations and learning experiences in an attempt to provide a starting point for reducing risk and avoiding negative consequences.

As I reflect on the escalating problem, I quickly realize that no one person could possess all the skills or answers, nor be an "expert" in this topic. However, the knowledge and experience to tackle this mammoth issue is out there if a risk consciousness is pervasive among the stakeholders of the organization's value chains. However, all stakeholders must be risk conscious—from the factory floor and back-office workers to the corporate offices, from the distant suppliers to those providing a safe and secure public infrastructure. How do you know if your organization is risk conscious? Here are just a few of the many concepts discussed throughout the book:

- Do persons in your organization communicate and engage in conversations about risk, especially early in process when change is about to/or has occurred?

- Has the organization defined a risk philosophy?

- Is the organization committed to a strong tone from the top, (i.e., a clear message, unified management pholosophy, funding, and a seat at the leadership table for risk management professionals)?

- Does management take the time to understand various stakeholder perspectives and motivations?

- Does management see the complete holistic risk picture? Do they design programs with the purpose of integrating risk practices into existing operational process flows, measure risk resource allocations and performance, test the results, and establish a dynamic risk model to support continuous improvement?

- Does your organization assume (but not verify) that all critical participants not under its direct control have the same level of risk sensitivity that it does?

When I began work on this book, I felt it necessary to go beyond the theory and math of risk management. Many books have been published about the quantitative aspects of effective risk management. However, risk management begins with behaviors, awareness, and incentives. Don't get me wrong, the analytics are required. One must be able to price, allocate, hedge, finance, and measure risk. But all that cannot happen without a keen awareness and the individual's willingness to address and measure risk in the first place. It is far too easy in today's busy world to just limit or ignore the risk conversations and quickly conclude, based on one's gut reaction, what risk should or should not be managed. My experience has also shown that many of the guilty parties who make these quick risk decisions should not be empowered to do so. For example, should a mid-tier IT manager make decisions about how risk to a customer's private data should be managed, or should an auditor have the final say on how the organization manages the risk of its suppliers? These are complex decisions with far-reaching impacts. One must collect the relevant data and perform the analytics—but, first, there must be a clear definition of who should be engaged in this process. Who are the stakeholders, who sets and executes the risk paradigm, what is the risk process that should be followed, and how does the organization know if those responsible for risk management have succeeded or failed in their risk efforts? Do the responsible parties cross their fingers and hope that the outcomes of their decisions do not become press-worthy or litigious?

The process of managing risk should be a well-thought-out, as well as an instinctive process. My goal is to communicate an executable, reality-based approach—one that is derived from the past interactions with a vast network of resources, representing many industries and geographies. I will provide perspective on the risk challenge through the various stakeholder lenses and the industries they operate within, identify specific issues facing organizations (or that they have already faced), and recommend approaches that address the growing risk exposure. Case studies, lessons learned, and self-assessment questions will be provided to facilitate education.

I present the material in three major sections:

Section One. Change, the Double-Edged Sword: Change always brings about both opportunity and increased risk. This is inevitable, and you cannot have one without the other. The greatest problem facing organizations today is the failure to recognize, prioritize, measure, and mitigate the range of risks up and down the value chain as change occurs, and the equally urgent failure to develop specific plans for how to assess and address those risks. Simply stated, the management of risk must be ingrained into business culture, operational processes, behaviors, and the governance structure by the organization as well as everyone who participates in the creation of value. And it's not just the "internal organization" that has to be considered. It is the extended organization—everyone involved with the creation and support of value. Every day we are losing more control over those processes and resources that we depend on to create value for our customers. All those who play a part in supporting the creation and delivery of the product or service, along the chain, are part of the new product or solution but also contribute to the risk challenge itself.

In this first section, I provide three chapters breaking down the critical aspects of our changed world from a risk perspective. The following key questions and topics are addressed in each chapter.

Chapter 1: Rapid Change, *Escalating Risk*
- The awakening: Three case studies of change and escalating risk
- What's changed and what risk has been brought about by change?

Chapter 2: Cause and Effect
- Six changes that have significantly impacted the risk profile.
- What factors are causing the chasm of risk to widen?
- What drives change and increased risk?
- Why should I care? Is this relevant to my organization (and me)?

Chapter 3: The Vulnerable Organization
- Why is every organization, regardless of size, more vulnerable in today's business environment?
- How does every level of change make my organization potentially vulnerable?
- How has change left others that I depend on vulnerable?
- What's wrong with today's strategies and solutions?

Section Two. Line of Sight/Obstructed Views: This section opens with an analysis of the problem through the leadership lens. It also defines the value chain and why it is important to begin using the "value" definition as the starting point for defining, identifying, and prioritizing risk activities. The value chain represents the organizational DNA. In this section we will look at the complete set of internal and external resources and processes that are needed to create and sustain value for the organization.

This section concludes with an introduction to the concept I call, "Value Chain Risk Management."

The key questions and topics addressed in this section are:

Chapter 4: A Leadership Crisis?
- Who is responsible and accountable?
- Why does weak top down leadership make organizations and their value chains vulnerable? What are the major leadership conflicts and pitfalls?
- Do I have the information I need to make informed risk related decisions?
- Am I efficiently managing or optimizing my risk management efforts across the extended value chain?
- What assumptions should I stop making?

Chapter 5: The Value Chain
- What is the value chain, and why is it important and relevant?
- Why do I need to view the management of risk differently (value chain context)?
- What is the focus of VCRM?

Section Three. Consciousness, Engagement, and Execution: Value Chain Risk Management: This section shows how your organization can develop an action plan, prioritize activities, budget its cost, execute the plan to manage a range of risks effectively, and create a risk conscious culture. Key questions and topics addressed in each of the three chapters are:

Chapter 6: Develop, Nurture, and Sustain a Risk-Conscious Culture
- What are the five tenets of a Risk-Conscious-Culture?
  ◦ Who needs to be involved?
  ◦ How do I get others to act and take responsibility? How can a culture be created that takes risk seriously and views it from a broad value chain and not from an isolated perspective?
  ◦ How do I ensure it will work in my industry and unique culture?
  ◦ How do I validate and continuously improve?

- ○ Who should be responsible? Accountable? Consulted?
- ○ What price should be paid for playing the *total denial* game and losing? What are the potential penalties?

Chapter 7: Diverse Stakeholders Views and Motivations Across the Value Chain

- Who establishes and sets the risk paradigm?
- Who are the stakeholders, and why must they be included in all critical risk discussions and decisions?
- What factors influence expectation setting?
- What actions should be taken to meet stakeholder expectations?
- What are the different stakeholder views?

Chapter 8: Executing The Plan

- What are the Six Steps to Successful Execution?
  - ○ Value Alignment
  - ○ Risk Identification, Analysis of Evaluation
  - ○ Risk measurement, Solution Selection of Pricing
  - ○ Risk Implementation, Financing of Mitigation
  - ○ Risk Solution Execution
  - ○ Program Monitoring, Measurement, and Continuous Improvement

As a business risk executive over a 30-year career, I have personally been at the wrong place at the right time many times and, as result, been exposed to hundreds of risk failures. I'd like to share with you my experiences and perspective in the hope that it will add a touch of reality to the much-published area of risk management. Some of my personal experiences include:

- Two major multimillion-dollar wire frauds
- Several externally sponsored/internally executed identity theft schemes that involved some pretty scary organized crime groups
- A night-shift data center operator who moonlighted as a serial killer
- Numerous hacking events originating in communist countries
- Several extortion attempts

- Dozens of hardware thefts, including the disappearance of the audit server from a heavily secured computer room
- A gun runner whose day job was, as a corporate vice president, to manage the bank's back office and who had the authority to wire hundreds of millions of dollars
- Hundreds of viruses and the mysterious deactivation and reactivation of a primary firewall where most of the funds transfer instructions passed through
- Theft of bank personal identification numbers (PINs)
- Thieves who posed as facility maintenance personnel so that they gain access to the executive vice president's workstation and e-mail

Even in light of these expanding risk realities, my message is *not* doom and gloom. I promote the cause of risk consciousness, which I define as the basic awareness of risk itself—by all stakeholders in the value chain—and the ability to address the risks that present the greatest impact to meeting the business objectives. Contained in this book is an honest summary of those risks, along with proven solutions that every organization and executive can put into action. I believe the message is relevant, timely, and presents real-world action plans already implemented by many progressive and risk sensitive organizations. We have reaped the rewards of a much more efficient and global business model. Now we must quickly and expeditiously confront the risk created while moving forward with the new risk-conscious culture to prevent a repeat of the past.

▉ ENDNOTES

1. "China Plant Played Role in Drug Tied to 4 Deaths." *Wall Street Journal Online,* February 14, 2008.
2. "Accused French Trader Ordered Jailed." *USA Today,* February 9, 2008; "Societe Generale's Fraud: What Now?" *BusinessWeek,* January 24, 2008.
3. "BlackBerry Service Out in North America." Yahoo! News, February 11, 2008; "RIM BlackBerrys Hit by Large-Scale Outage." *Wall Street Journal,* February 12, 2008.
4. "The Biggest Beef Recall Ever." *New York Times,* February 21, 2008.
5. "Sugar Soars Most Since June as Explosion Shuts Georgia Refinery." Bloomberg .com, February 8, 2008.

6. "Europe to Ban PVC Toys." BBC News
7. "Exxon Oil Cut Off From Venezuela's Oil." CNN.com/World, February 12, 2008.
8. Shirley S. Wang and Avery Johnson, "J&J Is Recalling a Pain Patch." *Wall Street Journal,* February 13, 2008.
9. "Federal Government Falling Short on Cyber-Crime." TechTarget (searchsecurity .techtarge.com/news/article/0,289142), February 20, 2008.

Change, the Double-Edged Sword

> *The only constant is change, continuing change, inevitable change, that is the dominant factor in society today. No sensible decision can be made any longer without taking into account not only the world as it is, but the world as it will be.*

—Isaac Asimov

You can view change as containing many important aspects, especially when talking about evolving risk and how to manage it. These aspects include: change resulting from innovation, competitive and investor pressures, organizational realignments, geopolitical events, societal shifts, and a variety of internal and external events. In this section, I look at what's at risk as a result of change, the cause and effect of risk brought about by change, the increasingly vulnerable organization, and how value chains are created and evolve over time.

My goal in this first section is to define change and its effect on an organization's risk profile. At the root of this challenge is the reality that an organization cannot completely control the speed of change, the timing of the change, or the cascading consequences of the many risks that arise as a result of change in our highly interconnected and interdependent global value chains. One thing is certain: with change comes risk. The challenge has always been, and will always be, to find the right balance between the "reward" that is afforded when initiating change and the "consequence" that is suffered when one poorly manages risk.

Risks created by change, and their unintended consequences, are a result of not being able to predict, forecast, or model all of the possible combinations of threats, vulnerabilities, external factors, and the many combinations of resources (labor/skills, technology and processing, physical assets, relationships) used to create value and support the value chain. The management of financial change and risk is an example of where risk is better understood, measured, modeled, managed, and highly regulated (e.g., foreign exchange, credit). To accomplish effective financial risk management the organization has to put in place strong governance, reporting, incentives, penalties, training, education, and clear expectations tolerances. However, the results of this analytical process are still subject to complex and many times unpredictable behavioral, environmental, operational, and societal influences that dramatically alter outcomes. *The primary focus of this book is on the operational view of these changes, resultant risks, and solutions to create and sustain a risk-conscious culture across the extended value chain.*

Change should not be a surprise to the organization, and neither should the risks that are associated with change. In most instances we typically find indicators, trends, signals—somewhere in the process or organization's memory (the seasoned employees with collectively hundreds of years of knowledge, experience, and intuition) - that warn us that change has occurred or is about to occur. A British psychologist, James T. Reason, came up with an accident causation model used in risk assessment referred to as the "Swiss Cheese" model. Reason hypothesizes that most accidents can be traced to one or more of four levels of failure. The theory looks at the cumulative act affect of contributory failures that have lain dormant for a long time. Simply stated, most big events don't just happen. There is typically something else that might have happened (and gone unnoticed or noticed and not reported). Something as meaningless as a small rounding error or a small amount of missing stock could be an indicator that there is a problem and that it could be much larger than anticipated. What is needed in the risk-conscious culture is the engagement of the masses to identify these symptoms and close calls and to report this upward to management for resolution. Once surfaced, appropriate filters which validate the information and exposure must exist. Confirmed risk must be escalated immediately and responsibility for resolution assigned. How informed and prepared we are—our ability to anticipate, predict, mitigate, and respond—or how quickly we learn of and communicate the potential for negative consequences is fundamental to successful risk management. Some organizations cause change, others react to change, and some are able to avoid change altogether—until others have proven it safe to proceed. Some organizations are change agents, such as Sony, Apple, Samsung, Virgin, Toyota, Procter and Gamble, Starbucks, Wal-Mart, Intel, GE, and, of course, Google. There are different risk implications for each, and by the nature of their size or global influences, all members of their value chains are impacted by any change. Some organizations seem to be more agile than others and aggressively implement risk avoidance practices. Others practice risk mitigation and possess a resiliency characteristic that allows them to "bounce back" quickly from an adverse event. Both of these attributes, agility and resiliency, are *necessary* for successful risk management. But how does an organization identify and manage risk associated with rapid change, and how do they achieve the correct level of resiliency and agility? With so much change under way—technical, social, geographical, environmental, economic, political, and operational—how does an organization implement a sustainable and comprehensive risk program without losing sight of its main purpose— value creation and social responsibility?

To answer these questions I will use case studies to deconstruct the change and associated risk process. These historical examples of change and ineffective risk management provide us with a starting point to better understand why significant risk resulted and what lessons can be learned. Change is dynamic, often unpredictable, and necessary as it fuels innovation, progress, and growth. However, the risk associated with change is potentially at a "flash point" whereby the realization of a single risk could cascade into a mega-crisis due to the nature of our interconnected, global society and mutually interdependent value and supply chains.

CHAPTER 1

Rapid Change, *Escalating Risk*

What are you doing, Dave?

—Voice of computer HAL in *2001: A Space Odyssey,* 1968

Change—inevitable and constant. What once were vertically integrated self-contained organizations are now mass assemblers, marketers, retailers, distributors, and service organizations. They rely on others to do what they once did in a global eco-network of human, manufacturing, logistics, and finance capabilities to fulfill their primary corporate missions. Change is taking place with greater speed, efficiency, capacity, ubiquity, and anonymity. Where does it end? In the well-known film *2001: A Space Odyssey,* the oddly-named HAL (advance the name alphabetically by one letter each and see what you get) senses that astronaut Dave is about to disconnect the system, so HAL (with a sense of self-preservation) kills Dave.

The sentient computer is the ultimate disaster of progress, and may remain in the realm of science fiction. But the idea is relevant here because it shows how progress and change can turn on us and even destroy us. HAL was a supercomputer of the highest order and a miracle of "future" technology. It ultimately destroyed its creators. They enjoyed the benefits brought about by change but failed to consider the risk. We can apply this lesson to modern-day risks that all organizations are experiencing.

THE ROOTS OF CHANGE

Change can be imposed on the organization from a variety of sources such as clients, regulators, investors, underwriters, competitors, suppliers, and of course, Mother Nature. A change can be unexpected or the result of some unanticipated event. The latter is much riskier because the assessment, reaction, and response time is severely limited. Unfortunately, there are many instances where an overreaction or incorrect response introduced greater risk than the original event. Negative outcomes often result from individuals making quick and uninformed ("gut") decisions. The worst case of all is when the unanticipated event has already produced an overwhelming catastrophic consequence that severely limits the organization's ability to manage the risk. This occurred during the September 11, 2001, terrorist attacks; European heat wave of 2003 that killed 35,000; Bhopal gas tragedy in December 1984, where several hundred thousand people were exposed to a deadly gas; and Hurricane Katrina, where 1800 people perished and there was an estimated US$18 billion in damage. Whether anticipated or unanticipated change, the organization will need accurate and current information about the potential impacts as well as a decision-making framework to provide options and actionable advice.

The organization can initiate change that adversely impacts others, accidentally, or purposefully. Poorly coordinataed changes (all participants in the value chain) could cause consequential damages if there is a negative outcome—hence the term third-party liability.

The point here is that with every change, there is a potential upside—an opportunity to grow, expand into new markets, and/or gain market share. However, there is the potential for a downside risk when unmitigated consequences are eventually realized. To strike the balance between risk and reward requires not only accurate and timely knowledge/data but also early intervention, risk assessment, and the care and feeding of a risk-conscious culture. The process cannot begin without a thorough understanding of an organization's business priority, value chain(s), and what's at risk.

Those that do not consider risk at the onset of change, or wait until after the important "change" decisions have been made, place the organization at tremendous risk. Any change—large or small, planned or unplanned—has the potential to create material risk to the organization and its stakeholders.

For example, the organization can initiate a change such as an organizational realignment. The intent of this change might be to improve operational efficiencies. However, this change has the potential to introduce significant and material *risk* if this strategy is flawed, poorly timed, or unsuccessfully executed (I think we've all experienced at least one organizational change that resulted in less-than-desired outcomes). The key to effective and efficient risk management is a pervasive culture that knows how to identify the value-based priorities, value chain processes and resources, financial/brand/strategy impacts, and risk treatment choices and associated implementation impacts (e.g., cost, service, quality, social). I've found it helpful to look at change from the vantage points depicted in Exhibit 1.1

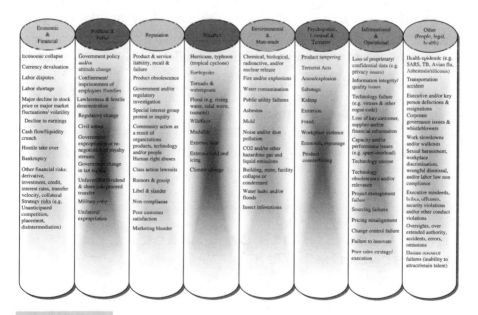

Economic & Financial	Political & Social	Reputation	Weather	Environmental & Man-made	Psychopathic, Criminal & Terrorist	Informational & Operational	Other (People, legal, health)
Economic collapse	Government policy and/or attitude change	Product & service liability, recall & failure	Hurricane, typhoon (tropical cyclone)	Chemical, biological, radioactive, and/or nuclear release	Product tampering	Loss of proprietary/ confidential data (e.g. privacy issues)	Health epidemic (e.g. SARS, TB, Avian flu, Asbestosis/silicosis)
Currency devaluation	Confinement/ imprisonment of employees /families	Product obsolescence	Earthquake	Fire and/or explosions	Terrorist Acts	Information integrity/ quality issues	Transportation accident
Labor disputes	Lawlessness & hostile demonstration	Government and/or regulatory investigation	Tornado & waterspouts	Water contamination	Arson/explosion	Technology failure (e.g. viruses & other rogue code)	Executive and/or key person defections & resignations
Labor shortage	Regulatory change	Special interest group protest or inquiry	Flood (e.g. rising water, tidal wave, tsunami)	Public utility failures	Sabotage	Loss of key customer, supplier and/or financial information	Corporate governance issues & whistleblowers
Major decline in stock price or major market fluctuations/ volatility	Civil unrest	Community action as a result of organizations products, technology and/or people	Wildfires	Asbestos	Kidnap	Capacity and/or performance issues (e.g. spam overload)	Work slowdowns and/or walkouts
Decline in earnings	Government expropriation or re-negotiation of royalty streams	Human right abuses	Mudslide	Mold	Extortion	Technology misuse	Sexual harassment, workplace discrimination,
Cash flow/liquidity crunch	Government change in tax regime	Class action lawsuits	Extreme heat	Noise and/or dust pollution	Fraud	Technology obsolescence and/or relevance	wrongful dismissal, and/or labor law non compliance
Hostile take over	Unfavorable dividend & share sale proceed transfer	Rumors & gossip	Extreme cold and icing	CO2 and/or other hazardous gas and liquid emissions	Workplace violence	Project management failure	Executive misdeeds, bribes, offenses, security violations
Bankruptcy	Military coup	Libel & slander	Climate change	Building, mine, facility collapse or condemned	Economic espionage	Sourcing failures	and/or other conduct violations
Other financial risks: derivative, investment, credit, interest rates, transfer velocity, collateral Strategy risks (e.g. Unanticipated competition, placement, disintermediation)	Unilateral expropriation	Non-compliance Poor customer satisfaction Marketing blunder		Water leaks and/or floods Insect infestations	Product counterfeiting	Pricing misalignment Change control failure Failure to innovate Poor sales strategy/ execution	Oversights, over extended authority, accidents, errors, omissions Human resource failures (inability to attract/retain talent)

EXHIBIT 1.1   Risk Triggers

I begin to expose you to your journey or, if you will, your odyssey, with three case studies of change, risk, and the subsequent consequences—the long view of risk. These are not examples of the occasional low-probability, high-impact threat, such as a catastrophic terrorist incident or mega-weather-related disaster, but rather real stories about risks that organizations face daily. Risk, brought about by change—whether planned or unplanned, the consequences remain the same. The business decisions made, or not made, and the associated risk were a reflection of the organization's culture, policies, and collective experience. Unfortunately, I have found that in most instances of risk failure the final decision was based on the individual's instinct—or worse—their incentives, rather than on a disciplined risk philosophy and approach.

The goal is to deconstruct and analyze these cases to better identify/anticipate change and to harmonize risk and change processes. The first case is about a major bank that decided to decentralize its global funds transfer capabilities and, as a result, fell victim to two separate $6 million wire frauds. The change created a risk that was exploited by an insider with the assistance of at least 12 members of an organized crime ring. The second case involved a global consumer electronics company that chose to outsource the manufacturing of a critical component of their flagship product to a supplier in a poorly regulated country. A fire ensued, the outsourced manufacturer's plant was destroyed, and production of the product halted. The third case is about a bank that was seeking to improve operating margins by reducing overhead costs in the mortgage origination process. They outsourced part of the credit reporting function and as a result became a victim of an identity theft scheme perpetrated from the inside and sponsored by a notorious Nigerian organized crime ring.

INSIDE LOOKING OUT: THREE CASE STUDIES OF CHANGE AND *ESCALATING RISK*

Like most cases, it was the greed and a careless mistake on the part of the perpetrators, rather than a comprehensive system of managing risks and executing critical controls, that prevented them from walking away with

CASE 1	RAPID CHANGE: ATTRACT NEW CUSTOMERS AND STRENGTHEN RELATIONSHIPS

RISK REALIZED: $12 MILLION WIRE FRAUD AND BRAND DAMAGE

When the phone rang late on a Thursday evening, the last people that I expected to be on the other end of the line were the CIO and general auditor of the bank. In two separate incidents, $12 million had suddenly disappeared from the asset management department's balance sheets. It wasn't immediately clear whether this was an isolated breach or a large-scale attack. The treasurers of more than 1,200 major companies used the bank's PC-based treasury management system to move billions of dollars daily ($400 million was moved daily on just one PC workstation in the internal operations area). During an around-the-clock investigation, we determined that an organized crime ring, consisting of 12 people, had carefully and systematically learned about flaws in the operational processes and computerized system (no system audit trail, easily retrievable passwords on the hard drive, ability to delete or replace audit records) and, as a result, easily made off with the money. The bank was caught flat-footed, completely unaware that it was so exposed.

$12 million. However 11 out of the 12 were able to walk away with their freedom. Could this potentially disastrous situation been prevented?

Many questions had to be answered quickly (*Note:* these questions should be considered as part of your first responder/crisis plan):

- What actually happened?
- What's our risk?
- Will we have to revert to a manual payment process until we determine if there is systemic risk or until the problem is fixed?
- What's our contingent risk and liability, and who else might be impacted by this event?

- Is this happening elsewhere (i.e., on other internal or external workstations)?

- How is management going to communicate to thousands of global 500 corporations that the integrity of their cash management environment might have been compromised and at any moment they could be defrauded of hundreds of millions of dollars (if they hadn't already)? Will they trust us?

- How will we handle the barrage of questions if this goes public? Could the confidence/trust of the payments systems be undermined? Who do we need to notify immediately (customers, regulators, directors, press)?

The bank, like most other organizations, was simply overwhelmed (and perhaps unprepared) for the risks it faces every day. The warning lights were flashing: The unobserved removal of the security and audit system two weeks prior; suspicious behaviors that had occurred and never been reported, questioned, or elevated to senior management; violation logs containing evidence that someone was trying to break in, had not been reviewed; and the technical support group had been cited by the audit group for exploiting a design flaw, but this activity was never discontinued because of need to provide customer support. This situation could have been avoided if someone had noticed that a similar scheme had taken place five years earlier at Prudential Securities. This scheme was publicly reported (Equinox/Discovery Channel TV special: *Information Superhighway Robbery*) and resulted in an $8.5 million theft under very similar circumstances.

LESSONS LEARNED *In the bank's zeal to cut expenses by reducing head count, they destroyed hundreds of years of corporate memory and the inherent "risk sensitivity" of long-term, experienced employees. These employees represented the organization's sensors, the first line of defense in managing risk. Somewhere a similar exposure was reported in the press or could have been obtained through a close/confidential relationship with an industry counterpart or law enforcement and/or government agency. This was found out later in the case—the insider had been suspected of wrongdoing at another major money center bank.*

Many of the more mundane operational risks are usually not properly addressed by the development, operations, and audit teams. In this case, the "sexier" external risks, such as capturing and altering a funds transfer message in transit, was the primary focus of the risk design team. Many of the internal, operationally based risks could have easily been uncovered during the system design phase if the assessment team focused on the value chain; key processes, resources, and the broader set of people, physical and electronic vulnerabilities. Too often, published information reflecting actual security/risk crises are not identified, analyzed, and acted upon by staff responsible for assessing or managing risk. They fail to ask the questions, "Do I have the same risk exposure, is the incident relevant to my business, and could it happen here?"

CASE 2

RAPID CHANGE: IMPROVE MARGINS; OUTSOURCE MANUFACTURING

RISK REALIZED: LOST REVENUE AND BRAND DAMAGE

"We've decided to outsource part of the manufacturing operation of our best-selling consumer electronic product," stated a product manager at a global Fortune 200 organization. Operational overhead will be reduced by 12% and delivery times shortened by a third. The supplier is located in Mexico, where labor is much less expensive, the tax systems, much more advantageous to business, and the environment is only moderately regulated. What could go wrong?

One day, a minor catastrophe occurred when there was a fire at the plant in Mexico. The facility suffered moderate damage, and that's when this company found out that its larger competitor was also sourcing parts from the same location. The supply chain was partially disrupted for a short period, but it wasn't a serious loss. However, a second fire occurred and this time it was a major fire, completely destroying the plant. The outsourced parts manufacturer's supply chain came to a screeching halt. Business interruption insurance will most likely cover the majority of the financial loss, although the carriers are challenging this assumption and asking a lot of questions about the company's risk management oversight and readiness. It appears that their flagship product will be off the shelves for at least six months. That includes their peak selling period, the holiday season, and NFL Super Bowl. Although this product does not account for a substantial piece of the overall revenue, this Asia-based company considers not having this particular product on the shelf, right next to their competitors, a catastrophic brand embarrassment. This is a true story, but let me explain a bit more. You see, when this organization decided to move the production of this critical component to an outsourced supplier in Mexico, they failed to consider that the low-cost labor and production facility was low-cost for a reason. One of these reasons was that the fire standards didn't require the building to have sprinklers, nor did it account for the lack of adequate water supply or fire protection. To make matters worse, this company also supplied a larger competitor. When recovering their facility and operating at partial capacity, the big question became: Who will get preferential treatment? (I call this contention exposure.) Thank goodness the workers were not injured or killed; besides the horrible personal consequence for the families, think for a moment about the brand and reputation exposure if this household brand were also exposing individual employees to unsafe working conditions.

LESSONS LEARNED   *Margins were squeezed as the number of competitors increased. Seeking a lower cost of goods sold, manufacturers were always on the hunt for ways to drive down labor and other production costs. All of this was predictable and obvious. However, the organization, in its quest to drive down costs, failed to apply existing property risk standards (fire) that were already in place at their facilities located in developed countries. The insurer failed to demand these standards as well. The moral of the story is that just because you decided to outsource a process in your value chain that it does not relinquish your organization's risk management responsibility. Initial risk assessment must be followed by routine and unannounced audits to validate that previously agreed risk practices are in effect. Here are several additional risk considerations. Critical risk information about the previous incidents did flow to those that could effect change. Following the first fire incident, no one performed a comprehensive risk analysis of recently discovered exposures. No steps were taken to mitigate this known and* *documented critical exposure. In addition, no one surfaced the inherent contention conflict that would result from being a less important customer of this outsourced supplier. These failures had a cascading effect that impacted current and forecasted production and many overseas jobs, lost revenue for all members of the value chain (transportation, retailers, etc.), and resulted in a major public embarrassment.*

| CASE 3 | RAPID CHANGE: STREAMLINE MORTGAGE ORIGINATION PROCESSES AND REDUCE EXPENSES |

Risk Realized: Privacy Breach, Identity Theft and Brand Damage

I received a call from our Legal Investigation unit requesting me to join them in following up on a tip provided by the FBI. It appeared that a disgruntled girlfriend was tired of her boyfriend's behavior—he was a contract employee of the bank—and decided to rat him out to the Feds. This was no ordinary boyfriend. It turned out that this individual was part of an elaborate Nigerian crime ring involved in defrauding consumers and the bank, by compromising thousands of individuals' identities.

I arrived in the office in midtown Manhattan to interview the manager of the mortgage origination business. The group consisted of 20 people who were responsible for originating millions of dollars in mortgages each month. The group had decided to keep expenses down by outsourcing one of the operations functions to a contract employee. The corporate memory and risk sensors had been lost when an experienced, long-term employee had been laid off to reduce cost. The contract employee was responsible for taking the mortgage application, which had been faxed or compiled during a phone call, and running a consolidated credit report from one of the regional credit agencies. He accessed the credit information via a PC and application provided by the credit agency. What was so ironic was that this employee had just been offered a full-time position because of exceptional performance. His fellow workers commented during the investigation process that "he worked day and night" and would come in on the weekends, just to keep pace with the work. At that moment I thought to myself, how much volume is the group doing and what is the extent of his function? I thought he just had to push some buttons on the computer, print off a credit report, staple the report to the application, and hand it to the loan officer. Was this a sensor or warning light that something was afoul? Needless to say, when I looked closer I discovered that only 50 to 60 applications were being originated per month. However, the accounting records indicated that between 600 and 800 credit reports were being requested monthly (by the way, the bank was being billed for each of these credit inquiries, but no one noticed—another warning light?). Something did not add up. As it turned out, we discovered that this activity had been going on for approximately eight months—more than 4500 unapproved individual credit inquiries!

LESSON LEARNED *The key questions that should have been asked were:*

- *Did the organization consider who and how risk would be managed when they were considering change (i.e., when reducing operational overhead via outsourcing the management of risk would no longer be performed internally)?*
- *Did they assess the risk of this change to the value chain, and did they track the flow of sensitive data through the entire value chain (i.e., from creation to destruction)?*
- *Did the organization define what constitutes sensitive data (i.e., the characteristics of the data that defined it as sensitive, e.g. regulatory requirement or privacy law)?*
- *Did the organization consider performing a threat agent assessment (i.e., a simple assessment to determine who would have the greatest opportunity—empowerment, means—to compromise the sensitive data)?*
- *Who reconciled the monthly billing against loan applications (i.e., should have surfaced the issue immediately)? In a risk-conscious culture a discrepancy like this would have immediately raised questions and been elevated to management.*

- *Why didn't a co-worker or manager notice, report, and question why a temporary employee was working hundreds of paid overtime hours— including weekends and evenings when the operation was closed?*

Management must create and nurture a risk-sensitive culture as well as train their employees and others in the field, on how to detect risk warning signs occurring in every critical process. Often, the observation of an unusual occurrence should be all that is needed to set off the risk sensors.
Guidelines for rapid report and escalation must be established. It is important that employees are incentivized and feel empowered to raise the warning flags. Management must be responsible and accountable to address and resolve all risk issues raised.

These are some of the many examples of risk assessment that could have easily helped to avoid significant brand damage, legal exposure, and financial loss. Why wasn't risk addressed early in the change process?

WHAT'S CHANGED AND WHAT RISK HAS BEEN BROUGHT ABOUT BY CHANGE?

These cases reflect that the identification of change is often elusive and difficult to spot. Like the old adage about the frog and boiling water—that is, throw the frog in boiling water and it will jump out, place the frog in the pan with heat increasing gradually and the frog might not realize the change, or its impact, until it's too late (of course, I don't advocate this behavior—it is merely used as a representation). You might not be aware of change or its impact on the processes and resources that support your value chain.

Processes change as they become automated; are improved for efficiency; are impacted by policy change; are adapted to organizational realignment; are migrated to outsourced partners; are transitioned outside of domestic borders; or are changed for multinational implementation. For example, the sourcing and importing of materials outside of domestic borders now is under close post-9/11 security scrutiny and new customs regulations apply for those seeking to be compliant with Authorized Economic Operators or U.S. Customs-Trade Partnership Against Terrorism (C-TPAT) standards (a voluntary supply chain security program led by U.S. Customs and Border Protection). This is a major change/risk to many organizations' value chains since it requires additional security diligence and, if not managed properly, will result in significant shipment delays.

Movement to offshore suppliers further complicates how work is done and, more to the point, how risks grow as well. Intellectual property theft, geographies more prone to natural hazards, availability of localized skilled labor, inferior product quality standards, and other risks increase exponentially when the value chain transitions from a vertically integrated, self-contained set of processes to a geographically disbursed linked set of relationships. This interdependent virtual eco-network consists of hundreds or thousands of public and private stakeholders. In most instances, these relationships appear to be strong and well defined. The reality is that when the perceived value of the relationship (we are all in this together) begins to diminish between, let's say, a supplier and the organization, these relationships dissolve and new ones are formed. New suppliers arrive on the scene and compete for the business. If the new vendors improve profitability or the return on investment/assets then the switch is made—or better stated—change occurs and risk is created. Unfortunately, pressures to change to more reliable partners, and the need to keep products flowing, often result in shortcuts being taken.

A few examples of the risks that arise as a result of this change are: 1) not properly deactivating physical or computer information access, or debriefing the former supplier, 2) failure to assess and integrate the new supplier's processes and technology, and 3) inheriting contingent supplier risk. In many instances the supplier relationship is not as important as having access to a pool of suppliers that can provide the raw material. As one senior executive at a high tech company recently told me "We don't really care about most suppliers, what we care about is the supply of the raw material. If our primary supplier fails, then we'll just find another. We only care when enough of the suppliers fail to cause a change in material price." The point here is to remember that you typically only have one chance and that inconsistent or unpredictable performance levels will be tolerated less and less as globalization continues to take hold. Although you might perceive that your organization has an unbreakable relationship with your customer, in today's global marketplace failure will not be tolerated, and there is always a competitor anxiously waiting somewhere—in India, Brazil, the United States, Vietnam, Russia, China, and elsewhere—to displace you.

One final point to remember about change: when your organization experiences change, you want to make sure the *improvement* is still viewed positively when long-term impacts are factored in. This requires consideration of the cost, service, quality, and social implications when implementing and supporting risk solutions. Also, the behavioral impact cannot, and should not, be underestimated when implementing risk solutions. To determine the long-term effectiveness of the control, ask yourself, "How likely will this control be accepted and adapted into the operational workflow?" Talk to your peers, public- and private-sector experts around the globe and within your industry, your risk-conscious network, and others who have experienced similar change. What you seek at this point is risk knowledge and a consciousness of what is at risk and how your particular way of creating value, possibly supported via a complex value chain, creates risk and risk resolution challenges. All too often, the net result of change (improvement less risk impact), viewed over the longer term, is just the opposite of what you desire: lower profits, loss of quality, and increased risk.

The past few decades have been nothing short of an economic, social, and technological revolution. Change has occurred on a massive scale, and it is this change that has allowed many to achieve prosperity and growth beyond anyone's expectations. However, the upside risk (sometimes referred to in the insurance industry as *variable risk*) experienced by so many may not have forced these organizations to assess just what type of vulnerability or downside risk was being created. Faster, better, cheaper—the recurring and continuously accelerating trend fueled by the increasing number of emerging economies that are participating in the global market. It is no wonder why the management of risk, what many perceive as a potential obstacle to achieving growth, has not been widely implemented as part of this "change" process. The result is evident by the recent rash of product failure (both design and manufacturing), environmental pollution, child labor issues, subprime lending crises, communication failures, and IT breaches. The change process is moving much too fast for organizations to try and retrofit risk management solutions. As a result, the vulnerability gap continues to increase as value chains grow and become more interdependent. Those that lack the risk-conscious culture and have failed to integrate risk activities into the change process will be more exposed than ever.

Change has to be managed carefully to ensure that the organization gets the return on change it seeks. The ultimate goal of any business is to quickly produce the highest-quality product at the least cost. This has sometimes been referred to as the "Fast, Good, Cheap" production paradigm. However, history has revealed that achieving and sustaining all three attributes is impossible. If it's fast and cheap, it can't be good; good and cheap, it can't be fast; and fast and good, it can't be cheap.

It is fair to say that the "unbalanced triangle," representing the three attributes—fast, good, and cheap—all too often excludes considerations of *risk*. If you expand the triangle into a pyramid, recognizing that the fourth point is often invisible and resides behind the three front points, you can begin to appreciate the real nature of risk. It is often invisible. The triangle is two-dimensional, whereas the pyramid adds the third dimension to the picture. (See Exhibit 1.2.) Once this fourth point is added, you are better able to quantify the concept of fast, good, and cheap in terms of the risks involved. The more you are able to achieve these three attributes, the stronger the risk element is likely to be.

1. Many leaders appreciate the advantages of improved technology, development of global markets, and the availability of low-cost labor and materials from other countries. At the same time, they have not confronted the corresponding vulnerabilities that this new environment creates, such as how to trust your reputation and business that you used to own to an unknown, one where the background of the workforce or supplier cannot be validated

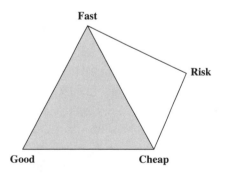

EXHIBIT 1.2   Unbalanced Triangle.

or actively monitored or one that operates in a part of the world with poor public infrastructure, political instability, or limited labor and environmental regulation.

2. Management typically lacks an unobstructed view (i.e., clear end-to-end "line of sight") of their product/service value chain. Here are a few questions to determine if your organization has a clear line of sight. What problems is the value chain solving? Where does the sourcing of our product/service begin (field, forest, farm, mine)? What are all of the processes in the end-to-end value chain that must be performed to create value? What resources are relied upon to create value—from the beginning of the process to the end (e.g., from the farm to the customer's mouth)? Is there a clear line of sight of all resources and associated risks? (*Note:* resources can be grouped into four categories: people/skills, technology and processing, physical assets, and relationships). Someone upstream or downstream in the supply chain management has *assumed* that someone else is adequately managing the risk.

3. Risk itself is a moving and evolving target. In our brave new world it is impossible to predict what events will occur or what risk will be realized. There is an opportunity to finance risk, via transfer products (e.g., insurance or catastrophe bonds), when there is a degree of certainty or predictability. However, risk financing is limited to that which can be clearly defined and calculated. For example, insurance/reinsurance carriers in the property market cannot create capacity in the market without a clear definition of a peril and knowing when the loss starts and stops. Therefore, the burden is on the organization and its stakeholders to mitigate (or knowingly accept) the ever-growing risk to labor, technology, processing, physical assets, and/or relationships. However, Wall Street and Main Street do not like, and will not tolerate, surprises or excessive volatility. My experience and battle scars have taught me that rapid change without a value-aligned, well-defined, disciplined, measured, operationally integrated, holistic process for managing risks and establishing a risk-conscious culture is a recipe for eventual disaster. Those without the "plan" typically find themselves trying to support inconsistent and duplicate risk initiatives. Most just need a place to start.

Also not considered by many organizations was, and still is, what I refer to as the long view—the long-term implications and subsequent impacts of the failure to effectively and efficiently manage risk. The short view typically reveals that all is fine and the risk of change was handled properly. The long-term view requires the organization to have the foresight to understand what risks are created by their actions. Unfortunately, the consequence of the risk that is realized later on is usually more significant since multiple value chains have been integrated and more organizations participate. Here are a few examples:

- Large money center banks, rapid loan portfolio expansion, and the subsequent multibillion dollar loan defaults by organizations doing business in lesser developed countries/LDCs (late 1970s/early 1980s).

- Overexpansion of the employment ranks by global financial institutions in the mid-1980s driven by technological change and deregulation of financial markets ("big bang" era). Then came the subsequent massive layoffs and business shutdowns.

- The proliferation of the e-business model and Internet businesses during the "dot-com" era (1990s) and the subsequent failed Internet start-ups (although there were some successes, such as Amazon and Yahoo) and massive financial market volatility. The impact extended to many secondary businesses such as advertising, recruiting, housing, and financial organizations.

- The rush to outsource key functions to create a lower-cost, geographically-distributed value chain causing enormous product quality and environmental issues. We are now beginning to experience rising labor costs in many of the major outsourcing countries such as India, and as a result there have been a few cases of reversing the process (in-sourcing[1]).

- The acceptance of subprime lending and the rapid creation, and subsequent failure, of a niche financial industry.

Some of those that have profited in the short term from the upside, the so-called rainmakers have reaped the rewards and moved on before the downside becomes reality. The masses are usually left to suffer the long-term impacts, such as loss of their employment/investments, buying power or worst case—their quality of life and/or health.

Many will argue that these so-called rainmakers were a necessary evil and that they were needed to spur economic prosperity and social growth. That's a matter of opinion and one's perspective, I guess, but it is my belief that the long-term ramifications of many of these risk-consciousless changes have not yet been realized.

KEY LEARNING POINT

Bottom line, the risk profile of the value chain is ever changing and therefore requires constant review, testing and a commitment to improvement. Everyone has a responsibility to participate and contribute in the organizations risk consciousness. The risk discussion should be deeply embedded, *early*, in the business change discussion. In the end, risk taking is essential part of the business.

As the chairman of a Fortune 500 company, points out: "Risk is like heat—too much and you get burned, too little and you freeze." Make no mistake, risk taking is essential.

ENDNOTE

1. Don Clark and Vibhuti Agarwa, "Some in Silicon Valley Begin to Sour on India," *Wall Street Journal*, Tuesday, July 3, 2007.

CHAPTER 2

Cause and Effect

Causality or causation denotes a directional relationship between one event (called cause) and another event (called effect) which is the consequence (result) of the first

—RANDOM HOUSE UNABRIDGED DICTIONARY

Over the past few decades, six mega-changes have significantly altered organizations' risk profiles. Each change spurred economic and social benefits as well as considerable long-term risk. These mega-changes are:

1. A globalized interconnected and interdependent economy
2. Just-in-time (JIT) inventory process improvement
3. Customer empowerment and pervasive access enabled by Internet technologies
4. Outsourcing and offshoring the labor force
5. Outsourced production and manufacturing
6. Virtualization and consolidation of the physical work environment

Now let's take an in-depth look at the vulnerabilities created by these mega-changes so that we can better manage risk.

SIX CHANGES ALTER RISK PROFILE

Change 1

A globalized interconnected and interdependent economy.

Risk: The evolution of a globalized marketplace has created massive growth opportunities and complexities. As is often the case, with greater complexity comes greater risk. Here are a few examples:

- **Supply-side risk issues (typically external risks):** sourcing and product quality risk, political risk (e.g., nationalization of companies), supplier soundness risk, labor risks, export/import compliance, raw material shortages, logistics, capacity, security, and the contingent risk created when suppliers outsource work to other suppliers without involvement of the buyer.

- **Operational risks (typically internal risks):** issues include intellectual property theft, counterfeiting, property-related exposures due to lower environmental/health and safety standards, technology/program/process failures and/or lack of interoperability, and disruptions due to facilities/labor located in high-natural-hazard locations.

- **Demand-side risks (typically customer facing risks):** unfavorable trade, legal or regulatory environment, language barriers, evaporating market, obsolescence, and lack of experience selling to customers in emerging markets.

Change 2

Implementation of JIT process improvement.

Risk: In an effort to improve the return on assets, JIT is a process to reduce inventory and its associated costs. Typically the JIT process is pushed upstream which results in Tier 1/first line suppliers also trying to reduce inventory. Although the efficiency of the investment has improved, a significant vulnerability is created throughout the value chain. Excess capacity/bandwith is eliminated. Safety stock, inventory buffering, and redundancy contingencies have typically been avoided. The flow of goods will be completely stopped if there is a significant disruption at *any* point in the chain; e.g. customs, transportation carriers, port operators, etc. This was the case for Apple when Samsung, a critical supplier of NAND flash memory chips was unable to produce product because of a power outage.[1] Flash memory is one of the many JIT components that are essential to the production of the iPod.

In another example, Ford Motor Company experienced border delays at the U.S. Canadian border that quickly increased from a few minutes to an extreme 12 hours after the September 11 attacks. Despite the fact that the attacks had no direct impact on the seaports and border crossings, the aggressive response taken by local, state, and federal governments across North America brought the transportation infrastructure to a grinding halt. Ford Motor Company was forced to intermittently idle production at five of its assembly plants due to parts shortages resulting from processing delays at ports and borders. Ford's production output for the fourth quarter of 2001 was down 13% compared to its production plan for the quarter. Similarly, when 29 western U.S. seaports were closed during a 10-day lockout of stevedores in the fall of 2002, the resulting port congestion did not dissipate for months, resulting in delays for virtually every company with exposure to West Coast port operations. Just-in-time supply chains were severely impacted.[2]

Change 3

Customer empowerment and pervasive access enabled by Internet technologies.

Risk: The speed, ease, and efficiency at which business is conducted can be attributed to rapid technology, networking, and processing advances. Also, an extraordinary amount of sensitive business and personal data was made available via the Internet. Industries, governments, military, utility companies, and Internet-based companies (Google, Amazon) became completely dependent on the Internet. Here are a few of the more dominant trends:[3]

- Wide-scale deployment of microprocessors (approximately 10 billion microprocessors were sold in 2007).
- Cost improvements (wireless systems cost per delivery has dropped from more than $10 in 1980 to less than 10 cents in 2007).

- Rapid technological advancements (transistors in Intel chips have increased from a little over 4,000 in 1970 to over 1 billion in 2007).
- Pervasive connectivity (1.6 million mobile phones are added every day).

To support service, quality, and cost improvements (and thus gain competitive advantage) organizations began to extend access, functionality, knowledge, and critical information to their stakeholders and their stakeholders' stakeholders. Wide-scale interconnectivity and Web-enabled applications created the opportunity to sell goods and services in a global, rather than local, marketplace. More efficient methods of sharing knowledge, via Web and collaborative technologies (e.g., blogs, wikis), have created empowered customer communities. Other applications include: home banking, Internet-based auctions/reverse auctions, integrated supply chain applications for forecasting, inventory, order entry/fulfillment,

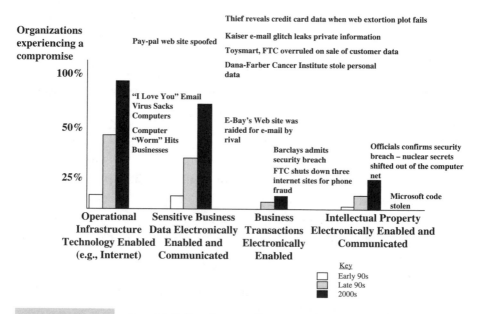

Business *change,* driven by technology (electronic) enablement, and *escalating* risk

EXHIBIT 2.1   **Rapid E-Business Change, *Escalating Risk***

SOURCE: Numerous Public data sources

integrated logistics and transportation applications, distance learning, and online retailing.

As quickly as new technology emerged, risks were exposed. Examples include: privacy breaches, electronic funds transfer fraud, hacked web sites, viruses, and denial of service attacks (which prevented the use of the servers and network). Exhibit 2.1 demonstrates this trend.

Companies leading the way, with the deployment of emerging technology, were especially vulnerable. As an early technology adopter, they were the first to experience many risk exposures not shared with other or never experienced by others. Unfortunately, many of the late adopters trying to desperately keep pace with competition could not take the time to effectively deploy risk solutions.

SIDEBAR   TECHNOLOGY: FRIEND OR FOE, THREE DECADES OF ESCALATING TECHNOLOGY CHANGE AND RISK

I first observed the expanding risk chasm in the late 1980s/early 1990s while managing Global IT risk at The Prudential and Chase Manhattan Bank. There was an upsurge in incidents that began to reveal the downside of the rapid technological advances in personal computing and networking. I subsequently published this hypothesis in a research note while at the Gartner Group. I asserted that "IT security risk would be unachievable for the emerging client-server environment over the five-year planning period," 0.8 probability. Client-server computing at the time consisted of desktop personal computers, local area networks, and application/system and network software and services, and is now the backbone of the majority of business environments. My hypothesis was based on the fact that the IT revolution and resultant change was happening more quickly than the organization's ability to manage the risk. I collaborated with hundreds of my peers to validate that technological change, although beneficial and necessary, was causing major disruptions as organizations were constantly in reactive mode. As the new technology became more pervasive, risks would become more obvious and the organization more concerned. Now the bad news: lurking behind every technological change was yet another technological change just waiting to be introduced by the overzealous vendors. Meanwhile, most organizations were still trying to secure the previously deployed technology—then, wham, IT would introduce the new technology and the organization would shift its attention to the new priority (after all, who would want to work with the old technology when they could be part of the next new thing?). Critical management attention, budgets, and resources would all shift. But here's the real problem that we still have to worry about: lingering vulnerabilities (that would later be exploited). In other words, *every change left in its path unaddressed vulnerabilities*; millions of potential land mines spread throughout the many value chains, which, if detonated, could have catastrophic social, economic, political, safety, and health consequences. Guess what—they are still out there. Beware of the explosions and aftershock!

Technology as Friend

In 2000, Goldcorp shared all of their geological data since 1948 with the world. This was unheard of in an intensely secretive industry. They launched the "Goldcorp Challenge" and made available $575,000 in prize money to the participants with the best methods to uncover potential locations. More than 400 megabytes about their 55,000 acre property was made available on their web site. As a result, the contestants that competed on the Internet identified 110 targets on the Red Lake property, 50 percent of which had not been previously identified by the company. Over 80 percent of the new targets yielded substantial amounts of gold—an estimated eight million ounces of gold had been found. Rob McEwan, CEO, estimates that the collaborative process shaved two to three years off their exploration time.[4]

The Goldcorp experience is an excellent example about an organization seizing the opportunity, taking risks, and achieving rewards. The CEO felt it necessary to reignite the exploration process by significantly changing the business processes. While this type of decision might be the norm in the future, as touted in the book, *Wikinomics: How Mass Collaboration Changes Everything*, one thing is certain: risk consciousness and assessment must be ingrained in the change process. Longer-term considerations should be further assessed, such as: what is the impact of making sensitive data available to the masses, and what lasting organizational impacts will outsourcing critical core business processes have to an unknown audience.

Technology as Foe

The bank's Legal Investigations team received a call from a very upset customer, a university professor, claiming that someone was withdrawing money from his bank account without approval. "How could this happen?" he asked. "My ATM bank card is in my wallet. How could someone be accessing my account?" Upon further review, the Legal Investigations unit had determined that a teller at one of the bank's branches had been involved with a small organized crime ring in an ATM fraud scheme. They were stealing personal and financial information (the individual's personal identification number [PIN], bank and card account number). Once armed with this information, members of the group created a legitimate duplicate of the ATM card. They would then use this card to make illegal ATM withdrawals. Ironically, the opportunity was created because of a need for the bank to address another risk, check fraud (at the time check fraud was running about $10 billion annually). To mitigate this risk the bank was piloting a newly designed check fraud prevention system. A PIN pad device (i.e., a small calculator-like device with a numeric keyboard) was installed at each teller station in high risk bank branches. The idea was to require the individual who was cashing the check to have in his possession a valid ATM card. This person had to also know the associated PIN in order to confirm his/her identity. The PIN was suppressed on the teller's display station, another security feature. Now here's how the scam worked (vulnerability exploited). The teller would instruct the customer to swipe their ATM card and enter the PIN. She would then tell the customer that their PIN didn't work and that they needed to reenter their PIN. Meanwhile, the check cashing IT-based application scrolled to the next screen. This new screen did not have the data suppression feature so the PIN was displayed when reentered by the unsuspecting customer. The teller would record this along with other information and then later send the PINs and bank card and account numbers to other members of the crime ring. Thanks to another technological innovation, e-mail, the process was extremely efficient. The criminal group purchased surplus card embossing/magnetic stripe equipment and then printed a duplicate ATM card. The rest was easy—go to a local bank and withdraw the maximum daily amount. They'd repeat this for a few days and then destroy the duplicate card. See, atyourownrisk.net for additional examples. Please send examples and articles, I will review and if appropriate, post for the benefit of others.

LESSON LEARNED *Any client/customer facing system that contains sensitive data should go through an independent threat assessment by an experienced security team. In researching this book, I interviewed Jim Woolsey, head of the Central Intelligence Agency in 1993 and 1994. He told me the difference between U.S. and Israeli strategies for identifying terrorists: "The Israelis are looking for terrorists . . . in the U.S. we are politically correct and randomly screen. Profiling is wrong in the U.S." As with the Israeli approach, corporations must aggressively identify their most vulnerable points, sometimes regardless of the political or social implications, and in a no-holds barred way do whatever is necessary to mitigate risk to a level commensurate to the value and in the best interests of the majority stakeholders. Leaders must be willing to do the same. They must think and act like the bad guys. When a vulnerability is uncovered, leaders must aggressively pursue its resolution despite the internal political ramifications.*

Organizations that handle very sensitive client or security data should implement a risk process that follows the movement of the data through the entire life cycle (value chain). Vulnerabilities should be assessed from the initial capture/creation of the data to its destruction/disposal. The scope of this assessment must analyze and evaluate the risk to the data in all its forms: intellectual, written, and physical. The value and relevance of data to financial institutions (e.g., bank, insurance companies, asset managers, and investment banks) is equivalent to the physical product in the nonfinancial services industry. The entire value chain, key processes, and support resources must be included in the scope of the risk assessment. Exhibit 2.2 is an illustration that presents the life cycle of data and examples of compromise when data is in various states (electronic, written, and intellectual).

Change 4

Outsourcing and offshoring labor.

Risk: In *outsourcing*, organizations seeking to improve operating margins have successfully reduced overhead labor costs by migrating production and back office functions to outsourcers. In o*ffshoring*, organizations have kept the function in-house but moved it to a less expensive location, such as India, or China, because of a less expensive labor pool and/or favorable tax structures. The entry of China, India, and the former Soviet Union into market capitalism has in effect doubled the world supply of workers,

Example of Compromises – Actual case used to demonstrate how sensitive data can be compromised at different points in the data life cycle

Origination/ Creation/ Capture	Access	Transmission / Transfer/ Move	Use/ Copy/ Process/ Update	Print	Store/ File/ Archive/ Backup	Dispose/ Destroy
——————————————————Data Life Cycle——————————————————						
Two sales executives responsible for originating accounts and supporting clients were capturing sensitive *physical* information and later selling to the Nigerian fraud ring.	Several support applications were implemented with shared/ generic *electronic* passwords. When the compromise occurred the organization could not determine prove who committed the compromise due to the lack of accountability.	Sensitive client information and unencrypted application passwords were being transmitted *electronically* via the network. An operator with network monitoring software was able to capture the data.	A temporary employee, hired to support loan origination, was actually a thief (*intellectual*). While handling loan applications and access, the individual would copy the sensitive data and later sell to a fraud ring.	A contract employee hired (*intellectual*) to service the HVAC unit over the weekend was copying and stealing physical reports and files that contained sensitive client information (*physical*).	A worker at the in-house offsite storage facility was routinely viewing archived documents, copying sensitive information, and selling the information to an identity theft ring (*intellectual, physical*).	Recycled hardware that was used to support back-office operations at this particular organization turned up during a raid by law enforcement of an identity theft ring's apartment (*electronic, physical*)

EXHIBIT 2.2   **Example of Compromises**

from 1.5 to 3 billon.[5] The trend does not appear to be ending any time soon. In November 2007, Pfizer said that it is looking to outsource as much as 30% of its manufacturing (in the United States and France) to Asia,[6] and Cessna Aircraft Company will become the first U.S. manufacturer to turn over complete production of an airplane to a Chinese partner, a move intended to cut production costs and foster a nascent private aviation market in China.[7]

Unfortunately, advanced risk management practices are too often not a prerequisite in the decision to offshore or outsource labor. The reason for this is clear; companies operating in emerging economies often lack the experience, time, capital, and resources to effectively manage risk. The organization's financial model may not support additional overhead such as the cost of a risk-conscious culture, risk management professionals, and technology. Keeping operating overhead low is core to many organizations' value proposition. Other critical risk challenges faced by inexperienced organizations include:

- Lack of adequate public records to allow effective worker background checks
- Miscommunication and errors caused by language interpretation issues

- Inadequate public infrastructure
- Product quality issues
- Changing attitudes toward and regulation of environmental and health issues
- Regulatory/statutory/legal violations associated with accessing sensitive individual data from a foreign country (e.g., accessing U.S. Department of Motor Vehicle records from India without consent/permission)
- Inability to control intellectual and/or sensitive data due to a weak social/legal/cultural environment
- Lack of available skilled labor

While visiting China-based clients in 2007, the operations manager of a Fortune 20 company told me that the issue of skilled labor was his biggest concern. He went on to say how this issue was forcing his corporate management, located thousands of miles away, to begin considering alternative sourcing strategies. He was not the only one concerned about the availability of skilled labor. In a survey of 600 chief executives of multinational companies with businesses across Asia, they stated that a shortage of qualified staff ranked as their biggest concern in China and Southeast Asia. It was their second-biggest headache in Japan and the fourth-biggest in India. Across almost every industry and sector it was the same.[8] The warning light has begun flashing, scarcity of skilled labor will lead to higher wages and a possible movement to other locations with less expensive labor pools (e.g., Vietnam). Let the risk process begin!

However, it's not all bad news. In the past few years I have noticed a significant change in this thinking, and as a result, the risk conversation has taken center stage at leading Asia-based organizations such as Haier and Taiwan Semiconductor Manufacturing Corporation.

Exhibit 2.3 reflects management's top risk concerns at a large business system process (BSP) outsourcing company. This company planned to offshore three critical operations to India. The business operations moved offshore were: IT application development/maintenance, the call center, and back office support. One doesn't have to be a financial wizard to see why the organization was motivated to make this change especially when the average cost per labor hour was between $7 and $15 in India while the same

Outsourcing *Change* & Escalating Risk

Business Operations	Disclosure of Sensitive Client Data	Security Risk Scenarios			Unauthorized Use, Distribution and/or Disclosure of Organization's Intellectual Property	Corporate Espionage, Embarrassment or Sabotage Due to Insertion of Rogue Code
		Violation of Statutory, Regulatory and Contractual Obligations	Disclosure of "Other" Sensitive Data Due to Access to Org. Resources	Disruption to Ops–Reliance on Offshore Support		
Application Development and Maintenance	*Identity Theft*					
Outsource Call Center						
Outsource Back Office Support						

Key

High concern
Moderate concern
Low concern

EXHIBIT 2.3   **Sample of Outsourcing Change and Increased Risk**

labor force cost $150 per hour (fully-loaded) in the United States. When you multiply this by several thousand workers . . . well, you do the math. But with this change came increased risk, such as: weak infrastructure; language barriers; no ability to conduct in-depth background checks; loss of past employees skills, knowledge, and experience; increased health exposure to pandemics (in a more risky region); natural catastrophe risks; data privacy, and physical security issues.

KEY LEARNING POINT

When outsourcing business operations the management of the organization should never relinquish responsibility for key risk decisions.

Change 5

Outsourcing of production and manufacturing.

Risk: In recent years, organizations capitalized on the opportunity to improve their return on assets by shedding their high cost, vertically

integrated factories and turning over control of their production operations to someone else. It is unfortunate that many organizations failed to
perform the appropriate degree of risk diligence. They assumed firms that
they were doing business with were adequately managing a broad set of
product, labor, environmental, and security risks. This assumption is still
prevalent today, as witnessed in a recent conversation I had with an executive at a large pharmaceutical company. He explained how aggressive they
have been in communicating their risk requirements and expectations to a
supplier base of 200 plus. However, he acknowledged that this strategy
might be flawed since they lacked a common risk language, and an active
program to audit or test compliance to the standards.

SIDEBAR

BusinessWeek magazine published an article on January 30, 2006 on
"The Future of Outsourcing." This article provided a perspective on the
magnitude of outsourcing in 2005. Here are the mind-rattling numbers:
global spending on outsourcing, such as modularizing the corporation
and its value chains, was over $546 billion in 2005. Leading the charge:

- Logistics and procurement, $179 billion (includes just-in-time
  shipping, parts purchasing and after-sales repairs)
- Electronics manufacturing, $170 billion (contract production;
  everything from electronics to medical devices)
- Information technology, $90 billion (software development, tech-
  nical support, web site design, IT[9] infrastructure)
- Customer care, $41 billion (call centers for tech support, air book-
  ings, bill collection, etc.)
- Engineering, $27 billion (testing and design of electronics chips,
  machinery, car parts)
- Finance and accounting, $14 billion (accounts payable, billing,
  and financial and tax statements)
- Human resources, $13 billion (payroll administration, benefits,
  and training programs)
- Analytics, $12 billion (market research, financial analysis, risk
  calculation)[10]

What remained? Distribution, final assembly, marketing, and some
servicing. All else, including the management of risk, was entrusted to
others in the value chain.

In 1996, the National Labor Committee, a human rights group, reported that sweatshop labor was used to make clothes for the Kathie Lee line, sold at Wal-Mart.[11] The group reported that a worker in Honduras smuggled a piece of clothing out of the factory, which had a Kathie Lee label on it.[12] Labor activist Charles Kernaghan spoke to the media and accused Kathie Lee Gifford of being responsible for the sweatshop management activity. Gifford addressed Kernaghan's allegations on the air, explaining that she was not involved with hands-on project management in factories. Gifford subsequently contacted federal authorities to investigate the issue, and worked with U.S. federal legislative and executive branch agencies to support and enact new U.S. laws to protect children against sweatshop conditions. She appeared with President Clinton at the White House in support of U.S. federal government initiatives to counter international sweatshop abuses.[13]

LESSONS LEARNED *Managing risk to an organization is as—if not more—important to an organization's brand and reputation as it is to its finances. The Tylenol poisoning and subsequent recall in 1982 has long been held as the one of the best managed (and scariest) events where an organization's brand and overall sustainability of their business was in question. Of course, the greater concern was the health and welfare of the general public. As it turned out, Johnson & Johnson took control, issued a complete and swift product recall, improved the security on the packaging, and even created a new tamper-proof gel cap. Their actions are still viewed as one of the best cases of how to effectively handle a recall. Tylenol's market share went from 35% to 8%, but because of their exemplary handing of the recall they were able to reclaim 92% of capsule segment sales.[14] At the heart of brand/reputation risk is trust and a level of customer confidence that sometimes takes years to establish.*

Organizations today have a social responsibility (sometimes referred to as CSR: corporate social responsibility) and a duty of care to fully understand the risks to an organization's value chain (i.e., the processes and resources that support the creation of value). They must have a clear line of sight of all process and resources up and down the value chain (regardless of whether they are performed internally or externally), educate and train their business partners on acceptable risk practices, and frequently assess/test/validate and report on the state of various risks. This line of sight/unobstructed view is necessary to avoid some recent and highly visible events such as: 1) the substitution of stated ingredients with cheaper variations (product risk); 2) workplace issues such as discrimination, safety standards, or child-labor practices (labor risk); 3) the effect to the community and natural resources as a result of the release of dangerous by-products (environmental risk); and, 4) the subcontracting of critical processes to less expensive and unapproved vendors (sourcing risk).

Change 6

Virtualization and consolidation of the physical work environment (e.g., IT facilities, warehouses, suppliers, and transportation systems).

Risk: Many organizations have consolidated their physical footprints and virtualized the officer worker to improve their return on investment. This concept of making an asset more productive was at the center of massive productivity gains in the 1990s. Some examples include eliminating expensive office space and virtualizing the workforce (remote/mobile access and computing), leasing capital-intensive assets, and consolidating and automating labor-intensive functions. As a result, single points of failure became more prevalent, thus increasing the risk profile. Here are a few examples:

- Factories and assembly lines became totally automated, increasing the dependence on sophisticated technology, concentrating resouces where many single points of failure now exist.
- Most manufacturing, assembly and testing was outsourced to the Asia-Pacific region in the 1990s, thus creating massive sourcing, transportation, and communication single points of failure points. For example, on December 26, 2006, a 7.1 magnitude earthquake off the coast of Taiwan disrupted 98% of Taiwan's communications with Malaysia, Singapore, Thailand and Hong Kong —almost no calls could be made to Southeast Asia.

- The workforce was transitioned from large central offices to virtual remote and/or home locations, thus creating heavy reliance on remote communications, systems capacity/throughput (e.g., firewall, virtual private network contention) and general public network bandwidth.

- Organizations, vital records were converted from physical hard copy to digital data, thus creating a technology-based single point of failure and concentration of sensitive personal and corporate date that can be illegally accessed at unsecured facilities. This not only presents hardware risks, but also software risks because the software used to access this information frequently becomes obsolete.

While these six mega-changes were taking place, one particular vulnerability was increasing: the failure by many organizations to align their strategy with this new operating reality. As a result, many were becoming exposed to greater losses and longer disruptions since most risk strategies focused on the facility/property and not the entire value chain.

> ### CASE STUDY
>
> A regional disruption had a significant impact on a large defense contractor, Northrop Grumman. They became a multibillion-dollar victim when Hurricane Katrina made landfall in the southeastern United States on August 29, 2005. Their technology, facilities, vital records, and 20,000 workers were all concentrated in a very small area in Mississippi as well as key external communications, public utilities, and logistics providers. As a result of the rising waters and wind damage, it was estimated by the company that Katrina cost it an additional 8 million labor hours on the 12 ships currently under construction. The company's insurer, the Factory Mutual Insurance Company, has denied payment on the ground that Northrop's policy did not include coverage for hurricane flood damage.[15] Here's an example of a regional outage that affected the Pascagoula, Mississippi, area as well as the entire southeast region of the United States. This was the hub of a collaborative effort with Navy and other contractors to build the next generation of warships for the U.S. fleet. The organization's data center consisted of 350 Unix, Windows 2000, and Windows NT servers; 5.8 terabytes of

data, and hundreds of man-years of engineering work. A disaster recovery plan was in place for many years; the organization regularly tested these plans. However, they were simply overwhelmed by the magnitude of destruction. Within 30 days of the disaster, 12,500 of the 19,800 workers in the ship sector returned to work. However, 6,582 did not return (i.e., eventually, 3,020 workers went on various forms of approved leave and another 3,562 did not go back). Another 715 were not accounted for 30 days after the hurricane. Production on 11 ships resumed in New Orleans, Gulf Port, and Pascagoula. Damage to the regionally centralized data center was extensive. In fact, the entire data center was lost. They later resumed operations in Dallas, deciding not to return to Mississippi. In addition, 33% of desktops were lost, and so was most of the telecom infrastructure; more than 200 servers; and the entire public communications, utilities, safety, health, and security infrastructure.[16]

Here are a few more examples of material consequences that occurred by aggregating resources or creating single points of failure:

- **Blackout at 4:10 PM, August 14, 2003:** Fifty million customers lost power in eight states; in Ontario, the Toronto Stock Exchange shut down; bank ATMs went down; and New York City cell phone networks became overloaded. Estimated loss, somewhere between $4 and $10 billion. Source: US Department of Energy and North American Electric Reliability Council.

- **Impact to telecom from Katrina:** Three million phone lines, 300,000 still without power one month later, 1000k cell towers to be restored. Cleanup costs exceeded $100 billion.

- **9/11 terrorist event:** $24 to $28 billion in property damage, loss of 6 buildings (13.42 million sq. ft.), 9 buildings heavily damaged (15.1 million sq. ft), 16 other buildings suffered minor damage (10 million sq. ft.), 36 miles of telecomm cabling, 300k phones, 4.5 million data circuits serving 140,000 Verizon customers, two major Con Ed electrical substations, MTA and Path trains $7.3 billion to repairs service, and $5 billion in equipment losses (IT, communications, furniture, software & services).

Unfortunately, the world of managing risk has not significantly progressed while all this change was taking place. Many organizations tried to solve this dilemma by deploying corporate-driven holistic enterprise risk management (ERM) programs. Those involved with the deployment of these programs have been and are still struggling to gain the support of executive management. Unfortunately, ERM is not a silver bullet. It has its place in providing a common language, protocols, and framework for managing organizational risk holistically. However, support might be diminishing. In a recent survey by The Conference Board, CEOs were asked the question, "How important do you consider ERM?" In 2004, only 39% of the CEOs and 30% of the COOs said it was important. When asked the same question in 2006, their enthusiasm appeared to further diminish since only 34% of the CEOs and 28% of the COOs said it was important.[17] As a result organizations find it more difficult to fund and implement comprehensive risk management solutions, and are left with tremendous risk.

Here are several trends that reflect the growing gap in an organization's ability to identify and manage the rapidly expanding risk universe:

- Rapid changes and accelerating risk caused by globalization, revenue pressures, competition, and regulation.
- Loss of direct control, geographical separation, communication gaps, and language barriers over key resources and processes that the organization depends on to create value.
- Growing pressure to improve margins by shedding activities that are not core to the business, reducing inventory and cutting discretionary spending.
- Increasing dependencies on other external entities (e.g., port operators, customs agencies, freight forwarders, outsourcers, job shops) across a global and disbursed value chain.
- Escalating empowerment of business partners, suppliers, and customers with inconsistent and sometimes conflicting risk standards, cultures, and expectations.

- Lack of critical and timely risk intelligence and the sensors/ listening posts needed to continuously collect and analyze the information.
- Inability to measure the impact of risk and the investment needed to manage this risk.
- Lack of a risk-conscious culture (attitude/philosophy, incentives/ penalties, education/training/awareness programs, metrics, urgency, engagement of stakeholders, etc.).
- Constant premature redeployment of risk investments and resources to activities perceived to be more important to the business.
- Lack of consistent risk policy and standards.

In Malcolm Gladwell's *Tipping Point: How Little Things Can Make a Big Difference*, he discussed the counterintuitive concept of how things can get out of hand very quickly. The tipping point becomes the flash point in the risk process, at which time systemic risk becomes unleashed and cascades wildly and blindly through interdependent value chains. The ramifications of these risk failures will continue to increase as organizations become more interconnected in the global marketplace.

A general manager of a major consumer packaged goods company described one such scenario where an unruly fan at a baseball game in the United States threw a glass beer bottle at a player on the field. Fortunately, it missed the player but the damage had been done. Next came the flash point. The commissioner of baseball, the owner of the team, stadium management, and the general public were appalled. As a result of the fan's action, glass bottles were banned at baseball games across the country. The beer industry quickly switched from glass to plastic bottles (and then to aluminum cans). Within days, the price of plastic/resin increased sharply, and within weeks there was a shortage of plastic since the beer companies quickly scoffed up the available supply of plastic. Unfortunately, this GM's consumer packaged goods company relied almost exclusively on plastic to package all of its products. Needless to say, they were a smaller company and needed to find an alternative quickly. As a result, they had to switch their production capabilities over to glass, thus driving up the cost of the product. Although somewhat of a simplistic example, the point is that this event caused a ripple effect impacting multiple industries. You need to look beyond your own value chain and consider competitive dependencies that arise when others rely on the same vendors/suppliers.

Management is typically forced to rethink they way they react and manage risk once the flash point is reached. Unfortunately, the initial reaction is typically one of overreaction, and not based on adequate investigation and factual information. My experience has shown that when an event occurs there is typically overmitigation before the optimal balance is found. To avoid this overreaction management needs:

- Timely and accurate data of the potential impacts being exposed (quantitative and qualitative)
- Mitigation options, costs, and implementation considerations
- Coordination and knowledge of potentially affected stakeholders
- Accountability (assignment of responsibilities)
- A decision process to support the "informed decisions"

An overreaction is costly and sometimes very disruptive since it introduces abrupt change that, in many instances, diminishes over time. A risk-based change (versus a market-based change) is usually the most difficult to gain support for, implement, and sustain since it typically has unknown stakeholder implications and does not *appear* to possess measurable and tangible benefits. This risk mitigation effort is often rejected or reversed over time because it is "too costly" or "it cannot happen to us." A wonderful excuse not to do anything else—maybe we should refer to this as the *sinking* point.

CASE STUDY **A TYPICAL RISK MITIGATION SCENARIO — "COMPLACENT DANCES"**

One Fortune 500 organization ran up $50 million in security costs over 18 months post-9/11. The deployment of guards, new procedures, background checks, and perimeter monitoring security were all part of the original allocation. Three years later, the guards had been laid off, background checks limited to only a few people, cameras were not being monitored, and entry to facilities was back to pre-9/11 procedures. By the way, that $50 million encompassed direct costs and did not include time lost (diversion of employees from other projects, manage time, etc.) or the soft costs involved in deploying the solution.

One might argue that the organization overreacted to the threat and then realized it did not need all these measures when it had a chance to more calmly evaluate them, post 9/11. Although I consider this partially true, what is certain is now the risk mitigation actions have shifted to the other extreme: limited risk mitigation. The security threat, whether terrorist or not, still exists. A simple business case analysis was needed early in the process. The analysis should have included an assessment of the costs to maintain these controls over a multiyear/multistaged plan.

One final note here: beware of the risk solution that attempts to eliminate the risk. These "extreme" tactics achieve the risk objective, but may not be financially or operationally feasible. One can typically find some sort of work-around when the operational or social interference is too great—for example, the organization attempts to address the problem of users' selecting weak passwords to gain access to sensitive systems by implementing complex password schemes: subsequently, users "sticky note" passwords to the monitor. A lesson I've learned over my long career is that the work-around does not take very long to appear and it *will* happen, for sure if the solution impedes an employee's ability to easily do his/her job. One of the most bizarre examples of a work-around that I personally witnessed was at a chemical manufacturing plant in Mexico. The organization had decided to implement security tokens on the shop floor that required the workers to not only enter their password but also to enter a random six-digit number that was generated every 60 seconds on this credit card–device. The purpose of this additional feature was to improve security and accountability since the sign-on also served as a time clock for the payroll records. One week after the company had made the investment in the new technology, the workers on the floor decided to tape all their cards and associated passwords next to the computer terminal. The first worker in the morning would then sign-on for all his co-workers. The lesson learned here is to evaluate the behavioral impact of any risk mitigation solutions.

WHY SHOULD I CARE? IS THIS RELEVANT TO MY ORGANIZATION (AND ME)?

As more mega-changes are introduced, risk will continue to increase at a rapid pace within a much shorter period of time. Exhibit 2.4 reflects the accelerated pace of change and the widening gap caused by the failure of organizations' risk management programs to keep pace with this change.

The question often arises, why should I care? Even when risks are explained, many fail to acknowledge the relevance to themselves or their organizations. The total denial and mutual denial so pervasive in organizations allows people to believe that "it won't happen to me." But consider a short list of reasons why everyone has a stake in addressing, preventing, and understanding risks:

1. **Corporate Social Responsibility (CSR).** It is not enough for organizations to merely be profitable; they also need to address the importance of social and community responsibility as a part

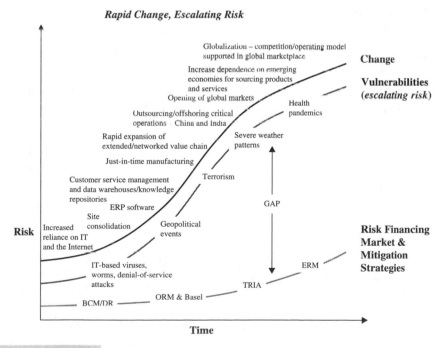

EXHIBIT 2.4   Rapid Change, Escalating Risk

of the culture itself. CSR goes beyond the brand. It's about more than purpose and why an organization exists—to create value for all stakeholders. Value includes not only economic benefits to investors and management, but also to the communities the organization serves. We are all in this together, and the mismanagement or ignoring of risk just creates a bigger impact later on. Some outmoded models of business life attempt to separate corporate functioning from personal ethics, but this is impractical and unrealistic. Just as the organization has an obligation to safeguard employees and their families, everyone within the organization has a corresponding obligation to society. This was demonstrated in past decades in emerging environmental awareness, reconciling the idea that it is not all right to pollute waterways in the interest of higher profits, or to fill the sky with toxins. This enlightened model—including awareness of and concern for society at large—is today a part of the global business family as well as simple operational mandates.

2. **To ensure the survivability of the ongoing concern.** Managing risk and ensuring that all stakeholders accept responsibility is not a one-time event. When those in charge completely ignore stakeholder risk and the risk is realized, then all involved are typically punished severely. We've witnessed this in the financial markets and at organizations such as Enron and Tyco. Managing risk has to be a continuing effort that involves and benefits everyone within the organization, including customers and stockholders as well as employees and their families. Losing stakeholder confidence and trust is the most damaging of all consequences.

3. **National and personal health, safety, and security.** In today's complex geopolitical environment, including the rapidly shrinking global business world, everyone has to be risk-conscious about the safety/security of their country as well as the personal health, safety and security of their family, and co-workers. Increasingly, organizational leaders are coming to realize that this is no mere platitude; it defines survival, both organizationally and personally. The threats of nuclear disaster, pandemics, and terrorist attacks are the most obvious threats. More subtle and invisible are cyber threats, potential

attacks on utilities, automation, and infrastructure, all complex and far-reaching in their implications.

4. **Personal liability, integrity, and damages.** Personal and organizational integrity is mandatory, and cannot be replaced with improved methodology; in fact, a real threat is that integrity may be lost in the shuffle of "improved" systems. Damage can occur at the individual or organization level, most commonly through employee or shareholder suits. The obligation of *duty of care* and *duty of loyalty* is not just directors' and officers' responsibility, but to be successful, must involve all stakeholders and is everyone's responsibility.

5. **Organizational implications of not addressing risk-related vulnerabilities.** The idea that "If I don't address risk issues, someone else will and that might impact my organization." Just as competitive companies have to continue to invent new, improved, more affordable products in order to compete in the future, they also need to develop new standards for effective risk management. Stakeholders will take aggressive action as they become more aware of the implications, especially if it suggests that there might be financial loss or personal liability. If the organization fails to take action when this occurs, then others might fill the void, such as regulators, nongovernment organizations (NGOs), special interest groups, and the media. Losing control of the decision to mitigate risk to outside regulators or special interest groups is a very dangerous situation because the financial, social, and operational impact of complying with these newly-imposed regulations will be an "unknown." The threat of regulation, versus allowing market pressure to dictate requirements, is something most senior executives are fearful of and therefore monitor closely. It does not matter if an organization does or does not want to implement the standards—they have no choice, as was experienced by publicly traded U.S. based organizations when Sarbanes-Oxley was implemented into law. The cost burden and implementation implications were something that publicly traded corporations were forced to manage. The threat of regulation typically follows a serious event such as product failure, environmental hazard, or natural disasters. Here are several examples that occurred immediately after the mishandling of the U.S.-based Hurricane Katrina disaster:

- House Committee on Science, Rep. Sherwood Boehlert (R-NY), Rep. Bart Gordon (D-Tenn) pushed for greater investigation into root cause of systemic failures in the context of the response and recovery to Hurricane Katrina.

- Senate Committee on Commerce questioned telecommunications executives about why the telecommunications infrastructure fared so poorly in the wake of Katrina (repeat of 9/11).

- Report in July, 2007 of 24 major agencies said to have "pervasive weaknesses in security practices" that could potentially cause a major failure of the infrastructure (run mostly by the private sector). A review by GAO stated that agencies have not yet conducted vulnerability assessments nor developed contingency plans.

This is one of the primary reasons why more and more organizations are taking the initiative to tackle the mega-risks such as carbon emissions, corporate social responsibility and organizational sustainability. DuPont, Wal-Mart, Virgin Group, and British Petroleum are all examples of "leaders" in this area. Here is example of changing security regulations that will affect the customs process and those organizations that are importing goods to the United States:

- A new U.S. law on maritime cargo scanning requirements will require foreign ports to scan every container they ship stateside by 2012.[18] Operators estimated average dwell time (the period during which a dynamic process remains halted in order that another process may occur) may increase to seven days from around five after 2012. These requirements affect approximately 700 ports around the world that ship goods to the United States. This is a case where managing the vulnerability/risk may create another risk and significantly increase expenses throughout the value chain. That is why the need to anticipate and monitor change and the "risk effect" is essential.

- New security accreditation systems for organizations' supply chains become part of the Authorized Economic Operator (AEO) recognized by Australian Customs Service. Premises and business procedures will be assessed against a series of security benchmarks (physical security, background checks, internal auditing of product movements). The United States has Customs-Trade Partnership Against Terrorism (C-TPAT) with three levels of accreditation. The EU introduced security accreditation criteria in January, Singapore launched theirs in May 2007, and New Zealand is testing one that deals only with exports. This unpredicted regulation will force all organizations that rely on transportation of cargo to totally rethink newly introduced supply chain vulnerabilities and impact on their bottom lines (impact to just-in-time delivery, customs/inspections, cold storage and perishable goods flow, inventory, storage/warehousing, etc.).

As additional mega-changes occur, the challenge for organizations is to create and sustain a risk-sensitive culture that encourages all individuals to take responsibility. For most organizations the hazard lights don't flash (or don't exist); negative information does not flow upward, is overly filtered, or is not aggregated to form a bigger risk picture; and those with the most knowledge and understanding don't get involved for fear of retribution or lack of incentives.

Many are afraid to challenge CEO or executive mandates for fear of being labeled "negative" or a roadblock. Many are also afraid to elevate risk issues when the sensors are activated (it's not for the lack of trying) and when they do, in many instances the bad news is suppressed. This becomes the *total denial* moment, when we all know what's at risk but choose to do nothing about it. Sadly, I am amazed at how frequently I still witness these total denial moments. I characterize this very common behavior in risk management as *event driven*, where an organization and people take action only *after* the risk has been realized. In 2006 and 2007 the world witnessed this extensively in the product recall, identity theft, and environmental risk areas.

Bottom Line

Change will *always* be accompanied by increased and broadened risk (as well as opportunity). Any time there is a change, a commensurate risk assessment and analysis should be conducted.

■ ENDNOTES

1. Samsung Halts Production of Chips After Power Outage, Bloomberg.com, August 3, 2007.
2. Georgia Institute of Technology and Massachusetts Institute of Technology, 2005
3. "A World of Connections," *The Economist*, April 28, 2007.
4. Don Tapscott and Anthony D. Williams, *Wikinomics*, Portfolio/Penguin Group, 2006.
5. "The New Titans," *The Economist*, September 16, 2006.
6. Ellen Sheng, "Pfizer Considers Outsourcing Up to 30% of Manufacturing," *The Wall Street Journal*, November 30, 2007.
7. Lynn Lunsford, "Cessna's New Plane To Be Built In China," *Wall Street Journal*, November 28, 2007, p. A14.
8. "Asia's Skills Shortage," *The Economist*, August 18, 2007.
9. "The Future of Outsourcing," *BusinessWeek*, January 30, 2006.
10. "The Future of Outsourcing," *BusinessWeek*, January 30, 2006.
11. "The Man Who Made Kathie Lee Cry," *Washington Post*, July 31, 2005.
12. *Zoned for Slavery: The Child Behind the Label*, New York: Crowning Rooster Arts, 1995.
13. http://en.wikipedia.org/wiki/Kathie_Lee_Gifford.
14. http://en.wikipedia.org/wiki/Tylenol_Crisis_of_1982.
15. http://www.corpwatch.org/article.php?id=13565.
16. "A CIO Discusses her Experience with Hurricane Katrina," *CIO Magazine*, April 15, 2006; "Opportunity from Disaster," *Unstrung*, May 26, 2006; "Four Disaster Survival Tips From Northrop Grumman," *Computerworld.com*, April 30, 2007; U.S. Securities and Exchange Commission. *8-K filing for Northrop Grumman Corporation*, 2005, EX99.1.
17. *Risk Business. Is Enterprise Risk Management Losing Ground?*, The Conference Board, Research Report R-1407-07-RR.
18. John W. Miller, *The Wall Street Journal*, October 25, 2007.

CHAPTER 3

The Vulnerable Organization

I don't trust anyone that works for this organization and neither should you. Keep looking and let me know what vulnerabilities you find!

—FORMER PRESIDENT OF A MAJOR FINANCIAL INSTITUTION

W hen someone tells you that you are at risk, it is logical to take action. You do not want to wait until the risk becomes a reality. However, at the organization level with its complex global reliance on subsidiary production and distribution, an unlimited number of constantly changing risks are often undetected or ignored. As a result, the resources that support the organization's value chains are vulnerable—it's people, technology and processing, physical environment, and relationships. In a litigious society, such as the United States, the directors' and executives' fiduciary responsibility create a duty of care and loyalty to their stakeholders. So how does an organization begin to shape its risk consciousness when facing the daunting task of managing their universe of vulnerabilities—the mismanagement of which can result in their personal fortunes being at stake? In other societies negligence is also viewed negatively, and the penalty is much more severe and seldom financial in nature.

A key component of risk, a threat or an impending peril, cannot be mitigated in the same way a vulnerability can, since it is beyond the organization's ability to control. The risk of a threat can only be avoided, accepted, and/or in some cases, financed (e.g., insurance). However, another component of risk, a vulnerability or point(s) of weakness, can be mitigated by the organization if it is identified and the impact understood. The organization may minimize the impact of vulnerability through effective mitigation and preparedness programs (establishing a viable risk management program). The goal of these programs is to build resilience (the ability to bounce back, i.e., survive loss or the unpredictable) and become more risk agile (the ability to avoid, move, change, and adjust rapidly to threats and vulnerabilities). Many organizations have programs in place to provide resiliency and agility. However, it is not uncommon for the operational units of a large organization to be executing hundreds of risk mitigation programs independently and at varying levels of effectiveness. The lack of integration and coordination among these mitigation programs (ineffective) and the possible misallocation of time and resources (inefficient) create significant vulnerability. Management believe that they are getting the job done since there is a funded program in place but the reality may be much different. But, are these programs effective, tested, and aligned with ongoing business priorities? The key is to stop wasting time and valuable management bandwidth guessing at what threat might actually occur and to establish a coordinated risk-conscious culture in which all employees and partners are trained and encouraged to recognize and report vulnerabilities. Organizations must also allocate their risk-related resources to the vulnerabilities that present the greatest potential impact to value.

WHY IS EVERY ORGANIZATION, REGARDLESS OF SIZE, MORE VULNERABLE IN TODAY'S BUSINESS ENVIRONMENT?

Are your organization's value chains vulnerable? Most would say yes, but others would argue that question is irrelevant—since there is no possible way to avoid being vulnerable. I would agree that value chains are vulnerable, but there are actions that can be taken to reduce exposure. The better questions are, "How is my organization's value chain vulnerable?" and "What would the impact to my organization, and its stakeholder's be if a given vulnerability was exploited?"

To operate in today's complex and competitive business environment an organization of any size must undertake risk, be lean, efficient, constantly changing, and resourceful. The solution is not, of course, for the organization to eliminate all risk. Instead, the business goal of managing risk should be to achieve balance—that is, the efficient and effective allocation of time, management attention, capital, and resources that will allow the organization to operate within an acceptable level of volatility.

All of this would be easy to achieve if the management of risk and the business environment were static. However, risk is dynamic and the elements of risk, threats, vulnerabilities, relevance, and probability are constantly changing (and in some instances, unknown). The organization's value chains are dynamic as well; the processes and resources that support the value chain are constantly being reconfigured and reallocated to achieve optimal efficiency and return. The always changing nature of threats and vulnerabilities and how they apply to the dynamic business environment is a primary reason why value chains are vulnerable. With this constant change comes greater complexity and more stakeholders responsible for the successful execution of the value chain, hence more points of vulnerability. All this is happening when the market for goods and services is much more competitive because of globalization. But with competitive pressures come greater business entrepreneurship and risk taking, creativity, and shortcuts. For example, what might appear as a simple, straightforward change—outsourcing a portion of the manufacturing process to a supplier located several thousand miles away—has the potential to expose an organization to dozens of new vulnerabilities. Without an active risk-conscious culture, the organization might not detect these vulnerabilities for years or even worse—not until they've become a reality. We don't have to look any further than the effects to health and safety as a consequence of not properly managing the risks to our environment. Of course, choosing a reactive rather than a proactive strategy to risk mitigation will always be more disruptive and costly. Remediation and retrofitting costs will outweigh preventative measures, not to mention the intangible impact of damage to one's profitability and reputation. That said, we must acknowledge that event-driven/reactive risk management is an operating reality that is difficult to reverse without a pervasive risk consciousness that initiates the risk process at the onset of change. Just take a look at the level of awareness and reinforcement/legal effort that is required to get the majority of people to respond to a personal risk such as wearing safety belts, managing financial risk, quitting smoking, and not drinking and driving.

Threats are everywhere—economic, financial, social, political, climate, environmental, and technical—the list is enormous. A product recall in China, and explosion at a major refinery, a tsunami in Indonesia could wreak havoc with worldwide supply chains and just-in-time, lean inventories. A labor strike by the port workers, a denial-of-service cyber attack on the Internet, a product or, worse, food recall or quality issue (e.g., Mad Cow, toy recall) are all events that if realized, can significantly harm the organization. But which threat is most important, which one should the organization worry about? Is it just low-probability, high-impact events that an organization should worry about? For the organization described in the following case study, it was not about a tsunami or earthquake, but the failure to understand the impact of the loss of a key resource—the skill set of the experienced worker.

CASE STUDY

VULNERABILITY

A simple decision to outsource production ("people change") in an attempt to achieve greater operational efficiency. The organization became vulnerable to quality risk issues when it lost its experienced worker—the corporate knowledge, memory and critical skills that produce industry-leading products.

RISK REALIZED: QUALITY SUFFERED—LOSS OF REVENUE, MARKET POSITION AND BRAND DAMAGE[1]

In 1993, Aris Isotoner, a manufacturer of gloves and slippers, was a highly successful division of Sara Lee Corporation. It was profitable, with sales of $220 million, 15% net profit, and high growth. Isotoner's plant in Manila, Philippines, was the crown jewel of the business. Highly skilled labor there had been turning out 27 million pairs of gloves a year at such low cost that even factories in China couldn't compete. One company executive later said that "The plant in the Philippines couldn't be duplicated. So many of the people had been there 15 years; they were so skilled. It was the lowest-cost producer in the world."

Trying to chase even lower costs, however, a new Aris Isotoner executive closed the Manila plant and sourced production to other Asian locales. As it turned out, the "low-cost" Asian suppliers Aris Isotoner chose to replace the in-house production ended up costing between 10% and 20% more.

Product quality plummeted. Aris Isotoner's sales also plunged. Three presidents later, the glove maker's sales had fallen by half, to $110 million. By 1997 operating losses had totaled $120 million, and Sara Lee had invested over $100 million to keep the company afloat. In late 1997, Sara Lee announced the sale of the once high-flying division to Totes Inc., a unit of Bain Capital, for a bargain price.

LESSON LEARNED *When the organization was considering change, did they assess the risk early in the change process (i.e., the vulnerability that would be created as a result of change)? Too often, organizations overlook the value of those employees that possess critical skills, intuition, experience, relationships, and knowledge resulting from years of employment. The impact of planned events such as retirement or carefully timed downsizing can be mitigated. Precipitous actions involving skilled employees may result in catastrophic risk exposure if careful planning and mitigation is omitted. Before personnel changes are made, a review of the value chain should be initiated to identify critical skills, relationships, and information that will be lost. It should also assess the risk implications and impact of such losses.*

Today, most companies know that it is critical to have succession plans in place in order to develop talent and consistently deliver strong financial results. Many of these companies fall into the trap of believing that these succession plans, which are extremely effective during the normal course of business, will also be sufficient during times of crisis. They also fall into the trap of creating succession plans that apply only to the seniormost management in the organization. The fatal flaw in that line of thinking is the fundamental fact that during a crisis it is not "business as usual," and these circumstances, which present elevated challenges, also require more sophistication in planning and preparation—and require the involvement at all levels in the value chain.

To better understand how to manage risk we must first identify/prioritize the activities/processes that represent the greatest value to the organization (revenue, quality, safety, etc.) and uncover the threats, vulnerabilities, likelihood, and consequences of a disruption. Here are key questions that represent a starting point in the process:

- How relevant is a particular threat to the organization's value chain? Can it be measured?
- How likely is it that a threat to your organization's value chain will be realized (e.g., probability of an earthquake damaging your facility)?
- How vulnerable is the organizations value chain(s), (i.e., a factor of the organization's risks consciousness, preparedness, agility, and resiliency, also contingent on timing of an event)?
- What is the impact/consequences of the threat's being realized?
- Where are the vulnerabilities, and which ones will hurt most?

Let's put the first two questions about threats aside for now since the likelihood of a threat's being realized and the relevance of a threat to your value chain(s) is, in most instances, difficult to estimate or calculate. Trying to predict the likelihood/probability of whether a threat might be realized is like throwing darts at moving dartboard, while blindfolded. Threat probability can be best calculated when there is historical/actuarial data (e.g., frequency of hurricanes in the past 50 years within a region), and even then it's a bit of a guessing game. Property insurance, as an example, is predicated on being able to model the impact of a peril. Although the probability that an event, such as a hurricane, will happen is also considered—the impact and value at risk are key to estimating coverage, premiums, and exclusions. If the loss and frequency of a threat can be statistically estimated with a reasonable degree of accuracy, then it is a candidate for risk financing (via a transfer or insurance product—underwriting property insurance to protect against fire and wind damage). Taking steps to soften the impact (backup generators, emergency relocation plans) or more drastic steps such as moving an operation to a safer location can greatly reduce the amount of risk.

So if the risk of a threat cannot be predicted and/or mitigated, then why do so many organizations exhaust an inordinate amount of energy on risk mitigation programs predicated on guessing when a threat might be realized? Or, worse yet, why are these same programs executed based on a narrow set of assumptions, such as defining a supply chain risk program that addresses security risk only while the goods are moving through customs—or a product risk program that addresses risk only during the manufacturing process, not the product design stage. The short answer—because a universal measure doesn't exist (i.e., globally accepted/consistent risk standard); it typically satisfies the auditors and compliance requirements, and it does not require additional effort, create conflict, or impose overhead.

CASE STUDY   SUPERFICIAL EFFORT = SUPERFICIAL OUTPUT

Avoiding Conflict And The Hard/Required Risk Work

One personal example stands out where a risk executive limited some important situational continuity work to a narrow set of assumptions and followed the path of least resistance. A very visible CEO of a Fortune 500 organization demanded that every operating segment within his empire be prepared for risk of a disaster. He wanted to ensure that each operating segment executive had a business continuity risk management program. The CEO designated a senior-level program manager to be in charge of this effort. The manager enlisted a consultant service provider to assist. However, the program manager viewed this task as an opportunity for personal advancement rather than an essential, but difficult, risk management effort. He believed that the operating segment executives, all of whom had just received the new CEO mandate, would perceive him as their savior if he were able to convince them that very little effort and investment would be needed to comply. He did not want to "rattle the cages" of those responsible for running the business, even if they were exposed. The fear was that he would get tossed out of their office if the initiative; a) took too much time, b) disrupted production, c) suggested any additional resource or capital investment, d) delayed the rollout of any new projects, and/or, e) required top management's involvement. In his defense, this is an age-old problem when the corporate folks enter into the world of the operating segments for the purpose of trying to gain support for a corporate initiative or sponsored program. The operating segment is where the money is made and the margins measured with laser-like precision, so it's only the extremely skilled and respected corporate few who can successfully influence the operating segments to invest any time, capital, or resources to managing risk. Realizing that it takes a lot to actually create such a program and make it succeed, the program manager simply promised the business unit heads that "this process would not take much of their time and *guaranteed* them that there would be no significant investment needed to complete it." What the program manager was *really* saying was that "we will check the box together to get to mutual denial and declare victory." He hoped to accomplish this with absolutely no alignment between value drivers and product processes, business cases, and real choices. He used a general approach to continuity that produced very large, well-organized manuals and addressed only a very small scope of predefined threat scenarios. For example, the plan assumed that the event would occur after-hours and the impact limited to just their facilities and operations, not the operations of those they depended on such as public infrastructure or their value chain partners.

Since the time that this situation was observed, three major disruptions occurred. A post-mortem should reveal the shortcomings of the existing continuity risk management program.

That is how many risk management plans work. Someone is put in charge of announcing that "we have managed our risk" and that finishes the job. In the case of the program manager, the real goal was a simple one. "All I really want," he explained, "is to make sure that the vendor I hired to create this continuity plan charges me rock bottom for the project and checks off the box that says we've put together a risk management program, whether it's a good plan or not. That would be a big plus for me with the top executives at the company. Nothing bad is going to happen here anyway." *He unilaterally made the decision on behalf of hundreds of senior managers on exactly how risk would be managed or, rather, unmanaged.* The bottom line is that there now is a false sense of preparedness and readiness that may in the future have catastrophic consequences. You have to wonder how many similar, equally dangerous time bombs exist in thousands of other organizations, which have been declared "risk free." Like a "recovered" drug addict rationalizing sneaking a fix now and then, many organizational risk programs often are delusional at best.

LESSON LEARNED *How should the project manager have assessed continuity risk and presented it to management? When given the mandate, he first needed to educate the CEO and operating segment executives of the level of effort required and potential project risks. If he did not have the experience/knowledge, then he should have reached out to his trusted network of peers or leaned more heavily on the consultants. He should have asked to describe "worst case" based on their experience working with similar clients. Examples of risks related to this project include the potential for capital investment related to additional mitigation efforts, liability created by documenting and acknowledging a vulnerability (starts the clock ticking), and potential for conflicting agendas within the operating segments. The project manager should work with executive management to devise a strategy on how to prioritize the business products and/or services. The project manager should analyze the entire value chain, that is, all the processes and resources needed to support the creation of value (inside and outside the organization) once all the priorities are understood. All vulnerabilities should be identified, assessed and their impact evaluated (more about this in the third section of the book). The vulnerable resources should be ranked according to level of risk management effort and impact. Those vulnerabilities requiring the greatest level of effort to mitigate and possessing the greatest potential impact from failure should be highlighted and elevated to executive management for a risk mitigation decision.*

A Note about Vulnerabilities and Resources

A resource is a component of the value chain that is a source of supply, one that can be readily drawn upon when needed.[2] The resource can be used to create other/more value and it can be physically, electronically and/or intellectually based.

RESOURCE

Understanding the *resource* concept is essential to managing risk in an organization's value chain because the resource is where the vulnerability exists.

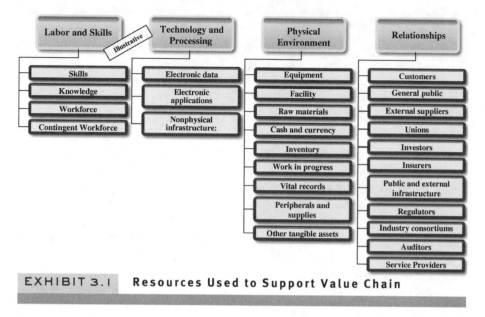

EXHIBIT 3.1   Resources Used to Support Value Chain

A process can also be considered a resource, but for now, I will exclude this from our definition. Exhibit 3.1 illustrates the four groups of resources that support the value chain and are exposed to risk/failure are:

1. Labor and the associated skill sets and knowledge
2. Technology and processing (that which is not physical)
3. Physical assets
4. Relationships

It's also where the risk lies.

WHY IS EVERY ORGANIZATION VULNERABLE (CONTINUED)

The Effect of Correlated Events in an Interdependent Ecosystem

Since 2005, I have been fortunate enough to have the opportunity to work with the World Economic Forum's Global Risk Network. During this process we studied 23 global macro risks to our interconnected society, political systems, and economies. A central tenet of the work was that global risks do not manifest themselves in isolation; their drivers, triggers,

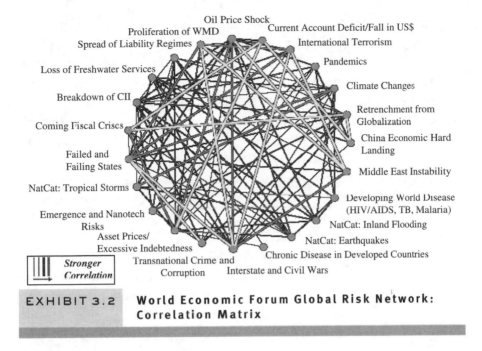

Oil Price Shock
Proliferation of WMD
Spread of Liability Regimes
Current Account Deficit/Fall in US$
International Terrorism
Loss of Freshwater Services
Pandemics
Climate Changes
Breakdown of CII
Retrenchment from Globalization
Coming Fiscal Crises
China Economic Hard Landing
Failed and Failing States
Middle East Instability
NatCat: Tropical Storms
Developing World Disease (HIV/AIDS, TB, Malaria)
Emergence and Nanotech Risks
NatCat: Inland Flooding
Asset Prices/ Excessive Indebtedness
NatCat: Earthquakes
Chronic Disease in Developed Countries
Transnational Crime and Corruption
Interstate and Civil Wars

Stronger Correlation

EXHIBIT 3.2   **World Economic Forum Global Risk Network: Correlation Matrix**

and consequences are interconnected. One of the exercises that the group engaged in was to assess the correlation between events (e.g., public policy of energy security and climate change). This was referred to as static interconnectedness or how heavily one macro-level risk influenced another macro-level risk. For example, one way to assess interdependent risk is to better understand the correlation between events such as transnational crime/corruption and failed/falling states.[3] This process can be applied at the organization/stakeholder level as well. This approach, although a bit esoteric, is extremely relevant to the discussion about understanding and modeling interdependency risk. There is a need to understand how the consequences of one risk can trigger a series of cascading events that result in a catastrophic outcome (see Exhibit 3.2).

How Does Every Level of Change Make My Organization Potentially Vulnerable?

The modern structure of organizations and their critical value chains that extend across the globe has made them more exposed than ever to maliciousness, errors in judgments, shifting organizational priorities and structures, and threats. One statistic is stunning: in 2003,[4] only 6% of Wal-Mart's merchandise came from abroad; today, more than 80% of the 6000 factories in Wal-Mart's worldwide database are in China.[5] Its imports increased from $9.5 billion in 2001 to $26.7 billion in 2006, an increase of 181%.[6] The concentrating of suppliers in one region of the world, that has a history of natural catastrophes (see Exhibit 3.3 on page 75), has placed the world's largest retailer and many others in a precarious position. The decision to rely so heavily on imports from China was also one of the primary reasons for the success of Wal-Mart, since it was able to procure goods at a price that was lower than anywhere else in the world. Fortunately, Wal-Mart is keenly aware of this risk and has been aggressively working to mitigate this geoconcentrational exposure. We don't have to look very far to uncover vulnerability in Wal-Mart's value chain. These shared resource providers, such as the port operators or maritime companies, create a vulnerability to Wal-Mart as well as thousands of other organizations that ship their goods through the ports in Asia. The resiliency and agility of the port operators and maritime shipper's value chains is essential to Wal-Mart's and others' success. Other operational vulnerabilities such as labor issues and transportation accidents in the Asia–Pacific region is a major concern and leaves Wal-Mart's value chain dangerously esposed especially during peak holiday periods, due to the high concentration of ports/carriers and limited shipping lanes. The migration of the value chain to be so heavily concentrated in Asia happened over several years, what many would consider to be a slow, incremental process. This is typically how a small risk turns into a very big risk. All those that benefit from taking the risk keep piling on (sorry, American football term)—let's say, keep adding to what was originally considered to be a small vulnerability.

Many operators of these supply/value chains indirectly or unknowingly support multiple clients as we witnessed in Chapter 1, Case 2. Often, the needs of each of these clients are in conflict when they face a reduction in capacity/bandwidth/throughput.

KEY LEARNING POINT

It is essential that the clients know their value chain partners and proactively understand what actions will occur if there is a risk issue (will they be in the front or the back of the line). The burden is on the client to take the initiative "to know" and take whatever action is needed at a time of crisis.

The March 2000 Nokia/Ericsson/Philips incident is an example that is frequently referenced when discussing proactive versus reactive risk management. Philips' manufacturing facility in Albuquerque, New Mexico, produced radio frequency chips (RFCs) for cellular telephone giants Nokia and Ericsson. A small fire broke out in the clean room, disrupting the manufacturing process for an unknown period. Nokia's response was two-fold—the company immediately created an executive-led "strike team" that pressured Philips to dedicate other plants to making the RFCs that Nokia needed. Nokia engineers also quickly redesigned the RFCs so that the company's other suppliers in Japan and the United States could produce them. The plan worked: through quick action, Nokia was able to meet its production goals and even boost its market share from 27% to 30%—a level more than two times that of its nearest rival. Ericsson, however, reacted much more slowly—the company did not become aware of the supply problems for weeks, by which time its ability to meet customer demand had been seriously compromised. And because Ericsson relied exclusively on the Albuquerque plant for the RFCs, Ericsson—unlike Nokia—found itself with nowhere else to turn for these vital components. Ericsson posted a nearly $1.7 billion loss for the year, and ultimately had to outsource its cellular handset manufacturing business to another firm.[7]

The port operator and maritime shipping industry serves as another very good example of a shared resource that, if failed, would have devastating consequences to those that did not take immediate and aggressive action to manage its risk. The 6 top container ports in the world are all concentrated in the Asia-Pacific rim.[8] They are: Singapore, Hong Kong, Shanghai, Shenzhen/China, Busan/South Korea, and Kaohsiung/Taiwan. In fact, of the top 11 ports in the world, these 6 ports handle 72% (110.3 million of a total of 153.3 million) of the units shipped. And unlike other regions of the world, there is little capability to reroute containers *en masse* to other ports via an efficient and sophisticated highway and inter-modal/trucking system. Clearly, this is a major vulnerability. But who is thinking about it? And what organizations, public or private, will be given preferential treatment if capacity is reduced 70%?

As change has occurred over the past two decades, the big question is whether Western organizations that rely on the Asia-Pacific region as their primary source of goods have assessed or responded to the aggregated risk picture. I recently asked the senior risk manager at a major global port operator "What keeps you up at night?" His response, "Singapore." He went on to say, "Most organizations do not realize, or consider, that when goods depart Asia-Pacific ports, a majority of these goods are transferred between ships at the Singapore ports." In fact, half of the world's goods, including manufactured items, energy resources, and IT components, ship through the hub port of Singapore. Its own vulnerabilities translate to every end user, supplier, and employee involved in buying and reselling raw materials. In Singapore harbor, working round the clock, a ship docks every two to three minutes, and volume of the movement of goods is unimaginable, with over 100,000 containers on site at any one time, generating an annual volume of 20 million containers from 122 countries. Yet, ships pass through one of the narrowest waterway channels in the world, and these are mega-ships 20 stories high and as long as 1250 feet (380 meters). As a hub, Singapore serves as port of exit for virtually all Asian suppliers; yet it faces numerous risks: traffic problems involving ships and trucks, crane operation, potential accidents on port and in the water (collisions are rare but they have occurred), terrorism, and even piracy (a piracy attack on a ship approaching or leaving Singapore occurs over 100 times per year).[9]

In this high-tech, complex international supply chain, a single event—a relatively minor one—could stop movement of goods completely. Even if the delay occurred for only a few days, the sheer volume of activity would have a rippling effect for several months and create potentially dire shortages everywhere, and affecting everyone from Wal-Mart and Dell Computer down to Mom-and-Pop operations in Muncie, Indiana. The vulnerability of this system demonstrates that supply chain operations must include an assessment of vulnerabilities and mitigation actions such as contingency plans, back-up suppliers and routing systems, and emergency-level inventories.

The risk manager presented two other types of risks that he is most concerned with—theft of goods and delays caused by pirates on the open seas, and the humanitarian issue of stowaways. In a separate conversation I had with a director on the board of a maritime shipping company, he shared his concern about the risk of pirates because of the threat to the safety of the shippers and the delays caused in shipping. For example, on October 28, 2007, a chemical tanker carrying up to 10,000 tons of highly explosive benzene was seized. Somali pirates hijacked more than two dozen ships in 2007, and they were trained fighters and in some cases linked to the powerful Somali clans. They were outfitted with sophisticated arms and global positioning systems (GPS) devices that led them to merchant ships, vessels carrying aid, and once even a cruise ship. This is an increasingly dangerous risk.[10]

Let's return to the Wal-Mart discussion about vulnerability that arises when relying primarily on others. I use Wal-Mart as the example because of their size and role in the bigger social and economic system. Many

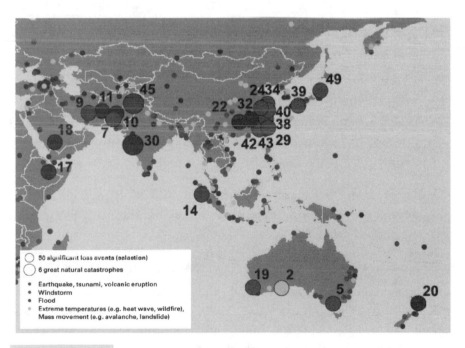

EXHIBIT 3.3   Asia-Pacific—A Risky Region

SOURCE: Munich Re.

others are dependent on Wal-Mart, so demonstrating interdependent risk and the cascading consequences of failure here is fairly straightforward. However, it should be noted that Wal-Mart in my opinion, is one of the most aggressive and progressive organizations in understanding and managing risk. Their corporate social responsibility and supplier audit and training programs are among the best.

I ask you to imagine for a moment a one-month disruption to Wal-Mart's Asia-based supply chain. Let's say the event was a pandemic outbreak of avian flu in the region (similar to the SARS outbreak in Hong Kong between November 2002 and July 2003, with 8,096 known infected cases and 774 deaths[11]). Now picture the direct impact and cascading effect (interdependent and correlated risks) it would also have on the Wal-Mart stakeholder base—the employees, customers, suppliers, investors, transportation companies, financial institutions, communities, and federal/state tax revenue. What would be the macro social and economic impacts to the:

- More than 7.2 billion customers who visit Wal-Mart stores every year, many who live on fixed budgets and rely on the availability of just-in-time purchases?

- 1.9 million employees and an estimated 3 million indirect workers who rely on the retailer?

- Global economic impact of the misstep of an organization that generates $345 billion in sales (2006) and operates more than 4,000 facilities?

These implications place a heavy burden on Wal-Mart, as well as other mega-organizations, to both protect themselves and the many participants in their extended value chain?[12]

Now maybe you are thinking that a pandemic is a bit of a stretch. However, the potential of an earthquake in the China region, resulting in significant consequences, is not. In 1995, the 7.2 Great Hanshin Earthquake in Kobe, Japan killed approximately 5,500, injured more than 26,000, and caused an estimated US$200 billion in economic loss. Supply chains around the globe were significantly disrupted when all 22 loading cranes and 235 out of 239 berths were damaged or destroyed.[13] An incident of this magnitude that affected any of the major Asian ports in Shanghai

(China), Shenzhen (China), Busan (South Korea), Hong Kong, and/or Singapore could be catastrophic to the global retail industry and all those who depend on it.

Although the above examples represent dramatic and catastrophic vulnerabilities, all organizations are faced with literally thousands of points of risk that, if realized, could have devastating and systemic effects to one or more parts of the value chain. Organizations have become more vulnerable as their business model sheds them of most of their past core competencies. The day of Henry Ford–like vertically integrated supply chains and direct control over all processes is long gone (with the exception of, e.g., manufacturing companies in China). As a result, they modularize components of their value chains and reestablish them as globally dispersed ecolike networks. For those exploiting these ecolike networks, lost is the direct control, and accountability, auditable quality standards, knowledge/experience, traceability, simplicity, and, most of all the foundation of properly managed risk—the known/trust factor, or what we might term the "know your global business partners" rule.

These exposures are similar in the fact that they refer to continuity risk. If the supply chain is disrupted, business comes to a grinding halt. But beyond continuity, the range of possible losses is vast. It is easy to focus on supply chain losses and threats to continuity because they are well-known. But consider the less obvious risks, too: cyber attacks, bacteriological or chemical terrorism, a nuclear explosion, weather catastrophes, disgruntled employee sabotage, theft or industrial espionage . . . the list is endless. Every organization is vulnerable to a host of possible risks. Even a narrow, short-term stoppage of operations causing continuity losses could effectively end an organization's ability to continue its operations. Many companies operate on a thin margin of working capital, and could not survive even relatively short downtime.

A broader shutdown, let's say a border shutdown, is not too farfetched, either. It happened following the September 11, 2001, terrorist attacks. The major automakers had to idle their plants since critical parts were sitting at the Mexican and Canadian borders. Ford Motor Company alone reported a fourth quarter 2001 reduction in output of 13 percent.[14]

But an incident does not have to be as catastrophic and obvious as a terrorist strike. While working at Booz Allen Hamilton, I was involved with a port security wargame where we simulated a dirty bomb entering the port of Los Angeles and being forwarded on to Detroit undetected. At the time, only 2% of the inbound containers were being inspected, so the scenario was not so farfetched. Once the bomb was detonated and traced back to Los Angeles port, the order was given to shut down all the ports in the United States. Now that was the easy part, as we found out during the game. The difficulty was figuring out who had the authority to officially reopen the ports. Since the repercussions were significant, all those involved were a bit hesitant to be the one to give the go-ahead to reopen. Meanwhile, the clock kept ticking and economic losses piled up.

How Has Change Left Others that I Depend on Vulnerable?

The challenge of managing an organization's vulnerabilities is further complicated by the concept of *interdependent* risk.

INTERDEPENDENT RISK

The weakest link concept, or the mentality that "if they are vulnerable, I am vulnerable."

Many organizations today have a false sense of immunity since they believe that all they have to worry about is only the risk they can see or directly control. I witnessed this over the past three years as I watched organizations declare victory when preparing for a health-related risk such as a pandemic (i.e., the avian flu). The majority of the several hundred pandemic preparedness strategies and plans that I reviewed or was exposed to were thorough in that they addressed important people issues such as hygiene, benefits, travel, and emergency actions. However, only a handful of these plans addressed the broader external scope of the organization's value chain. They simply failed to address the economic resiliency of the interdependent value chain. More than 90% of these plans assumed that pandemic preparedness was being provided with the same thoroughness by someone else, including those in the public sector. They chose to assume that someone else understood their risk needs and was effectively managing them. What I also discovered was that although some of these organizations communicated their pandemic risk preparedness requirements to their business partners, they were not willing to invest any more time or effort to validate or test that these partners were complying with their requirements. In other words, they were willing to assign the management of risk of their value chains to others. They were also willing to "assume" that others understood their risk requirements and successfully implemented a risk mitigation solution and risk-conscious culture. Outsourced logistics, customs, upstream suppliers, downstream distribution and warehousing, communications, public infrastructure, insurance, and other aspects of the organization's value chain—the management of risk all left to others and chance. Is that any way to assure continued success of the business? Is that an effective level of diligence and reasonable care? If you rely on others (outsourcers, energy providers, communications companies, public sector customs and border protection, transportation carriers, underwriters, banks), assume you are vulnerable. However, if they have implemented a risk mitigation strategy that is in sync with your expectations, and requirements, then the result is different. Be sure to validate that it is in sync with your program (if you are a small organization, then your requirements may matter less). The more difficult task is to identify where you might be vulnerable and how to prioritize vulnerabilities in a way that deals with the greatest impacts first.

Vulnerabilities have been and will always be present throughout an organization's value chain; the key is to be able to quickly prioritize which ones, if realized, will cause the organization the most harm. A terror attack in India could disable the customer service operations of hundreds of financial, technology, and telecommunications organizations. But are these vulnerabilities where what I refer to as the Risconomics (i.e., the allocation of precious time, management focus, resources, and capital) process should begin? Is customer service the most critical process to creating/providing value? What is my risk profile and tolerance for this critical service? For a large insurance company, the claims service and call center might just be at the top of the list of "most important" value drivers.

AUTO MANUFACTURES DISCOVERS THE "REAL" VALUE OF $1.50 PART TO ITS MULTIBILLION DOLLAR SUPPLY CHAIN

On July 16, 2007, at 10:13 A.M. local time, a 6.6 magnitude earthquake occurred. Riken, a key supplier in the automotive supply chain, lost its production facilities as a result of the quake. Riken produces piston rings that are sold for approximately $US 1.50. As a result of the Riken failure, Toyota had to temporarily shut down 12 domestic production lines and delay shipment of 55,000 vehicles. This was just-in-time production, and the failure of a key supplier meant failure of the supply chain. But the disruption did not idle just Toyota's supply chains. It also forced closure of nearly 70% of Japan's auto production. Automotive manufacturers such as Honda Motor Company had to close a plant that produces Civic and Fit models. Nissan Motor Company, Mitsubishi Motors Corporation, Mazda Motor Corporation, Suzuki Motors Corporation and Fuji Heavy Industries Ltd (Subaru) all also stopped or slowed down production.[15] All of these manufacturers had a supplier/supply-based vulnerability that if realized, was going to result in significant impact to the value chain.

LESSON LEARNED *Organizations must take the time to fully understand their extended value chains, and they cannot assume that someone else is addressing risk. Even if this were true, the way others are addressing risk might not meet/exceed the organization's expectations, or risk mitigation/financing efforts might not be performed in the most efficient way possible. A clear line-of-sight is needed before risks can be holistically identified, measured, and eventually treated. Traceability back to the source is required by many countries if the product produced is a consumer or food product. Executives should be asking questions such as "Where does my supply chain begin—the farm, mine, forest, fields—and who/how is risk being addressed." Other questions that should be asked are:*

- *Does the organization have a clear and documented understanding of all of the key processes and resources (i.e., farm to fork) that are needed to create the product?*
- *Is that program consistently implemented across the product/service value chain?*
- *Is it being tested and monitored on a routine basis?*
- *Is there a risk-conscious culture deployed where everyone who interacts with the value chain feels empowered to push "bad news" upstream as quickly as possible?*

WHAT'S WRONG WITH TODAY'S STRATEGIES AND SOLUTIONS?

To this point we've discussed how change impacts risk, the shortcomings of a threat-based risk program, the challenge of trying to address the massive points of vulnerability that exist in an organization's globally distributed value chain(s), and the need to prioritize risk mitigation activities (Risconomics). Now I would like to introduce one more concept that typically leads to significant vulnerability, and as such, must be addressed in the risk program. It is the concept of the "assumption." A few of the most commonly used risk mitigation planning assumptions and observations are described below.

ASSUMPTIONS

Most are not explicitly stated but they are, in my experience, implied, and exist in almost every organization. I believe most of the assumptions are flawed, and the lesson learned here is that they should be avoided.

Commonly Used Risk Mitigation Planning Assumptions and Observations

- I can manage and mitigate threats.
- I need only to manage what's in my immediate perimeter.
- The organization has the capacity (time, resources, management attention, and capital) to address and respond to all risk.
- Organizations not under my direct control have the same risk-sensitive attitude that I do.

- When the organization responds to risk, it does so by deploying solutions without first identifying, assessing, measuring, and pricing risk.

- Organizations do not factor in the cost of risk when implementing lean, Six Sigma, or supply chain optimization efforts, or when quantifying cost savings of those efforts.

- Negative events and event-related impacts do not always provide the impetus or motivation for an organization to focus on addressing its supply chain risks.

- The process for choosing "critical" suppliers is often flawed—sometimes it is important to consider aspects of one's internal operations as being suppliers and manage them accordingly. Additionally, infrastructure, such as ports, roads, and rail lines used in the supply chain, must not be overlooked.

- Lack of visibility beyond "tier 1" or primary suppliers creates significant supply chain blind spots from which unexpected risks can emanate—line of sight from raw material source to the end customer is essential.

- Demand volatility can have significant supply chain impacts—most companies focus on financial volatility and fluctuation within set tolerance ranges from a pricing perspective, not including considerations that the resources in question may become completely unavailable (i.e., demand shifts caused by a use of the resource for other than the intended purpose).

- Assumptions in supply chain risk management are often too narrowly defined (focusing on the expected, known and controllable).

- More risk gaps. Unfortunately, the response by many organizations is to propagate the strategy of reactive, silo thinking, that is, managing the risk of the latest threat by a small group of people in the organization, usually detached from the broader (corporate) risk management program (see Exhibit 3.4).

The scope of risk thinking is a narrower, more segmented, more reactive (last event, latest priority), and event-driven management philosophy. It includes deployment of risk solutions without understanding operating, social, economic, and/or financial implications.

To summarize, the scope and relevancy of threats and vulnerabilities are greater than ever before. Your organization exists in a global environment,

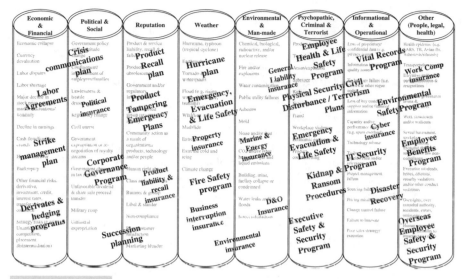

EXHIBIT 3.4 **Typical Risk Response — Segmented Risk Mitigation Programs**

whether it is affected directly or indirectly by globalization. If your organization uses the Internet to communicate (e.g., e-mail) or to support the business (e.g., ordering, servicing, procuring goods)—you by default are *interconnected* into the global infrastructure. If you rely on customers, suppliers, financers, insurers, or public infrastructure outside of your immediate control and geography, then you are *interdependent*. Being interconnected and interdependent increases the scope and relevancy of threats exponentially. If you turned over control of processes and resources to others, or those that you rely on have turned over control to others (perhaps without your knowledge) then you are more vulnerable than before. Different business models and organizational cultures, cross-organizational integration issues, increased complexity, communication barriers and interpretation issues, and loss of risk knowledge and memory are just a few of the issues that contribute to being more vulnerable.

ENDNOTES

1. Section excerpted from: Gillmore, Dan. "First Thoughts: Worst Supply Chain Disasters" Supply Chain Digest Jan. 2006: http://www.scdigest.com/assets/FirstThoughts/06-01-26.cfm?cid=57&ctype=content; with permission.

2. http://dictionary.reference.com/browse/resource.
3. World Economic Forum, *GlobalRisks 2007,* A Global Risk Network report, p. 13.
4. Ted Fishman, *China, Inc.,* NY: Scribner, 2006.
5. *Wal-Mart's Imports Lead to U.S. Job Exports,* www.aflcio.org/corpwatch/walmart.
6. *The Wal-Mart Effect,* Economic Policy Institute, Issue Brief #23, June 26, 2007.
7. Knowledge@Wharton 2006.
8. As measured by the Port Authorities/Marketing Information & Services in term of millions of 20-foot equivalent units shipped in and out combined, 2006.
9. "World's Busiest Port," National Geographic Channel, August 23, 2007.
10. Mohamed Olad Hassan, "2 Somali Pirates Arrested in Hijacking," Associated Press, December 13, 2007.
11. World Health Organization (WHO), www.who.org.
12. *Wal-Mart Effect* and *Corporate Fact Sheet, www.walmart.com.*
13. University of Washington website: http://www.ce.washington.edu/~liquefaction/html/quakes/kobe/kobe.html.
14. Yossi Sheffi, *The Resilient Enterprise.* Cambridge, MA: MIT Press, 2007.
15. Amy Chozick, "Toyota Keeps Sales Targets Despite Delivery Delays," *Wall Street Journal,* July 23, 2007.

Line of Sight/Obstructed Views

It is always wise to look ahead, but difficult to look further than you can see.

WINSTON CHURCHILL

Ah, the good ol' days—manual processes, vertically integrated factories, large corporate offices that housed the majority of the workforce, geographical boundaries that inhibited competition, and central oversight of risk. Long gone are those days, and with it the organization's ability to centrally and holistically identify, assess, and manage risk. Now the organization and its leadership, are confronted with two major challenges:

1. Understanding what resources are needed to support their value chain—one that extends far beyond the four walls of their organization and as a result depends on the successful risk management of others.

2. Motivating numerous stakeholders with diverse interests to engage in a risk consciousness that is consistent with the organizations business risk objectives.

The value chain refers to all processes and resources needed to create value. It begins with a concept and continues until the final product/service is delivered to the end consumer. As value is added along the way, today's managers must be adept in dealing with a series of interdependent value chains. Each of your outsourcers/suppliers may in fact have to depend on other interdependent value chains to produce and deliver the product or service you need to satisfy your customers. Once you understand the full scope of the value chain, you can begin to understand how to protect against most forms of risk. A word of caution: all members of a value chain have their own stakeholders and business objectives and may not share your risk sensitivity. Failure to address these issues is fatal.

"A Leadership Crisis" is a description of how specific change has created uncertainty and potentially placed what the organization values, and those associated with it, in harm's way. Traditional methods, such as audit or compliance-driven checklists or insurance if a market exists, simply are ineffective and inefficient by themselves for managing operations and financial risk. The traditional risk mitigation and management approach may not reflect the way the business actually operates; therefore, the solutions are typically superficial and often not sustainable. Many risk management approaches do not take into account the priorities, incentives, and motivations of all stakeholders. Maintaining current checklists that reflect changes over time and at key points in the value chain is often not done, making the use of checklists ineffective. As a result, management may have a false sense that risks are being properly managed. For years, I've heard senior executives state: "I am managing my risk because I have a plan or a risk register, checklist, and insurance." However, most risk-related plans and checklists tend to represent a static snapshot of the problem that was highlighted when a potential risk was first identified. *These tools and reports may not represent a practical, actionable, measurable, and sustainable solution, one that is dynamic and designed in a way that reflects how the value chain currently operates.*

KEY LEARNING POINT

Unfortunately most organizations focus only on the risks that are under the direct control of their organizations, do not identify and engage all internal and external stakeholders, and too often assume that all stakeholders are as sensitive to risk as themselves.

And yes, the risk register is a vital governance tool but it does not usually reflect the connection between "broad" risks and the operational processes and resources of the value chain (i.e. operating companies, the shop floor, outsourcing partners, logistics providers, port operators, and the dozens of other stakeholders).

To address this challenge, leadership must begin by expanding their view of all aspects of the value chain. They must also be willing to clear the barriers that would prevent them from possessing an unobstructed *line-of-sight* view of the risk up and down the value chain. This takes time and courage, but it is an essential first step to determining where the greatest risks might lie in the value creation process. As part of their mission, managers must not assume that all stakeholders in interdependent value chains share the same level of risk sensitivity as you do. Managers must have in place qualified risk management staff that are able to deal with the complexities of geography, language, culture, and business operations. To do this entirely one must begin by understanding the leadership responsibilities of each entity in the chain and creating clear and auditable risk policies and procedures that are checked and rechecked on a routine basis.

CHAPTER 4

A Leadership Crisis?

You know what your problem is? You care too much! Stop surfacing all these risk issues!

—SVP AND CIO OF A FORTUNE 100 COMPANY IN A
CONVERSATION WITH HIS OPERATIONAL RISK OFFICER

Do executive officers and directors actually think about mitigation of risk? When they outsource major components of their value chains, do they assume that the external party is responsible for managing risk? Do they assume that the internal party (chief risk officer, chief financial officer, head of supply chain or IT, etc.) is managing risk efficiently and effectively? For that matter, do the rank-and-file and other stakeholders ever pause to ponder risk-related questions? Or does our culture—dependent on audit compliance and stock price performance—accept the notion that if something has not yet happened, it is just fine to not think about or plan for it? Since the culture is set and behavior themes are generated at the top, this is where an effective risk management program must originate as well. In a litigious society, executives and directors who fail to exercise due care could lose their reputation, their job, and their freedom and saddle their organization with enormous liabilities.

This modern-day culture too often overlooks or is unaware of the very real risks we live with.

I am always surprised and amazed to discover that so many top executives live in *total denial* about their organization's risks. If the topic even comes up, it is usually dismissed as someone else's responsibility, or just an overzealous worker making something out of nothing. Even worse, when an executive discusses risk with other stakeholders, a phenomenon of "mutual denial" often dominates, and the core issue is—once again—swept aside. Of course, no one wants to document bad news for fear of implicating themselves or starting the "timer" for action. However, clear direction is needed from the top to establish risk consciousness and maintain alignment between the priorities and risk activities.

Here's an example of mutual denial. Recently, a member of the contract pursuit team at an organization bidding on an assignment noticed that there was significant operational risk not being addressed in the request for Proposal (RFP—a vehicle describing the specifications and requirements for an open bid). The risk would have made the IT systems and network vulnerable. Although the network was not classified as Top Secret, the data was considered sensitive and the availability of the network essential. The manager from the bidding company felt that it might be a considerable exposure and additional expense so he raised the concern to the procurement officer of the organization that had issued the bid. The procurement officer stated that because the issue had not specifically been identified in the RFP it was at the bidder's discretion to include it in their response. The bidder thought about it awhile and realized that if he submitted the proposal without requiring all other bidders to address the same issue then this extra cost would place their organization at a price disadvantage. He decided not to do so because he found out that the procurement officer did not alert the other bidders to the problem and that he strongly believed that the competitors were not going to address this exposure in their bids. The RFP issuer did not want to reissue the RFP, fearing personal exposure (oops, he forgot the important risk exposure and this would delay the process—make him look bad). The pressure was on, so in the end, the person who issued the RFP and the bidder who found the flaw decided mutually to do nothing about the issue at this time. That exposure was an 800-pound gorilla in the room.

This example should not surprise anyone who's been in the risk business because denial is so prevalent. The solution, to be effective, has to involve all stakeholders and employees at all levels in the company. The big question is "Who owns the problem"? The answer: We all do. Risk ignores function and organizational charts, and this is why risk management sensitivity and adequately funded programs must be treated as a corporate priority.

Two behaviors that I have repeatedly observed are:

1. In many instances, management simply does not have a sense of urgency or sensitivity, a clear risk "expectation" (what are acceptable or unacceptable behaviors, decisions, and tolerances, and most of all, what is expected by investors and other key stakeholders) or, worst case, they assume risk is being addressed by someone else. In many instances they lack the skills, processes, information, talent, technology, or the proper attitude to understand the range of risks they and their organization face. They don't know what critical risk questions to ask. Without understanding that there is a problem and a willingness to place value on the risk process, how can anyone begin to develop a solution?

2. Those who do acknowledge risk are often unwilling to pursue it through to resolution, lack the business case, and/or fail to acknowledge and respond to change. One way to detect this behavior is if the organization has misaligned management incentives that are narrowly focused on the bottom line and their individual performance and rewards, the stock price, and ultimately the decision-maker's own incentive compensation.

The approach to managing risk must be comprehensive while also being flexible enough to allow the business to continue to focus on goals, exploit opportunities, and pursue the strategy within their risk tolerance.

WHO IS RESPONSIBLE AND ACCOUNTABLE?

The starting point for anyone with a broad view and an executive mind-set has to be, *Who owns and is accountable for risk?* Managers and directors are now more than ever required (go-to-jail-time) to understand and manage the risk across their extended value chains. As we have witnessed recently in the area of labor practices, environmental safety, and product quality, the actions of the outsourced supplier are now considered the responsibility of the organization facing the public. This comes at a time when critical people are being released and the "corporate memory" and intuitive knowledge erased as the result of outsourcing. The corporate memory and intuitive thinking represents hundreds of years of knowledge—those who can sense change and are proactive in the way they react and respond to risk.

Therefore, risk consciousness among all stakeholders must be pervasive throughout the value chain, upstream (origination/source) or downstream (ultimate destination). That assumes one of the basic risk-conscious principles has been defined: well-defined philosophy, common terminology, and standard goals/requirements. If your organization benefits from the products/services that move through the value chain, then every senior leader in your organization must propagate a common risk consciousness to all participants/stakeholders in the value chain.

Underlying this changed or expanded thinking is a major trend that is resulting in a leveling (or "flattening"[1]) of risk standards among developed and emerging economies. Both private and public sector organizations are driving this change for greater accountability for achieving the management of risk and risk consciousness. The private sector is being driven by market, regulatory, and non-government organization (NGO) pressures, as well as a greater sense of corporate social responsibility. This sector is now, more than ever, being influenced by legislation and public policy. There is also a growing acceptance by both the public and private sectors for greater collaboration and cooperation on difficult social and economic issues. Both realize that the consequences of mishandling these critical issues could be catastrophic to all. Public-sector (cooperative) organizations that act as leaders in bringing these issues forward, raising awareness, and fostering cooperation between the public and private sectors are: APEC (Asia-Pacific Economic Cooperation), WCO (World Customs Organization), WEF (World Economic Forum) Global Risk Network, WHO (World Health Organization), and the UN (United Nations). The market and public policy pressure continue to increase on the global stage (as well as the cost of mitigation), albeit slow but inarguably definitive in areas such as labor health and safety, environmental protection, product quality, port security, customer information privacy, and intellectual property. The cost advantage of conducting business in a riskier environment—one without standards—will quickly diminish. This change combined with higher labor cost will drive sourcing from such mega-producers as China, to such emerging economies as Vietnam and Indonesia.

The result—it is totally unacceptable for executive managers and directors to ignore risk issues by: 1) denying they exist, 2) assuming that an outsourcer or partner is equally risk conscious, and addressing the issue, or, 3) worst yet, burying/concealing them in a remote geography. Even if the legal framework or financial incentives do not currently exist in that country, the adverse impacts on the organization's survival/reputation/brand have become so great that action is no longer considered discretionary but rather mandatory. There are legal consequences for companies that ignore risk; if a vendor fails to supply a component part to a manufacturer because of an unanticipated supply chain problem, the vendor may have to pay the manufacturer the increased price the manufacturer had paid to get the component from someone else. The risk discussion must be occurring early in the change process. This acknowledges that change is inevitable to remain in business, such as outsourcing to China, since the decision to outsource is about maintaining low prices and strong margins. Many executives that I have spoken with have expressed a concern that a change (e.g., outsourcing) is non-negotiable since the alternative is not being able to compete. The rules of the game have changed!

This leads to the beginnings of solutions, especially when few believe that risk planning is their responsibility and the scope of planning, limited to the four walls of their organization. In fact, there is no simple fix; the process can take enormous effort, focus, and financial resources. But there must be a starting point. Those familiar with process-based improvement programs such as Six Sigma know that there must be a generating force to cause action—such as beginning with a design structured with the customer in mind and an organizational commitment to create and maintain the solution. The same approach is required to address the risk question with the exception of regulated mandates such as those that are in the interest of national security, health, or safety (must do it). The problem today in most organizations is that *ownership* of risk is often vague or undefined and therefore seldom structured or consistently implemented. The motivation or incentive to resolve risk issues is weak at best. Everyone knows that risk exists, but few take ownership—especially in horizontally or network-aligned value chains where there are significant interdependencies, multiple stakeholders with varying cultures, priorities, and multiple points of control. While working on this book, I interviewed the CEO of a large venture capital organization in the Asia-Pacific region. I asked him, "Who influences and/or sets your risk paradigm?" His response; "I hadn't really thought about it." He went on to say that he probably should perform a closer assessment of non-financial risk. He said that the reality is that his investors, primarily large pension funds, set the risk paradigm. Unfortunately, they define the risk paradigm as that which could be protected via insurance. He went on to say "They tell me what type of insurance I need to carry, limits, and acceptable deductions. That's it. That's all they expect." The full spectrum of the risk paradigm did not include that which could not be insured.

Getting individual stakeholders to engage in the problem is an obvious challenge. An equally difficult problem is that high tolerances toward risk are evident in many organizational cultures. An organization's corporate division might define the standards, but their expectation is that the operating groups will access and surface risks, and understand and implement these requirements with a minimum of costs and/or disruption to service, quality, and social environment. Operating groups, however, may not know how to implement the requirement without causing significant disruption or incurring excess expense. As a result, these groups will often just do the minimum to get the box on the risk checklist ticked. As a result, lots of pretty risk checklist binders sit on the shelf and collect a whole lot of dust.

CASE STUDY	RAPID CHANGE: BUSINESS DOWNTURN

RISK REALIZED: ILLEGAL AND NEGLIGENT PROTECTION OF CUSTOMER CONFIDENTIAL INFORMATION

The *Wall Street Journal* published an article ("Dumped Mortgage Files Invite Identity Theft," October 23, 2007) describing how a maintenance worker at an apartment complex in Atlanta made a discovery inside the complex's dumpster: a cache of 40 boxes of loan files containing Social Security numbers, credit reports and other data on customers of the Ameriquest Mortgage Company. In another somewhat related case, Bob Segall, a reporter at WTHR-TV in Indianapolis, tried to get a sense of how bad the problem was around central Indiana. Over three days, he peered into 40 dumpsters behind loan branches and title companies that handle mortgage documents. In nearly half of the dumpsters he looked into, 18, he discovered sensitive information about borrowers. This situation most likely arose as the result of the 2007 subprime mortgage crisis, the rapid reduction of employees, and financial distress, which led to the lack of compliance with records retention and destruction polices.

LESSONS LEARNED *Every public corporation has a legal and ethical responsibility to protect the confidential customer information they gather, store, process, and utilize through the life of the value chain (including the disposal, destruction, or deletion phase). Privately-held organizations, at a minimum, have ethical— if not inferred legal—right to offer the same degree of protection on sensitive customer data (not to mention that they won't be in business too long if they don't). There is a growing trend of laws and regulations requiring companies to protect confidential information. Each company and its executives are legally and contractually obligated to develop and adhere to a stringent records retention and management program that protects these important information assets (both corporate and potentially personal liability if found negligent—standard of care). The growing trend in the European Union, United Kingdom, Canada, United States, and Australia is to continue to evolve strict individual privacy laws and regulations, the violation of which carries with severe financial and/or criminal penalties. Here are a few examples:*

- *United States—Health Insurance Portability and Accountability Act (HIPAA) and Children's Online Privacy Protection Act*
- *Canada—Personal Information Protection and Electronic Documents Act (PIPEDA)*
- *European Union—Article 8 of the European Convention on Human Rights (ECHR), Directive on the protection of personal data*
- *United Kingdom—Data Protection Act 1998*
- *Australia—Federal Privacy Act*

> *Clear responsibility must be assigned for the establishment, execution, and auditing of corporate record retention, privacy, and management programs. This is especially critical in distressed companies (bankruptcy, financial difficulties, legal/regulatory investigations, etc.). Internal and external audit and compliance departments must continuously validate that these important processes are implemented.*

In the future, it is realistic to believe that global standards will be developed to govern value chain approaches to risk management. The genesis of these standards will most likely be attributed to those financing the risk, such as the large insurance/reinsurance carriers.

How else can the global economy even function? The *global standard* of the value chain has to include four crucial elements, at the very least. These are:

1. Labor—the consistent methodology for employee working conditions, compensation, and benefits.

2. Environment—the very difficult but essential theme being that all centers of economic and industrial activity face a broad set of common risks that cannot be different among disparate countries.

3. Security—in recognition of the global threats everyone faces and unlike past perceptions of security risks, which often were described and quantified in terms of national problems.

4. Product Quality—offshoring of production has to be accompanied by the value chain standards ensuring consistency of quality and security for the entire structure of joint venturing to survive.

Of course, this global standard requirement also defines risks for every organization seeking a realistic/achievable strategy as well as acknowledgment by the investors, regulators, and other stakeholders for compliance with these global standards. In defining the kinds of risks you face, reflecting on terms of supply chain is quite helpful and essential to moving toward solutions. Not every risk environment or value chain is the same, however. What does "risk" look like in your company? What is its paradigm? The answers to these questions define who is responsible and to what degree. While everyone in the organization plays a role in managing (or at least identifying) risk, how do you get from the defining point to an effective action point?

To begin this process, decision making itself needs to change. When it comes to risk, the model of the top executive passing orders down the chain does not work well. That assumes that risk is simply an "issue" that can be solved through delegation. Delegate, forget, of course never measure, and pray. The effective alternative is to create a procedure for measurement, illumination, and informed decisions *involving* everyone in the direct or indirect value chain, and creating knowledgeable executives and a risk sensitive culture. And the trigger for initiating the risk process must be "change." Whether the change is being considered by those at the corporate level or on the factory floor—the time for risk engagement is at the onset of change initiated internally or observed somewhere in the extended value chain. This should be non-negotiable.

■ EXAMPLE   In one example, the CIO of a major bank was frustrated by an obstructionist executive vice president (EVP) who refused to support corporate risk management policy. He walked into the private banking EVP's office and dropped a huge printout on his desk. The CIO stated, "Here is a list on the Internet of all of your private banking customers, their balances, and personal information such as address and phone numbers." The EVP saw the end of his career. The CIO then proceeded to ask, "What did you do to protect the identities of your most precious asset?" Such a breach of security would put this company out of the private banking business. The EVP looked up and said "I thought that was your job." The CIO expected this response, shook his head and said, "No, it's *your* job." What he meant was that he was the custodian of the information and most impacted by any failure. The EVP got the message (enlightenment time) and became a risk management champion. A risk management program was implemented at every level of the organization. (P.S. The stack of paper was blank!! Point made.) ■

So what is needed is a new class of true believers who "find the religion" of risk management by realizing that their ways of the past were blind, and that they had refused to see and seek resolution to even the most basic of problems. The nature of risk is vastly different today than in the past due to globalization, connectivity, pervasive use of Internet-based technology, and greater dependence on partners not under direct control. So a new approach in management itself is going to lie at the core of an effective new agenda, the salvation for these new believers.

SUCCESSFUL PRACTICE: IMPROVED VALUE/SUPPLY CHAIN AND ETHICAL STANDARDS

Ten years ago, few were talking about ethical standards programs; today, more and more companies are addressing combined issues such as worker conditions, environmental conditions, and collaboration with suppliers. Wal-Mart conducted 16,700 audits in 8,873 factories around the globe encompassing every phase of its value/supply chain. The purpose was to ensure compliance with product standards and processes while recognizing that simply enforcing rules was not the answer. In its 2006 report, the company wrote that "The only effective way to achieve our objective is by moving beyond monitoring factories, increasing collaboration with stakeholders and capacity building." The program and its audits include provisions for health and safety, environment, compensation, labor hours, underage labor, discrimination, compliance with numerous rules and laws, workers' rights, and more. Wal-Mart also requires suppliers to sign agreements to abide by its standards for suppliers. By past standards, this series of audits and ratings is revolutionary. The range of risks it addresses and eliminates or mitigates is noteworthy.[2]

The Wal-Mart program is a good example of how management can better and more effectively manage risk, even in a complex global value/supply chain. A 2007 problem faced by Mattel in its value/supply chain in China and numerous toy recalls makes the point: not only is immediate and apparent risk often ignored, but managing risk itself has evolved and therefore the approach needs to change.

A good product risk program requires at a minimum: traceability to origin, reverse logistics, and crisis/stakeholders communications. Measures, incentives, and penalties should also be included as part of the program although sentencing a regulator to death for taking bribes might be a bit extreme![3]

Moving toward a refreshed, disciplined, and responsible methodology of problem solving is the only way to begin effectively managing risk. A risk-conscious culture is not easily produced overnight, and it cannot simply be commanded from above. It has to be worked into the organizational culture as a dramatic change in thinking. Fundamental is a risk philosophy/consciousness that begins with identification of what the organization values the most and then defines who is responsible for making risk decisions about how to evaluate, measure, and finance/mitigate risk to this value. Policy, incentives, penalties (career threatening), and a broad set of metrics that define risk standards and measure effective compliance with these standards are tools to enable and empower the risk-conscious culture.

The historical problem evolves from the methodology within the organization itself, set up much like a military command structure. The executive levels oversee "field commanders" (managers), who order the troops to execute *functions*. While this kind of structure is essential to the day-to-day operations, budgets, and orderly process in the corporate culture, the risk paradigm has to be approached in a revolutionary way.

How do you make the business case for approaching this problem in a different way? In the process of Six Sigma or similar programs, the business case or motivation for becoming involved in a team is normally the greatest challenge to the success of the project. The same is true in the management of risk, which may be thought of as a large, permanent, and often intangible project. However, the fact that it is intangible in many of its aspects does not diminish its crucial importance. It is often a difficult case to make, both to management and to the rank-and-file. When you consider the *years* of internal education it took to instill Six Sigma standards into the organizational culture, not to mention the financial commitment required to train everyone from the top down, the scope of changes (notably intangible changes such as risk management) is considerable.

The "chicken and egg" of this issue is profoundly difficult to overcome. The lack of a business case translates to not having the right people involved in the solution. The people responsible for risk activities simply may not own the business case, and lack the skills and authority to really change things. So often, this risk activity is underfunded and staffed, limited to the business as usual, compliance-related checklists, "awareness lectures," and important but simplistic actions such as posting safety bulletins in high-hazard areas. That is just scratching the surface of the broader risk universe.

LESSONS LEARNED   *The executive problem and fix includes:*

- *Acknowledging the issues*
- *Deciding what needs to be done*
- *Allocating the resources*
- *Empowering others to act and report*
- *Communicating the process to others*
- *Determining what the end result looks like*
- *Continuously checking, monitoring, and measuring the program*

If this approach is applied to mitigating the consequences of risks rather than an attempt to eliminate specific risks, it is going to be far more effective than the traditional approaches.

A Note About the Board of Directors

While everyone has an obligation to ask the right questions, it is those at the top, in executive level or board positions who are ultimately accountable, who can set the tone and drive change. The board in particular is responsible for challenging executives and using their experience to ask the right questions and uncover risk that could create a catastrophic situation if not dealt with properly and early on.

The board in many organizations is involved minimally in operational problems and solutions, and usually concentrates only on "big decisions" such as major corporate initiatives; acquisitions; divestitures; declaring dividends; approving high-executive pay packages; and complying with audit, compensation, and policy requirements imposed by regulators. The board's role in a comprehensive risk oversight program should be one of actual leadership. This should not be a revolutionary idea but in many organizations, it is just that. The board needs to set responsibilities and accountabilities for managing risk. With so much emphasis on bottom-line thinking and profits, risk-related matters are too often ignored, and this is where the board's role is so critical. Protecting the asset valuation and net worth of the company (whether expressed in accounting terms or as the stock price) requires operational leadership as well as long-range vision from the board. An organization cannot ensure future profitability and capital strength unless the board sets and enforces risk management policies.

WHY DOES WEAK TOP-DOWN LEADERSHIP MAKE ORGANIZATIONS AND THEIR VALUE CHAINS VULNERABLE? WHAT ARE THE MAJOR LEADERSHIP CONFLICTS AND PITFALLS?

When top-down leadership is weak, it is, in practice, no leadership whatsoever. By definition, leaders have to lead and not follow. The top-down leader completely delegates accountability, but does not demand a penalty for failure. Applied to risk, this is a reckless approach. If you apply the combination of no accountability and no penalty for failure removed, what is the outcome? First, risk preparedness lacks because urgency and concern are removed. Second, nothing is done until after a risk has occurred. Third, no one is going to be held responsible because there is no leadership anywhere up or down the chain of command. The sad truth about top-down management is that it often fails. So the popularity in past decades of evolved-sounding management styles (management by walking around, management by exception, one-minute management) were short lived. In moments of real need, when budgets have to conform to risk rather than the other way around, these "new-age management" techniques are dismal.

These discussions demonstrate how pervasive the leadership crisis is within organizations. In fact, the intrinsic risk issues organizations face today will only continue into the future. A new, enlightened point of view is needed, not only at the operational level, but all the way up to the board of directors. Without this change, no risk mitigation will be effective. With this change, the modern organization will not only survive; it will thrive.

How do you know if your organization is risk conscious? Here are a few questions to ask:

- Do persons within the organization communicate and engage in conversations about risk, especially early in the process when change is about to occur, or has occurred?

- Has the organization defined a risk philosophy and invested to create a risk-conscious culture? Is the organization committed to a strong tone from the top?

- Does management take the time to understand various stakeholder perspectives and motivations?

- Does management see the complete holistic risk picture?

- Is the risk conversation included during the onset of change?

- Does the organization learn from experience (and the experience of others)?

- Does the organization have a process in place to gather external intelligence of the risk facing others (competitors, peers, etc.)? Is there a process for analyzing this data to determine how it might apply to the organization?

- Does the organization clearly define what it values (such as a set of goods and/or services, type of market segmentation, behaviors, etc.) and communicate to all stakeholders of the value chain?

- Do they design with the purpose of integrating risk practices into existing operational process flows, measure risk resource allocations and performance, test the results, and establish a dynamic risk model to support continuous improvement?

- Does the organization routinely measure its risk consciousness? Are exceptional behaviors rewarded?

- Is every employee (lowest-level employee to executive) encouraged to report any observation or change that represents an unresolved or apparent risk?

CASE STUDY   **HOW NOT TO PROMOTE A RISK-CONSCIOUS CULTURE**

Executive management contracted a reputable external management consulting firm to conduct an information protection (security, integrity, privacy) risk assessment. The manager in charge of information assurance and continuity was designated as the person responsible for leading this assignment. Within the first 72 hours of the assessment, the team had uncovered major control

deficiencies that they immediately elevated to the executive directors. The reaction of the two executives was one of "total denial."
This was unexpected and did not promote one of the basic tenets
of a risk-conscious culture—escalate and address bad news
quickly. Here's a small sample of what the team found within the
first 72 hours:

- Patient health care diagnosis and other sensitive data in shared
  publicly accessible directories
- An e-mail password change facility that allowed any user to re-
  set any other person's password
- A publicly accessible database (with global read permission—
  anyone could read the contents of files) that contained the personal identification numbers (PINs) of the individual enrolled in
  the employee retirement plan
- Electronic funds transfer systems that moved millions of dollars
  daily did not use an industry standard control to authenticate
  critical and large-scale funds transfer outbound transactions
- 2.4 million active user accounts for an employee base of 80,000
  (why so many?)
- A list of 9,500 user accounts with access to a sensitive trans-
  action that allowed for the retrieval of patient insurance case
  files (again, why so many?)
- Traders with electronic privileges (i.e., access rights) to delete
  the funds transfer activity and audit logs
- Sensitive and proprietary network and system architecture information that identified vulnerabilities, made available erro-
  neously via the Internet by an outside contractor
- System exits, which were critical to prevent electronic funds
  transfer transactions from remote locations, were disabled and
  went unnoticed for months

How should the two executive directors have reacted to this
potentially harmful risk news? In a risk-conscious culture negative
information flows quickly to, and is addressed quickly by, the responsible executive(s). That happened. However, once the news
reached the two executives sponsors they were simply overwhelmed (hence the reason they slipped into "total denial" and
took a defensive rather than offensive position). They became distracted from the ultimate risk issue/goal and instead began

conjuring thoughts of how much pain this was about to cause them. "Was this another Year 2000 risk mitigation effort?" they thought. The organization recently had been engaged in a massive Y2K remediation effort to reduce the risk from a potential programming bug that would roll the clock back to the beginning of the century, paralyzing the IT infrastructure and all applications. This risk forced the entire organization to become "risk conscious" in a very short period of time and, worst of all, allocate 20% of the annual IT budget to the remediation effort. At the time, this represented approximately $200 million per year for the three years leading up to the millennium. It was this thinking that distracted and discouraged the risk executives.

High costs, a potentially disruptive remediation process, and damage to their personal reputation from the embarrassment of not detecting these exposures or taking action sooner—all potential motives for the two executives to exercise reckless risk behavior. They stopped the flow of negative information, isolated the news from other executives, and tried to erase/discredit what had been discovered. They immediately terminated the contract with the management consultants and demoted the internal manager in charge of the engagement (they later forced him to leave the organization).

LESSONS LEARNED *These were obviously significant and potentially value-, compliance- and brand-threatening risks that needed to be resolved swiftly. Unfortunately, that was not how the two executives responded. They worried first about their personal careers and the effect this negative report might have on them. They struggled and failed to immediately disclose these electronic and operational vulnerabilities to the business products managers, senior executives, and stakeholders who were at risk. They should have validated the findings, prioritized the impacts, outlined remediation steps (possibly a multiyear effort), and then notified the individual executive stakeholders responsible for the business products and services that were affected by these control deficiencies. They also* *should have enlisted and notified and engaged senior leaders (audit, compliance, and risk committee) and appointed a leader and cross-functional remediation team. They failed to acknowledge the urgency and they needed to act quickly since the organization was potentially noncompliant with federal privacy (Health Care Insurance Portability and Accountability Act) regulations.*

Years later, these executives began to correct some of these risk deficiencies. Much of this risk might have been passed on when they sold part of the company and other risk transferred when they outsourced their IT operations. Regardless, the original organization is still responsible for the risk and could be held potentially liable for the consequences of their inactions or negligence. Two other points:

- *Much of the Y2K risk remediation strategy, process and execution work could have been leveraged to identify, assess, measure, and report on many of these risk violations*
- *The risk awareness/consciousness that was created as part of Y2K remediation effort could have been used as the foundation for building a sustainable risk-conscious culture.*

The organization should always check its internal risk "inventory" first to determine what other program initiatives, strategies, architectures, process, technologies and competencies can be leveraged to propagate a risk-conscious culture. If the organization is in a regulated industry, such as banking or pharmaceuticals, then it is more likely that a general risk consciousness already exists (many know the risk and consequences of failing to meet regulations). The key is to expand the scope of these regulatory standards to the entire value chain (not just the portion of the chain that is subject to regulation).

One other lesson learned applies to the consulting team and manager responsible for the engagement and the results of the report. When presenting this type of negative and potentially "damaging" risk information, there should always be a "connection" and "alignment" to the specific impact. For example, the impact should be clearly articulated in terms of the product/service revenue stream, the organization's cash position, asset base, specific compliance requirement and violation (and which stakeholders are directly affected), strategic value, and/or brand/reputation. The executives correctly asked for an independent assessment of their risks but failed miserably to acknowledge the results and then take action. Risk-consciousness is, in this case, a core institutional and individual behavior, not simply a veneer.

As you can see by this case study, risk assessment is a critical step in the overall risk management process. Leaders must insist that assessments be conducted on an ongoing basis understanding that they vary in type (e.g., internal versus external—audit, unannounced test, simulation, live) and scope (narrow, very specific to much more broad based—full value chain). However, all too often the organization will fail to follow through and not assign responsibility for resolution of all "discovered" risks. Almost every organization I've been exposed to has at least one, if not a dozen, processes to identify risk. This is where the so-called internal Holy Wars of risk management begin and the distractions occur. Those involved with conducting the assessment and those on the receiving end will typically argue indefinitely about which assessment methodology is the best, whether the impact calculations are correct, whether a risk event could actually happen, and what will be actually impacted. If organizations do not treat risk by way of discovery, mitigation, financing, acceptance, or avoidance, what good is it to prepare yet another report? It is too often the case that the assessment is bound up in a report with a handsome cover, distributed, filed, and forgotten. I call this the "AADD" syndrome—Assessment, Analysis, Debate, and Drop. I wish I had a dollar for every time I returned to a company that had paid for the assessment and analysis but never acted on it—even many years later. Don't get me wrong—I believe the assessment is necessary and should be used to identify risk exposures. However, it's the prioritization and execution of mitigation activities that all too often fails.

The current attitude toward risk and business discontinuity among top executives and directors—CEOs, COOs, CIOs, CFOs, chief risk officers (CROs), global value/supply chain managers, operations managers, product managers, procurement officers, back-office service personnel, and chief security or compliance officers—determines the effectiveness of an organization's risk program. The level of executive knowledge concerning modern-day threats, the degree of their concern, whether they believe it is a priority, and what types of resources they feel should be used to mitigate risk is sadly lacking, in my opinion and experience. It is a competence issue; it's also about desire and motivation. Too many individuals who are appointed to manage various aspects of risk are usually low level and chosen for the "don't rock the boat" qualities. Many of my colleagues agree but also recognize that they need to earn a living, and if "rocking the boat" is going to penalize them, then why do it in the first place? In most instances, management has a very limited line of sight (scope) about risk—usually that for which they are responsible, as evidenced, in a recent example of a pharmaceutical executive stating that the risks of producing his blockbuster drug were being addressed since they had a hurricane plan for the manu-facturing site in the Caribbean. After reviewing his value/supply chain, he quickly realized that by sole-sourcing the active product ingredients from a country in the Pacific Rim, he had failed to consider the extended value/supply chain and all the participants in his risk planning process (logistics, IT, order flows, transportation systems, port operators, etc.). His actions were based on flawed assumptions (as if to say, "I have a plan, so therefore I am prepared") where the extended chain, all process and resources neces-sary to create value were part of the risk assessment and design process. In most instances, even after losses occur, it is unlikely that anyone will ask, "How can we prevent this from recurring?" The more common question is, "How much did we lose and what's the probability of it happening again—should we spend any money or waste any more time to fix it?" It is essential that those driving the risk process must provide management with a full view of the value chain. Management can then decide what risk management activities should be in scope, and at what speed these activities will be executed and over what period of time. Exhibit 4.1 illus-trates this point.

In a report by the Aberdeen Group which surveyed 150 companies, 82% of the respondents stated they were concerned about value/supply chain resiliency and risk but just 11% were actively managing it.[4] The report went on to state that 82% of companies had experienced value/supply chain disruptions that caused them financial hardship within the past 24 months. Most would say that they've conducted the assessment but have not addressed or implemented the solutions. Here are three important considerations that will increase the likelihood of successful execution:

1. **Stay focused—remain aligned**. The business case for risk miti-gation and financing activities must be built before the final decision makers are engaged. Here are a few important questions that should be included in the business case for risk:
   - What business value is at risk and why (e.g. product, market, ser-vice, etc.)?

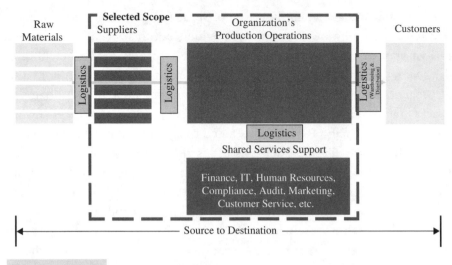

EXHIBIT 4.1   **Scope of Risk Management Activities**

- What are we currently doing and why is that not enough (gaps)?
- What are others doing about this issue?
- How much will the solution cost and who will be impacted,
- Where does this fit it in the broader set of business priorities (i.e. how urgent is this matter in the context of other business issues)?

In conversations with directors, investors and senior executives I find that most executives are far too lax about the true risks that their companies face and are generally unaware of the potential material costs to the businesses that these risks represent. They don't create an adequate level of fear for failure to take responsibility. They choose to react, not ask for details, and draw rather simple conclusions very quickly—calling it "decisive response." It's the back-of-the-napkin analysis, and in most instances is considered acceptable and at the same time dismissive to anyone suggesting the need for further analysis. They lack an operational risk philosophy, discipline, measures, and details to form these quick and unsubstantiated conclusions. As a result, they downplay the problem and often neglect it rather than address it. To avoid these situations, prepare the business case for risk activities and ensure it is aligned with what management considers of greatest value (usually a product(s) or service(s)).

2. **Be persistent, prepared, and thorough when tackling the difficult but most important risk issues—show courage**. It's important that a fact-based analytical approach to analyzing risk implications be adopted and that the final decision makers do not rely on hearsay, intuition, or unsubstantiated analysis of employees. Decision makers demand the intelligence needed to anticipate risk and question past assumptions that may have been appropriate at one time but are no longer because of dramatic change to the operational model. Also, listen and entertain dissent from the stakeholders. Who should be encouraged to present their beliefs about risk (even thought the most common beliefs, are that "it is not my problem" and "it's not likely to occur"). Sanity checks by outsiders that are considered "expert" should be performed in the normal course of business.

The strategy must address the risk mitigation that requires a high degree of effort and represents a high potential impact. **WARNING**! Here's a trap that many leaders fall into when making critical risk decisions about which vulnerabilities to mitigate. I refer to this trap as "Avoiding the Top Right Quadrant" or avoiding the tough mitigation decisions/work that represents the greatest impact ("x" axis) and require commitment and investment ("y" axis). Here's how it typically plays out: Most will do a good job identifying and assessing vulnerabilities. However, subconsciously they will begin to prioritize which vulnerabilities should be mitigated based on what will cause the least pain or will require the least investment in terms of effort, time, management attention (political capital), and capital to their organization. For example, a manufacturing organization that I did work for avoided the top right quadrant by limiting their review of supplier risk to only 15 of the 450-plus suppliers that accounted for the top 10% of payables. However, to produce the high-tech electronics product they failed to acknowledge that they were equally dependent on all 450 suppliers (not just the top 10%) since the product could not be shipped without the contribution of each. In contrast, an automobile manufacturer might be able to roll the final product out with only the majority of suppliers that produce the 24,000 parts. Some of the parts such as the cigarette lighter, floor mats, or even the radio could be temporarily omitted if they were unavailable for an extended period of time. For

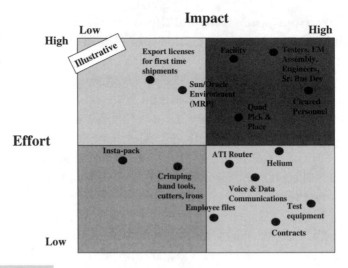

EXHIBIT 4.2   **Prioritized Resource Failure List for Service Business**

this electronic product, *all* parts were mandatory; therefore, it was necessary to consider all of their suppliers in the risk assessment process. What is the result of not addressing the top right quadrant? Significant exposure (by definition—high impact)! The tough risk decisions are avoided and for the financial types, it is poor Risconomics (i.e., ineffective and inefficient allocation of scare resources to manage risk). Exhibit 4.2 represents an organization that effectively and efficiently prioritized their vulnerabilities by impact and effort, as part of the overall risk management process.

3. **Think long-term, not quick and disposable risk resolution.** It is my opinion that the primary reason why risk solutions fail during execution is the failure of the deployment to consider the long-term operational implications. Since the risk design and deployment team is typically reacting to an event, often they do not consider the long-term impact of the risk solution and whether it is scalable and sustainable. An effective risk management solution must include effective planning, successful deployment, checking/validating, and continuous improvement. Standards bodies such as the International Standards Organization (ISO) describe this as Plan, Do, Check, and Act although I believe this was first communicated

via early Chinese philosophers. An unsustainable program demonstrates the ultimate irony: the initiatives often create more risks than they mitigate.

A final note on the consequences of failure. Every manager of a major financial services institution knew that failing an audit or failing to surface a known risk exposure was a potential career-ending event. Appearing on the " BUM of the month" list was avoided at all cost. This risk sensitivity was pushed down to all levels of the organization. Is creating an atmosphere of fear an appropriate tactic? I think so. Any tactic that increases risk sensitivity and encourages all employees to participate in the risk process is valid.

A BEST PRACTICE! HAVE THE INFORMATION NECESSARY TO MAKE INFORMED RISK-RELATED DECISIONS

Here's an example of a leadership team that I worked with that went beyond the traditional thinking. A senior business strategist and the continuity leader at a major manufacturing company were faced with the prospect of another request by corporate audit for organizational compliance with industry business continuity risk standards. These leaders had been asked many times to be compliant with standards that did not reflect the organizations realities. Although this was a multibillion dollar organization, it did not have unlimited time, resources, management bandwidth, or capital to address the full universe of business continuity risks—no organization does. They began the process with a discovery exercise that involved interviews with 45 senior executives. Some of the questions that they were trying to determine whether corporate and operating segment executive management understood included:

- How should we efficiently and effectively allocate scare resources, time, capital, and management attention to managing continuity risk?
- How should the management of operating segments continuously identify risks to their business and value chains?
  - Do they know the specific processes, resources, and key stakeholders needed to support the value chain?

- Do they know what vulnerabilities will have the greatest impact to the operating segment's value chain(s)? Are they aware of peak risk periods where the time of day or, year, or sequence of events places the value chain at greatest risk?

- Is there a process and technology to perform real-time monitoring of threats? Are industry and law enforcement contacts being leveraged? Do I have current and accurate information about my existing state of risk mitigation controls and gaps?

- Do risk-related issues quickly flow up, side to side, and down in the organization? What is the process for resolution? Are there rewards, incentives, and penalties for good and bad behavior?

• How should the organization measure and price risk; that is, the impact of risk against the cost of risk mitigation and financing options? Do I know what risk mitigation and financing options are available to address identified threats and vulnerabilities?

- Is the information available to support effective and timely decision making and modeling when a risk is realized?

- If the threat can measured, what are the likelihood of a specific loss occurring?[5]

- Do they have monitor the risk project deployment (plan), the execution of the solution (do), validation that the solution works as designed (check), and information about how to continuously improve the risk solution (e.g. optimization—act).

The overall goal was to identify business risk priorities, expand the scope to include all resources and stakeholders in the value chain, and, most importantly, acknowledge the prevailing corporate culture and the way the business actually operates. After input was solicited in a structured way from the entire executive team, we then began to deploy a fully integrated value/supply chain-oriented approach to continuity. Some of the key changes included:

1. Migrating from a threat-based (i.e., trying to plan for every event) to an impact based risk management approach.

2. Prioritizing programs that represented the greatest business value and expand the scope of risk activities to address their specific needs.

3. Reallocating resources to risk mitigation efforts that represented the greatest impact.

The operating unit (part of the operating segment) president summarized the results, stating, "I finally had what he needed, a fact-based business case for risk investment—to communicate a clear request to my client (i.e., buyer/stakeholder)."

You cannot make your organization bulletproof from operational failures, data theft, internal sabotage, or terrorism; but you can initiate measures to reduce exposure. You can look for signals or, at the very least, the lack of diligence on the part of the current executive mind-set. But the question, "What is the exposure?" has to involve at the very least the prioritization and alignment of risk activities against that which create the greatest value to the organization. Just as a security guard moves through a building checking to make sure all doors are locked, the risk-conscious organization instills in its staff a sense of diligence and purpose. No one judges the security guard negatively because he does not find a thief every night; but he would lose his job if a theft occurred and he had *not* gone on his rounds. That is all anyone can ask: prioritize that which creates value, identify associated risks, assess current capabilities, and implement solutions that mitigate/finance identified risk.

As a closing self-assessment risk leadership exercise, ask yourself the following:

- Would you delay the deployment of a market-killing product (i.e., sure thing) if all critical risk issues were not addressed and/or resolved?
- If the CEO "mandated" a deployment date, would you challenge it if substantial unmitigated risk were present?
- What risk intelligence programs are in place to identify today's and tomorrow's risk exposure?
- When you think about managing risk, what actions come to mind?
- What do you consider the greatest risks you face today? Has accountability been established and progress tracked?
- Who is responsible/accountable for risk management?
- Do individuals responsible for risk management have a seat at the management discussion table?

- What consequences are there for risk failure caused by management inattention, negligence, or ignorance?

- Can you, as the executive, name your top risks, and do you know what is being done to address these risks?

- Is a risk-sensitive culture present that expects and encourages every employee (clerk to executive) and stakeholder in the value chain to identify and report their risk-related concerns?

ENDNOTES

1. As referred to by Thomas L. Friedman in the book, *The World is Flat: A Brief History of the Twenty-first Century.* NY, Picador, 2005.
2. Wal-Mart, "2006 Report on Ethical Sourcing."
3. Andrea Ang, "Chinese Regulator Sentenced to Death," *Washington Post,* July 7, 2007.
4. Aberdeen Group Global Value/Supply Chain Benchmark Report, June 2006.
5. An actuarial study of loss can identify probabilities and their relevance to specific scenarios. For example, the probability of death is 100%, but you cannot know when that will occur; thus, you buy insurance to offset economic losses to your survivors for the time period when death is not affordable. This is the perfect example of transfer, in knowledge of the outcome but not of the timing. Insurance companies, like casinos, always have the advantage. The cost of insurance is based on actuarial averages, and by investing premium dollars during a policyholder's lifetime, they will always come out ahead of the game: claims paid will be less than the combination of premiums collected and investment income. In other words, insurance companies understand their risks quite well, and build the costs into their premium structure. By further excluding specific types of losses and imposing time constraints within policies, insurance companies make sure that losses do not take them by surprise; the contingencies are built in to the system. Most losses are not so clear. A fire is unlikely to occur in your warehouse, statistically speaking; but you buy relatively cheap casualty insurance because a loss would be so catastrophic in comparison. All losses need to be analyzed in a similar manner in order to better understand the exposure. For most people in responsible positions within organizations, an awareness that many losses might happen is troubling; but once you quantify the exposure, it is easier to determine how to manage it. No capacity in the market exists when it isn't clear and the house (insurance carrier or casino, for example) cannot get the advantage. Then the organization either is unable to operate or has to depend mostly on very extensive mitigation controls or luck.

CHAPTER 5

The Value Chain

The weakest link in the chain is also the strongest. It can break the chain.

—Stanislaw Jerzy Lec

An interesting and comprehensive way to understand the problems of unaddressed risk is to analyze the fabric of the value chain from end to end. The value chain consists of all processes and resources that are required to create value. It also includes all internal organizations, outsourcers or any entity touching or adding value to the product before reaches the intended customer. It is the organizational DNA.

An organization will typically have many interdependent value chains, each supporting product(s)/service(s). Although it is easy to visualize the organization's value chain in the context of its products and services, the reality is that the organization typically will play a role in other organizations' value chains and they will have interdependent value chains—making the picture more like one of an eco-network of linked processes, people skills, technology and processing, physical assets, and relationships. Efficiency has driven the change in ownership of a value chain from a proprietary state to more of a virtual cooperative state. If an opportunity exists to reduce cost such as outsourcing, then at the blink of an eye, the scope of risk expands and a potentially vulnerable link added to the value chain.

WHY VIEW VALUE CHAIN RISK MANAGEMENT DIFFERENTLY?

The value chain can be very complex and convoluted, and most organizations have more than one—sometimes hundreds of value chains. For this reason it is not uncommon for the managers at all levels—including product/service, procurement, and logistics managers—to admit they do not know all the participants or resources in their value chain. If they don't, who does? How the organization defines the scope of its specific product/service value chains, and the associated risk, is critical since value chains can have: 1) very long tails (or a lot of interconnected links that are outside of the organizations control, such as a small job shop in a faraway location); 2) very long legs (tremendous amount of resources that provide the infrastructure required to create value); and 3) many "shared" owners of their processes and resources. These overlapping value chains sometimes introduce conflict or a contention exposure since competitors are vying for the same resource. Remember, what is important to your organization might not be as important to those supporting your value chain (e.g., common transportation provider, port operator, subcontracted manufacturer) in other words, your organization might be less of a priority than other organizations when there is a reduction in bandwidth/service.

Most organizations attempt to manage risk from two perspectives: through the corporate lens (e.g., enterprise risk and insurance management programs) or through an event/functional lens (e.g., security, continuity, environmental, health, and safety). However, these programs seldom engage the operating segment managers who are responsible for creating value. Instead these top-down programs are too compliance/checklist oriented (i.e., do not acknowledge the operating realities such as need for an integrated and sustainable risk solution) while the bottom-up event-driven programs are far too tactical and inefficient to maintain or scale. For example, early in my career, I managed IT security for several large organizations. It was many years later when I realized that IT security management was just one of the many risk-initiatives competing for valuable management time and investment. These functional programs have a place, but must connect to other such risk programs as enterprise risk management (ERM) and value chain risk management (VCRM).

The solution: the organization can more efficiently and effectively allocate its scarce resources—time, management attention, skills, and capital—to the management of critical risk by taking a *value-based* approach. This approach, which I refer to as value chain risk management (VCRM) looks at risk through the value lens by: 1) identifying the product(s) or service(s) that create the greatest value; 2) defining the specific resources and processes used to create and support this value; 3) assessing the impact of risk being realized so that informed risk decisions can be made; 4) prioritizing risk activities and investments (e.g,. mitigation, financing) based on the business case; and 5) continuously monitoring and measuring the business risk environment.

WHAT IS THE VALUE CHAIN AND WHY IS IT IMPORTANT AND RELEVANT?

In military strategy, it is not necessary to completely destroy an army in the field; it is more effective to destroy the enemy's ability to continue fighting. In other words, the supply line is crucial to an army, which requires ammunition, supplies, medicine, food and water. So a smart war is fought not to sacrifice lives, but to prevent the enemy from advancing their goals. In other words, "The object of war is not to die for your own country but make the other poor bastard die for his."[1]

I apply the same philosophical idea to risk management. In war, you prevent the enemy from advancing. In risk management, you prevent the risk from having a catastrophic impact on people, assets, revenue, profitability, process, liquidity, strategic value, or the "brand," while simultaneously protecting the organization's ability to create value. You create value by executing the plan that benefits the community and all its stakeholders.

To achieve this sensible and realistic goal, we need to apply the principles of preserving the value chain to all processes and resources (internal and external) that add value to the product or service. Just as an army cannot survive if its supply chain is cut off, the organization cannot create value if its value chains face risk that exceeds the organization's tolerance. In the military supply chain the value of each category of supply is not created equal, and as a result, the risk impact from one, such as food or water, might be greater than another, such as clothing. Therefore, understanding and prioritizing the impact of a risk being realized, for each type of resource, is critical step in the VCRM process. For a high tech manufacturing firm, which I did work for, it was the calibration equipment, specialized packing material, electromechanical engineers, export filings, cleared personnel (U.S. Top Secret Clearance level), pick-and-place machine, and crimping tools with special plates that were considered the resources that would have the greatest impact, if unavailable. The firm didn't really care about the type of threat, or what caused the risk at this stage of the process. The firm addressed threat-assessment as a separate and later process to create scenarios that were used to test/improve the current plans.

In the end, this does not mean that risk should be avoided altogether or even that it can. Being in business and earning profits means taking calculated risks. But every effective CEO understands that there are balances between the opportunity to grab market share and profits on the one hand, and the unexpected consequences on the other. The key is to have a precise view of the far-reaching value chain and associated processes and resources, for each product or service. To guide the decision-making process when a risk is realized, the organization must also have a clear understanding of "impact" and options/implications for risk mitigation and financing. Armed with this knowledge, management can make "informed" and educated risk decisions. General Robert E. Lee was once described as a successful general for one reason: He never got into a battle that he could not win—and he had the knowledge to know what it took to win. Thus, on a corporate level, the organization is expected to take *smart* risks, which will result in certain wins and small chances of losses. No one in a position of responsibility should be taken by surprise when unintended consequences occur. The realization of an unanticipated risk is a symptom of a poorly conceived plan.

What is the value chain and VCRM concept? The value chain is about creating value and includes all processes and resources that are required to fulfill a need and/or service demand. I will oversimplify the value chain concept so that we have a starting point for our discussion. Picture the value chain as a straight line moving from left to right. The starting point is an action and/or a location from which anything is derived—the *need*. This is usually the vendor, client, or customer. An order is placed, a product purchased, or a service consumed (in-person, Internet, telephone, fax, mail). The connection is then made between those who create demand and those who can supply any part of the finished product. The current scope of risk activities typically is limited to what the organization can see (or what it wants to see) and what it can manage: the internal facilities, production/

service lines, employees, and a handful of critical external suppliers. Risk transfer products such as business interruption insurance provide only a partial solution. The scope of these products covers only the loss from property related hazards that impact the supply chain (e.g., flood or fire versus health crisis such as a pandemic outbreak).

In the new efficient and modularized business model, the ownership of risk is still the organization's responsibility, and it cannot be passed off to others with the assumption, or hope, that they will manage it. The value chain concept defines those who support the value chain as the custodians of "value," not the owners or ultimate individual with decision-maiking authority and accountability. As custodians, they have the responsibility to implement and maintain the risk policies and strategies that have been defined by the owner. This is why the owner must clearly communicate risk policies, standards, strategies, expectations, and tolerances. This concept of custodianship applies to all internal and external providers of the process and resources that support the value chain. Sometimes the risk requirements of a custodian are imposed by external parties, such as regulators (e.g., port operators customs security and inspection standards). Of course, the owner must comply. These externally imposed responsibilities can come from any external party, anywhere up and down the value chain. In some industries, such as the manufacturing of appliances, the value chain stretches further, continuing through to the disposal or destruction of the product (the same is true for the service chain and the destruction of information). The value chain does not stop once the sale is completed. Either the existing value chain is extended to address the service and maintenance process, or in some instances, a separate value chain exists.

What are the components of a value chain? The value chain resources consist of five key components:

1. People, skills, and knowledge
2. Technology and processing
3. Physical assets (including raw materials)
4. Relationships
5. Processes

Exhibit 5.1 illustrates a single product for a product-based value chain. Exhibit 5.2 illustrates a single service product (insurance policy) for a

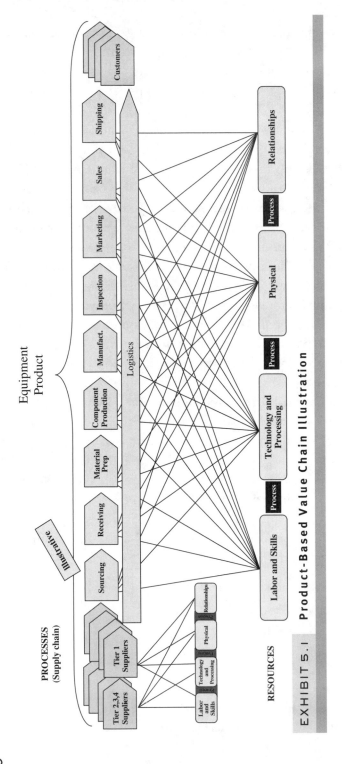

EXHIBIT 5.1   Product-Based Value Chain Illustration

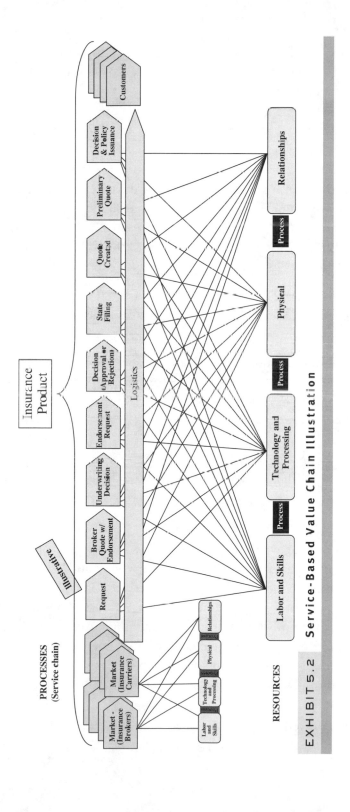

EXHIBIT 5.2 Service-Based Value Chain Illustration

service-based value chain. As you can see by this illustration, the links in the chain represent an *interdependent "point in time" eco-network* rather than a linear set of relationships.

As you can see by the illustrations, the scope of the value chain includes all internal and external resources that provide the infrastructure. For the manufacturing of a new-generation aircraft the value chain might begin in the mines of Australia, Brazil, or Africa with sourcing of raw materials such as aluminum, titanium, or iron ore. If the organization produces petroleum-based products such as cosmetics, bandages, bubble gum, golf balls, plastic bags, panty hose, or crayons, then the source of key raw materials might be located in Russia or the Netherlands, the top two exporters of petroleum products.[2] The value chain may include those who:

- **Source** the ingredients/raw materials (e.g., farming/agriculture, fishing, mining, forests/lumber, energy/oil/gas fields) or services

- **Create** the interim state products (suppliers) or services

- **Move** the goods (public and private transportation and logistics providers, such postal service, shippers, truckers, rail operators, port operators, airlines, etc.) or services

- **Support** the entire life cycle of goods and services by providing public and private infrastructure (telecom, electricity, water, health and safety, law enforcement, customs, etc.), as well as the internal shared services infrastructure such as human resources, logistics, information technology (IT), finance, legal, and compliance

- **Store and distribute** goods (distribution and warehousing)

- **Protect and provide** the health, safety, and security of the stakeholders of the goods by regulating, overseeing, and/or monitoring the social and economic environment (e.g., U.S. Federal Trade Commission, Food and Drug Administration, and U.S. Consumer Product Safety Commission; European Environment Agency, European Medicines Agency, U.K. Financial Services Agency, and Medicines and Healthcare Products Regulatory Agency; Japan Pharmaceutical and Medical Devices Agency; China Administration of Quality Supervision, Inspection and Quarantine)

- **Market and sell** the goods and services (retail, wholesale)

- **Service** the goods and services (service providers)

The point here is that a broad definition of the value chain must be adopted. This is often not the case, as I experienced while participating as a panel member at the World Customs Organization meeting in Brussels. The common thread throughout the conference was the need for greater security against terrorism and enhanced facilitation of the inspection and customs process. However, both the public- and private-sector organizations assumed a very narrow view of the value chain. They defined supply chain risk only in the security context and limited the view of an organization's value chain to the logistics and customs process (and legislation around authorized economic operators; i.e., government approved). This is a very important topic; however, it is not the only risk that an organization needs to actively manage, nor should the scope be limited to just the logistics/customs portion of the value chain.

THE FOCUS OF VALUE CHAIN RISK MANAGEMENT

Understanding the processes and resources that support your product/service value chain is a critical first step in VCRM. However, the prerequisite or first step in the VCRM process is to define which product or service (or group of products and services) will be the focus of the VCRM activities. Executive management must rank value; that is, determine which of their products/services are considered to be of greatest value (discussed at length in Chapter 8). *The transition to a risk-sensitive culture begins by understanding the business priorities.* For a manufacturer, that might equate to one set of catalog products versus another, or their top three corporate contracts (i.e., versus the 500 others, especially if it is an original equipment manufacturer); for a beverage company, the focus might be bottled water products versus 450 carbonated beverages; or for a bank, it might be a wholesale banking service, such as global payments, over a retail service such as home mortgage origination and servicing (probably not a good example today when looking at the subprime loan crisis). For an apparel manufacturer, Target may be the only priority.

Let's use a utility company to further illustrate the first step of the VCRM. We begin by identifying how the business creates value—exploration, generation, distribution of power, and trading services. Exhibit 5.3 illustrates this segmentation. Our goal is to align risk

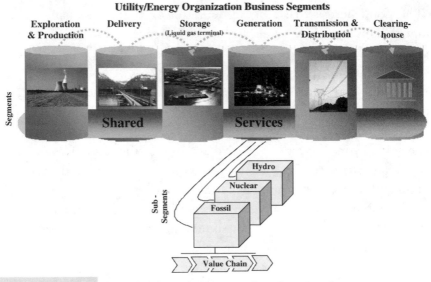

Utility/Energy Organization Business Segments

| Exploration & Production | Delivery | Storage (Liquid gas terminal) | Generation | Transmission & Distribution | Clearing-house |

Segments

Shared   Services

Sub-Segments

Hydro
Nuclear
Fossil

Value Chain

EXHIBIT 5.3   **Utility/Energy Organization Business Segmentation and Value Chain**

activities with the service value chain. To meet this objective, we will then need to determine which services create the greatest value to the organization and its stakeholders. For utilities, we have to consider the regulatory requirement (U.S. Department of Homeland Security) that might require our organization to provide a specific service such as the "power distribution," even if we don't consider this the greatest value to our organization. For this example we will assume the management team has determined that "power generation" is the service that creates greatest value. Once the product/service has been selected, then a further granulation of the value assessment should continue until the management team believes that they have identified the finite product/service that represents "value." In this example, there are at least three different product lines that support power generation, which—fossil/coal, water/hydro, or nuclear—creates the greatest value. Once management has agreed on the product/service, power generation via fossil fuel (because it represents 85% of their client base or 90% of the revenue), then the processes and resources across the entire chain allocable to fossil fuel generation can be mapped and the impact of risk assessed.

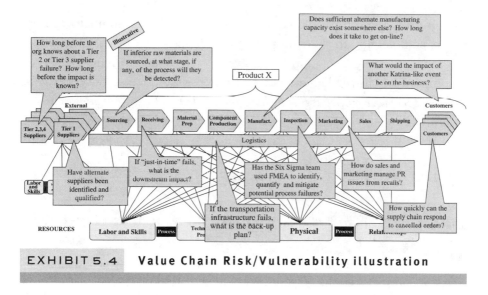

EXHIBIT 5.4   **Value Chain Risk/Vulnerability illustration**

In this particular example, the power generation value chain might begin in the coal mines in Australia (of course, it starts with the customer demand and service order, but again I simplify to make my point). Assuming others have not outbid you for the raw resources, you must now move to the value chain issues. As we move through the value chain, we identify critical processes and resources, skills sets, technologies, facilities and transportation providers and processes (e.g., customs).

As we move through the value chain, one can quickly see that vulnerabilities are present throughout—machinery, qualified labor, facilities, technology (refer to Exhibit 5.4). We also assess the consequences of a risk's being realized in order to prioritize impacts. In our example, we have identified our relationship with Class 1 railroads as critical because they move 66% of the coal. We've also identified the skills sets of the yardmaster and conductor as having the greatest impact if lost (e.g., to a health pandemic). Since we have only a four-day supply/inventory of coal, we will elevate this exposure to the top of our risk mitigation list.

Each process and resource represents a point (or node) where something can go wrong or a risk can be realized. And if that's not a scary enough prospect, each connection or point of interdependency represents yet another level of vulnerability. There are literally hundreds, if not thousands, of points of vulnerability along any value chain. These potential exposure points combined with the risks previously discussed (constant change and the speed of change, relinquished control of the management, loss of the organizational knowledge/memory, and increasing threats) show *why value chain risk management represents perhaps the greatest and most important business challenge over the coming decades.* This is also why a focused process is required that quickly prioritizes risk activities and then allocates the organization's limited risk resources efficiently and effectively.

CASE STUDY   **PRODUCT FAILURE IN THE SUPPLY CHAIN**

Here is example of the penalties an organization might encounter as a result of product failure anywhere in their supply chain.

Defective crankshaft design blamed for small-airplane engine failure. Product Liability.

FACTS AND ALLEGATIONS

Plaintiff is Interstate Southwest Ltd. (ISL), successor company to Interstate Forging Industries Inc. (IFI). Between 2000 and 2003, a number of small-airplane engine failures occurred when crankshafts manufactured by Lycoming Engines, Williamsport, Pennsylvania, broke in flight. The failures resulted in 11 deaths. Lycoming is an operating division of Avco Corporation, a subsidiary of Textron Inc. The Federal Aviation Administration (FAA) issued three airworthiness directives that resulted in the grounding and recall of numerous Lycoming engines. Lycoming conducted an investigation and concluded that the crankshafts failed because of subsurface metallurgical defects caused by IFI overheating them during the forging process. Accordingly, it demanded that IFI pay it for losses associated with the grounding, recalls, and settlements reached with the wrongful-death plaintiffs. IFI refused; and ISL—on behalf of itself and IFI—sued Lycoming, alleging that Lycoming breached its contract with IFI, that IFI was fraudulently induced into signing the extension of the contract in 2001, and that Lycoming conducted a fraudulent investigation. The plaintiff contended that the crankshafts were underdesigned. Lycoming denied the allegations, contending that there was nothing wrong with the design and that IFI overheated the crankshafts.

RESULT

The jury awarded plaintiff a total of $96,120,413, including $86,394,763 in punitive damages (Case: *Interstate Southwest, Ltd. v. Avco Corporation and the Lycoming Reciprocating Engine Division of Avco Corporation*, No. 29,385, Court: Grimes County District Court, 278th, TX, 2/15/05).

LESSONS LEARNED *We can see that the supply chain involved raw material providers, forgers, manufacturers, and installers. Failure could have occurred during any of these processes, again reinforcing the need to:*

- *Map the entire supply chain and all critical resources needed for support.*
- *Assume resource failure/risk being realized for a resource.*
- *Implement rigorous quality control processes.*
- *Analyze and evaluate the impact.*
- *Measure and price mitigation and financing options.*
- *Prioritize investment based on those risks with greatest impact.*

Let's take a look at another value chain example. This is a specific example of a poultry/food producer's value chain that I evaluated several years ago while helping them with pandemic preparedness. In this example, the poultry producer's value chain begins at the the farm, (source) and ends at the customer mouth (referred to as "from farm to fork"). I've eliminated the customer and the order process for simplicity. Exhibit 5.5 provides a partial view of the producer's value chain.

As I mentioned, this is a simplified and partial view. Not included are several critical processes and resources such as transportation services, logistics, ordering/forecasting/reporting, and finance.

Most customers don't think about the value chain when they enter the grocery store to purchase goods. They just expect a quality product at the

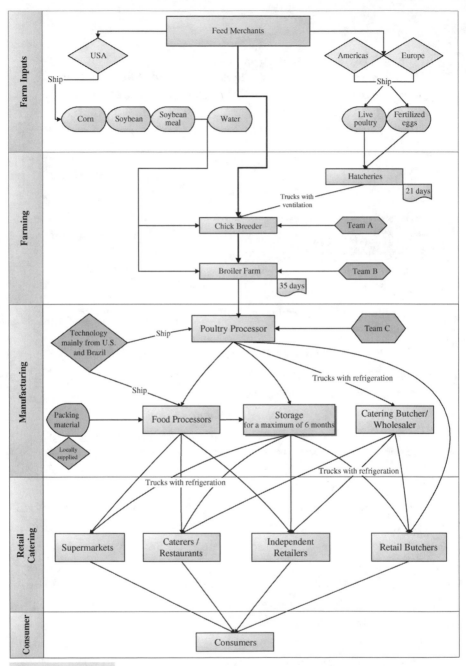

EXHIBIT 5.5   **Poultry Producer's Supply Chain (Illustrative Only)**

lowest possible cost. They really don't care about the risks in the value chain unless something goes wrong and it directly affects them or someone they know. They begin to care if the product quality standards have slipped or if the product they want is out of stock—especially if it's a critical prescription or ingredient (no cheese for the pizza store). But what if one of the worst possible risk scenarios becomes reality for the poultry industry? What if a highly pathogenic virus, such as the H5N1 (avian flu), were detected in a poultry facility and all major customers shut down import licenses? The value chain would naturally come to a screeching halt, product would be recalled, and the source of revenue—the poultry—would be culled. Demand would plummet resulting in severe economic consequences.

Many stakeholders in the value chain would be impacted and in this case, it might take a long time for demand to recover. Here are a few examples:

- **Truckers and freight forwarders**—no revenue and excess capacity
- **Government (customs)**—loss of tax revenue from sales of product and additional economic consequences such as increased unemployment
- **Investors**—possible loss of investment or downgrading (not achieving expected level of returns)
- **Gas stations/energy companies**—loss of revenue from decreased trucking
- **Suppliers**—loss of revenue, disposal/destruction costs of contaminated poultry and loss of confidence in product that could result in a long-term demand shift to other products such as beef
- **Retailers**—loss of revenue, unproductive shelf space, limited selection of goods, limited product for such retail outlets as Kentucky Fried Chicken
- **Consumers**—poultry would probably find its way into the country, but the cost would most likely be significantly higher because of the demand-and-supply imbalance and additional cost to move the goods from another location

As you can see, even with a simplified view of a value chain, the stakeholders are numerous and the processes complex. By the way, this risk scenario is not fictional. It happened in Colombia, South America, in

September 2005 (conversion of the H9N2—LPAI, bird flu). Colombia was a major exporter of poultry to Venezuela, Ecuador, Peru, and Bolivia. But the risks in the value chain can extend far beyond adequate and reliable supply. In this particular case, Colombia poultry farmers got a taste (no pun intended) of another risk—how demand can be impacted by political risk. The original health problem was resolved swiftly, and the outbreak of the virus was a low pathogen in December 2005. However, restrictions were maintained by Bolivia, Ecuador, Panama, Peru, and Venezuela for political rather than technical reasons. As a result, Colombia struck back by halting imports of rice from Bolivia and Ecuador.[3]

Now let's take a look at two critical dependencies in this value chain—the essential feeds (and water) that are needed to grow/farm the poultry and the logistics/transportation providers that move the goods. Another critical link, early in the poultry farmer's chain, but late in the grower's chain, essential feeds include corn, soybean meal, and soybean. As we see in Exhibit 5.6, the producer's value chain (in Colombia) depends on the ability to source and move corn primarily from the United States, and source and move soybean meal from Bolivia. Failure to obtain the feed can lead to failure to produce the end product (poultry) and bring the value chain again, to a screeching halt. Therefore, how and when orders for these ingredients are communicated, competitive bidding and how these goods are moved (is there an adequate transportation infrastructure in place?), the political situation, and the current state of security (what is the process for inspection/customs?) are all key considerations when managing risk of the poultry value chain.

Let's take a look at the second interdependency risk, vulnerability to the logistics/transportation provider's value chain. Depending on the method of transportation, the vulnerability can be different. Exhibit 5.7 illustrates some of the different types of logistics and transportation and the vulnerability that may exist.

VALUE CHAIN, ENTERPRISE AND FUNCTIONAL/ISSUE-BASED PROGRAM RISK MANAGEMENT

The VCRM concept takes a different view of risk than the traditional ERM and what I will refer to as the "issue-specific" risk mitigation programs (e.g., business/disaster recovery, IT security, environmental health

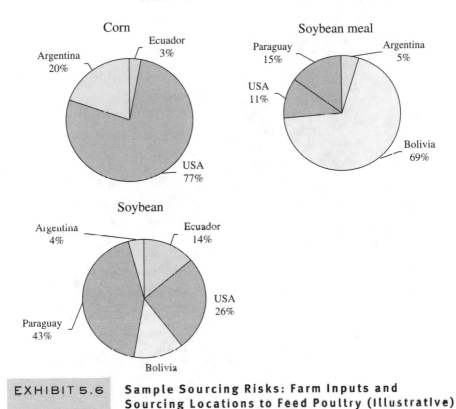

EXHIBIT 5.6   **Sample Sourcing Risks: Farm Inputs and Sourcing Locations to Feed Poultry (Illustrative)**

and safety, product risk, and/or security). ERM programs have come to be an accepted norm in the regulated industries such as banking, although successful global execution is still an open question. However, the non–service industries such as retail, manufacturing, and distribution have struggled with large corporate-driven non-revenue-producing initiatives that have a direct impact on margins with no immediate tangible returns. The top down programs (e.g., ERM) are important but require large investments and a great deal of time to deploy, and are typically biased in that they view risk through the eyes of corporate and financial management rather than the divisional perspective or operations management. The bottom-up issue-based specific initiatives are important as well, but are typically limited in scope and application to mitigation of a specific risk issue such as IT security or environmental health and safety. Many of these programs and their sponsors lack alignment with that which creates value and

EXHIBIT 5.7 Sample Logistics Risks

Illustrative

Lines of Business

Customers

Ocean Services
- Avian flu
- Open seas piracy
- Volatile fuel prices
- Changing international regulations
- Terrorism/ civil unrest
- Stricter port and customs regulations
- Language barrier
- Broken equipment (cranes, loading)
- Damaged cargo
- Weather & natural disasters (hurricanes, typhoons, earthquakes)
- Labor strikes & worker shortages
- Open seas risks

Rail Services
- Disruption of service due to regional health issues
- Regulation of transportation of hazardous shipments
- Tampering
- Loss of power
- Weather & natural disasters
- Damaged cargo
- Derailments
- Freight theft
- Accidents & hazardous materials

Truck Services
- High fuel prices
- Disruption of service due to regional health issues
- DOT compliance
- Insurance costs
- Safety
- Aging Workforce
- Weather & natural disasters
- Damaged cargo
- Fatigue
- Temperature flaws
- Fuel prices
- Drive recruitment and retention

Tracking and Tracing
- IT System Failure
- Navigation/ communication issues
- Tampering
- Privacy
- Piracy

Distributions & Warehouse Services
- Absenteeism of key employees due to pandemic
- Other labor shortages/ strike
- Contamination
- Utility shortages
- Weather & natural disasters
- Access failures (accidents, emergency situations)

Information Technology
- Utility Failure
- Corruption of data
- Hacking
- Data integrity issues
- Denial of service conditions
- Privacy
- Worker shortage
- Physical threats such as weather & natural disasters

Customers

lack the line-of-sight view needed to evaluate and manage risk across the extended scope of the value chain.

As the Scope of Value Chain Expands, New Risks Appear

Earlier in this chapter we stated that the scope of the VCRM process begins at the source of the value chain (e.g., mine, farm, oil field) and extends through to the hand-off/sale of the product to the customer. However, as value chains are constantly changing and becoming more complex—as the sourcing methods and location of suppliers frequently change—so is the landscape of risks. In fact, General Electric's ecomagination[TM] program states, "GE's commitment to imagine and build innovative solutions that solve today's environmental challenges and benefit customers and society at large." The program began by asking the question, "How will our products impact the environment?"[4] The program even goes as far as using this information to determine what products and services they will sell. With growing concerns about the environment and the changing climate, we now have to extend the scope of the value chain to include disposal through the entire product life cycle—in this instance, through the disposal of hazardous materials. This will be one of the more challenging risks to organizations in the products business—how to dispose of these materials efficiently, economically, and in an environmentally friendly manner. The European Community was one of the first to consider this environmental risk and as a result put in place the "Restriction of the Use of Certain Hazardous Substances in Electrical and Electronic Equipment" (RoHS) and Waste Electrical and Electronic Equipment Directive (WEEE). To prevent the generation of hazardous waste, Directive 2002/95/EC requires the substitution of various heavy metals (lead, mercury, cadmium, and hexavalent chromium) and brominated flame retardants (polybrominated biphenyls [PBB] or polybrominated diphenyl ethers [PBDE]) in new electrical and electronic equipment put on the market after July 1, 2006.[5] The directive imposes the responsibility for the disposal of *waste electrical and electronic equipment* (WEEE) and the *cost* of disposal on the manufacturers of such. So when organizations map and analyze risks in the extended value chain they must look beyond the client, customer, and consumer and into the disposal and destruction of the products—including the costs of such a program.

One can only imagine that in the Western world's litigious society it won't be long before we have to apply this requirement to other industries such as automotive and pharmaceuticals and that an imbalanced application of a disposal standard globally will only be tolerated for so long. This will continue to push forward the "flattening" concept discussed in the previous chapter. If one wants to do business with the European Community, then one must comply with its environmental regulations. If that community has not adopted a particular regulation, then a competitive cost advantage will exist. The cost advantage will begin to diminish once the requirement begins to take hold through market, NGOs, and consumer groups, and the standards for due care will begin to flatten or become equally applied throughout. The United States, China, and others will find themselves playing catch-up if they want to continue to have access to the European market as well as maintain a positive reputation for being environmentally friendly. Activate the sensors; change has occurred, and as a result, the organization may be exposed to greater risk and additional costs.

WHO IS RESPONSIBLE FOR VALUE CHAIN RISK MANAGEMENT?

Risks can be broad and overwhelming across a value chain, therefore disparate views of the way risks may be managed exist. The plant manager worries about the risks to the plant from bad weather; the procurement officer worries about supplier risks such as failure/integrity; the corporate services managers worry about the risks to their shared services (finance, operations, IT, and or human resource) such as hardware failure, increasing labor costs, and the like. On the surface these diverse views might not appear to be an issue, but in reality they raise a number of concerns. Beware of the following pitfalls:

- Increased risk—since risks brought about by interdependencies assumptions and failure to communicate expectations typically fall into a gray area where ownership of risk management is assumed by no one (I thought someone else was accountable for managing the risk)
- The lack of standard risk processes that are leveraged across the value chain. Avoiding stand-alone tactically-focused risk assessment since they adversely impact the overall efficiency of managing the risk investment

- Conflicting priorities/agendas and poor communications may be widespread since risk mitigation activities are being managed by separate parts of the organization. The lack of standardization reduces the likelihood that the risk solutions (assess, test, and measure) will be sustainable and scalable.

A great deal of ambiguity exists as to who is responsible for ownership of risk. Unfortunately, there is extensive partitioning of value chain activities by different parts of the internal and external organization, leading to fractured business and risk ownership (e.g., procurement, operations, warehousing, risk-management). I've been able to identify a few instances whereby someone in the organization could actually articulate the process, resources, and owner of their most critical value chain. Value chains have evolved over time and are typically a hodgepodge of technologies, networks, suppliers, organizational cultures, and management philosophies. Participation and ownership by a large group of senior managers is needed to have a viable value chain risk management system. I've found a few good examples in the pharmaceutical industry in which a product manager acknowledged this responsibility and had the power to direct all resources toward a common goal. He drove the risk process and led the deployment of a risk-conscious culture. I believe that the trend to find someone to ultimately "own" the full scope of risk for a product or service line will slowly increase over the next three to five years as broader ownership becomes commonplace. Breaking the responsibility into pieces and managing them separately is just too inefficient (no one has ultimate responsibility and accountability), creates too much ambiguity, and results in gaps that leaves the overall management of risk for a critical product/service to chance— and a prayer. In the poultry/food service example, we see that these partitioned/silo managers assume someone else is managing the risk. The retailer of the poultry assumes that the manufacturer is adequately managing risk. The manufacturer assumes that the farmers are managing risk, and the farmers assume that the suppliers of soybean, soybean meal, and corn are adequately managing risk. However, it is those types of assumptions that might result in a corporate failure and land the senior management squarely in the middle of a major lawsuit or, worse yet, jail.

This is where value chain analysis can become most valuable: by identifying how and where disruptions are likely to occur, the value chain exposure can then be measured and priced against various risk financing and mitigation solutions. They can include modifications for greater security, policy and procedures, testing/quality control, pass-around contingencies, alternative routing, insurance, alternate financing vehicles (e.g., catastrophe bonds), and emergency response; or diversified with secondary chain routes (more expensive, less efficient, temporary—but intended to keep the value chain moving forward).

I believe regulation has begun to change this silo/portioned approach to VCRM. As the organization attempts to comply or perform its diligence with the far-reaching mandatory or discretionary regulations across geographic borders (e.g., by country regulators such as U.S. Food and Drug Administration, Customs and Border Protection; U.K. Food Standards Agency; China State Food and Drug Administration, and General Administration of Quality, Supervision, Inspection and Quarantine), the need to respond/comply with a specific regulation becomes a starting point for more efficient leveraging of common risk processes (e.g., common value chain mapping and risk profiling/assessment) across the value chain. It also begins to define who might/should take responsibility for championing the VCRM effort. In financial organizations it might be the chief risk officer. In a mid-size retail organization it might be the chief financial officer and in a technology, telecom and pharmaceutical organization it might be the product manager. However, it does not infer that risk can be, or should be, managed by this one person. Instead, success requires a risk champion and the involvement of all contributors along the chain to create a risk-conscious culture. Regulated industries will take the lead, especially those considered core or root industries such as farming/agriculture, mining/extraction, water, energy, and lumber. Being at the root, or point of origination (i.e., closer to the earth), presents unique and multiple risk challenge and exposes these industries to much greater scrutiny and, in most instances, regulation. An example is presented in the case study, "The Mining Industry: Being at the Root of Risk."

VCRM represents a significantly different approach to holistically managing the organization's risk along its far-reaching value chain(s). It assumes that the organization does not have unlimited time, management attention, resources, and capital to allocate against the large number of risks. Therefore, it needs to align risk activities with business value and then prioritize actions and decisions against that which creates and supports that value.

However, to be truly effective the organization must broaden its view to include the perspective and incentives of other stakeholders. As Arthur Schopenhauer stated, "Every man takes the limits of his own field of vision for the limits of the world," so in our next chapter we will look at these diverse stakeholder perspectives and incentives for the purpose of understanding what it will take to get others to part of our risk conscious culture.

CASE STUDY   THE MINING INDUSTRY: BEING AT THE ROOT OF RISK

VALUE CHAINS DEPEND ON THE MINING INDUSTRY TO EFFECTIVELY MANAGE RISK

- The mining industry is a diverse, complex industry and is a core dependency within most supply chains. It is of vital importance to the global economy. Examples of industries that could be directly and materially impacted include: manufacturing (e.g., machinery), utilities (e.g., coal), transportation (metals), and defense (metals and uranium).

- The mining industry has been managing risk for many years. These risks include: political (national and local governments, international and local NGOs, community groups), regulatory (Kyoto protocol, Kimberly Process, bioterrorism statute requiring traceability of product to source, i.e., which mine?), environmental (air and water pollution—CO_2 emissions, chemical waste), and safety (ventilation, methane drainage). Other risks requiring attention, such as: informational, criminal/terrorist, social, reputation, economic, weather, people, legal, customer demand, and interdependency risks, present significant challenge to the profitability and success of the industry.

- Mining, unlike most industries, faces *variability* risk—that is, the risk presented by a constantly changing environment. In mining, the ore reserve or deposit (the feedstock) is fixed in the ground and extremely variable, but the mining system (akin to the factory in the manufacturing system) is mobile, moving through the input feedstock, or ore-body, encountering a constantly changing environment.

- "Social responsibility" is an important concept for big-brand companies. The mining industry has been under intense political, environmental, and social scrutiny over the past decade. Historically there have been industry issues such as asbestosis/silicosis. There are now International Labour Organization (ILO) requirements, for example, child labor in third-world countries.

- Examples of risks in the mining industry include:
  - **People related**—rapidly increasing global demand resulting in increased number and frequency of injuries and illness (exposure: lead poisoning, respiratory disease, mercury poisoning), exploding wages, loss of critical skills due to aging workforce, terrorist attack, health crisis (e.g., epidemic/pandemic), fire, labor strikes and/or other adverse event that results in significant loss of workforce or critical skill.

  - **Technology and processing**—accidental or malicious destruction of critical geographical, financial, or other data; theft of sensitive mining, financial, or other critical business data; accidental or malicious destruction or denial of networking or computing services (e.g., viruses, worms, denial of service attacks).

  - **Physical**—mine failure due to unpredictable/unknown nature of the underground mine, loss of key equipment for extended period caused by loss of long lead or sole sourced suppliers (e.g., girth gear; 6–12 months to acquire, 3 to install).

  - **Relationships**—failure of transportation and logistics (e.g., due to inclement weather)—rails, trucking, maritime, failed/strained relationships with local governments and communities (e.g., nationalize mines), loss of investor confidence, Noncompliance—inability to trace source of material (i.e., bioterrorism statue).

- Specific threats include:
  - **Economic**—labor strikes affecting prices, loss of transfer capacity—inability to insure, inability to secure mining rights resulting in decrease supply.

  - **Environmental**—pollutants from heating metals and mining (e.g., CO_2 and mercury emissions, uranium, asbestos, radioactive gases, arsenic), hazardous material (e.g., cyanide and sulfuric acid/acid mine drainage), other waste. Ecological damage could include pollution of air, drinking water, rivers and soils and loss of vegetation); exposure (inherent dangers in metal (e.g., uranium, lead) and abandoned mines.

○ **Political and Social**—disputes with governments (e.g., Oxus Gold in Uzbekistan and Kyrgyzstan) and community opposition/special interest group objections (nationalize mining concessions (e.g., Glencore and Boliva); indigenous traditional landowners claims either as to mining or royalty payments (e.g., Australia and South Africa); increased regulatory awareness and more demanding assurance (i.e., mine reclamation and associated financial assurance levels required for a permit to operate mine)—limits exploration (i.e., inability to secure mining rights); potential curtailment if Kyoto protocol moves forward globally; corruption, civil unrest/ethnic conflict; reputation; human rights abuses (e.g., Anvil Mining DR Congo) and safety issues (United States); corporate image/ethics/management—negligence, corruption, fraud.

ENDNOTES

1. *Patton*, 1970 (never actually spoken by General Patton, but attributed to him in the film).
2. International Energy Agency.
3. Experts: Banning Imports Won't Stop Bird-Flu Threat, NewsMax.coM, Wires, Saturday, Oct. 29, 2005.
4. http://www.ecomagination.com/news.
5. European Commission WEEE page, http://ec.europa.eu/environment/waste/weee/index_en.htm.

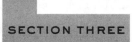
Consciousness, Engagement, and Execution

VALUE CHAIN RISK MANAGEMENT

Focusing on the "value chain" and defining risk in terms of organizational resilience and agility are essential in understanding our growing risk exposure. This requires a consciousness by all, as well as commitment to consider risk in every aspect of the business decision making process. Left to a few who do not understand risk-management processes or exposures, or viewed through a single lens, the risk effort becomes nothing more than a feeble and unsustainable attempt to address exposure. In the modern, globalized and digital world, the new and expanded risk paradigm has overwhelmed most organizations. It is time to regroup and redefine, to expand the organizational *line of sight* about potential risk throughout their value chain and engage the masses with this constant and expanding challenge.

Just as significant changes in past technology threw the world into chaos, today's new environment is also transitional. Access to low cost labor, new and emerging markets, and pervasive communications through the Internet created new opportunities *and* new chaos, obscuring old visions of what is required to create value. The highly efficient and modularized interconnected economy is doing the same thing to every organization today. Much needed risk information and responsibilities is being dispersed into the hands of many others. Equally challenging is locating, retaining, supporting, and valuing experienced "risk-sensitive" talent. These are the individuals who can be deployed by organizations and will be devoted to worrying about the impact and potential consequences of change. Also missing are the evangelists of the message (risk awareness is everyone's responsibility), the integrated risk processes, a sense of urgency, and, most importantly, the attitude, training programs, and resources necessary to establish a risk- conscious culture. In the absence of this talent and acknowledgment that this is a real business issue, the result is that many executives, employees, and business partners do *not* think *nor* do they take responsibility for creating and sustaining a risk-sensitive culture that treats risk identification and management as a corporate priority across the organization's far-reaching value chains. Whether the reason is one of awareness/ignorance, lack of accountability, malice, lack of motivation/incentives, and/or leadership, the issues can no longer be avoided. I contend that we can no longer live with the imminent negative risk profile or the idea that "it's not my job," nor can we "assume" that all stakeholders (e.g., employees, clients, suppliers, outsourcers, regulators, investors, or insurers, etc.) in a value chain will take responsibility for addressing risk. Every change introduces unknown factors as well as potentially new and undiscovered risks. And *every* change leaves in its path unaddressed vulnerabilities; millions of potential land mines spread throughout the many value chains, that if detonated could have catastrophic social, economic, political, safety, and health consequences. By confronting these realities with creative proven approaches in place of *Total Denial*, the process of overcoming these problems intelligently and methodically can begin—thus creating a risk-conscious culture.

CHAPTER **6**

Develop, Nurture, and Sustain A Risk-Conscious Culture

If everyone is thinking alike, then somebody isn't thinking.

—GENERAL GEORGE S. PATTON

How can an organization establish, implement, and sustain a risk-conscious culture in a rapidly and continuously changing environment (markets, geopolitical, regulatory, climate, social, and technological)? As if the challenge of keeping one's eye on the value-creation ball is not enough, the organization is now faced with rapidly escalating risks brought about by the increasing type and frequency of threats (weather, environmental, political, reputational, informational, economic, people-related, health, and terrorist) and changes to business operations—leaving the organization more vulnerable than ever. This is the Big Question. The Big Answer is that by employing the specific tools of intelligent management, and improving preparedness, resiliency, and agility, our risk consciousness may be expanded and actions can become properly aligned and harmonized with the business model.

However, the problem seems overwhelming, with too much to digest, no obvious or affordable solutions. As with all big problems, though, the solution is to adopt a methodical approach, set priorities, and use the "first aid" approach. Before doing anything else, stop the bleeding (eliminate glaring, immediate risks), restore breathing (get everyone revitalized about working together to attack the problems), and elevate the feet (analyze the high-impact, high-probability vulnerabilities and devise specific strategies to manage the risk). As big as the problem is, organizational survival depends on a dramatic and revolutionary change in corporate culture and in management thinking. The budget, as a risk management tool, is useless by itself. Rather than the budget and the audit checklist dominating the decision-making process, these have to be relegated to tools in the hands of effective, action-oriented management that can think outside of the bureaucratic box. This can be achieved, but true leadership is demanded and "buy-in" by all is non-negotiable. With that, there is hope—a risk sensitivity that becomes ingrained in behaviors rather than an afterthought, after an event.

THE RISK-CONSCIOUS CULTURE

What is a risk-conscious culture? According to Craig Goldman, former CIO of Chase and director on many boards, "A risk-conscious culture means that every employee and member of the value chain is encouraged, incentivized, and feels empowered to escalate/surface perceived risks, no matter how small, up the management chain for analysis, prioritization and correction." It is a culture where:

- Risk leadership begins at the top and includes all internal and external stakeholders and directors/officers (from CEO all the way down to the low-level stakeholder).

- Truly enlightened leadership—containing ethical and farsighted people—is able to look beyond self-interests and prioritizes risk programs and expenditures based on what's best for the corporation as a whole.

- Risk management professionals are an integral part of the decision-making process (a seat at the leadership table).

- All employees and business partners have the responsibility to surface risks. The risk "thinking" and actions are not considered optional and, as such, are factored into critical business decisions—before, during, and after decisions are made.

- The risk discipline—identification, assessment, measurement, treatment, mitigation, and optimization—is integrated into the business objectives and value chain management.

- A long-term focus and disciplined approach is needed. It requires hard work, significant resources, investment, and management attention. It is not produced overnight; however, in the long run, creating such a culture will prove invaluable to efficiently and effectively managing risk. Risk-related issues flow up, side to side, and down to all stakeholders throughout the value chain (not just the organization). These issues are quickly analyzed, prioritized, and resolved.

- There are rewards for success and serious consequences for failures caused by controllable factors.

What is a risk-conscious culture, and how does an organization go about establishing one? I begin our discussion with a real-life story of how the actions by a group of business leaders, following a tragic event, created a "best practice" of how to build a risk-conscious culture. At a tactical level, these leaders improved their disaster preparedness. However, the benefits went far beyond developing just a process. What occurred instead was a contagious awareness of the risks and appreciation of how individual decisions and actions affect others.

The incident was a Category 5 hurricane named Ivan, and the place was the Cayman Islands (the fifth-largest banking center in the world). Ivan damaged more than 95% of the buildings[1] and disrupted essential value chains such as food, water, shelter, supplies, communications, and energy, and its core revenue generators—financial services, and tourism. Everyone on the island was affected both behaviorally and financially. However, after it was all over, the impact of Ivan then became the genesis for another great phenomenon. A risk-conscious culture emerged, born from the desire by the business leaders to proactively, rather than reactively, manage risk. In all my years working for/with hundreds of organizations, I had never witnessed such an example as the one I was exposed to in the Caymans. I have a profound respect for Gene Thompson and Paul Marchena for bringing together a set of diverse leaders for the purpose of learning and addressing those vulnerabilities. The result was improved preparedness, greater resiliency, increased participation by a much broader community of stakeholders, more effective alignment of risk investment with business priorities, and most importantly—a risk-conscious, sensitive, and responsive community of business leaders.

Hurricane Ivan: Gaining Strength from a Devastating Event

Several months after the devastating Category 5* Hurricane Ivan (Exhibit 6.1), a community of business and social leaders came together in what was originally a postmortem meeting. Their individual frustrations motivated them to engage in a conversation about the economic and social impact of Ivan and what could be done differently next time to reduce the exposure. After three meetings it was clear that the theme had shifted from a limited view of their own businesses to one of a communal economy. They recognized the need to begin a dialogue about risk issues long before an event could occur (e.g.,

BEFORE   AFTER

EXHIBIT 6.1   A Grand Story of How the Caymans Established a Risk-Conscious Culture

---

*An unofficial report from the fire station at the airport was that there were 190 mile per hour winds, with gusts of up to 211 miles per hour.

hurricane, pandemic, or other natural disasters). They realized that they had a symbiotic relationship, which had advantages and disadvantages.

With the help of Gene and Paul, the group rallied another dozen or so leaders to the first meeting. Prior to the group's getting together, Gene requested that I survey some of the executives in order to identify what worked and didn't work, what close calls were avoided, and what their individual priorities were. What I discovered was that communication between the government and business was a major issue, as well as between the business leaders, the general community and their international customers. I also found that the leaders behaved as if the storm affected only them, instead of harnessing the power of the interdependent community.

My assignment was to lead the research and facilitate the sessions. The leaders demanded action and they got it—a risk consciousness among the group emerged. They inventoried their competencies and capabilities, and then began to determine how they can benefit from each other. Initially, resources were pooled, valued, and exchanged on a bartering system. For example, satellite phones were made available so that the executives could stay in touch with each other and their overseas customers, high ground was allocated for the storage of critical vehicles, special fuel delivery was prearranged, prearranged delivery of lumber was offered to critical sites, a web site was created, employees became more involved in the preparation, heavy-duty transportation vehicles were identified, and emergency response procedures were shared. The group went as far as building a bunker so the leadership team did not have to evacuate the island during a crisis. When Hurricane Dean hit in 2007 these new capabilities were activated. Fortunately, the storm took a southerly turn and spared the island. Regardless, they were ready to manage the worst possible outcome. From my home in New Jersey, I was able to watch the action firsthand via the security cameras mounted on one of the participant's buildings in the Caymans. Remote monitoring was one of many improvements that was implemented and activated. The leaders listened to each other, understood the collective needs, and then agreed to who would contribute what to ensure economic and social resiliency. Fortunately, the CEOs and other senior leaders at the Thompson Development Group, Hurley's Groups of Companies, Cayman Water Company, Cayman Utilities, Workplace Environments, A.L. Thompson's, Brown's Mobile Fueling, Foster's Food Fair Supermarkets, Marsh, and others have taken action and benefited from the lessons of

Hurricane Ivan (ironically, the storm first made land on September 11, 2004). They are proactively managing risk both individually and as a community.

HURRICANE IVAN	GAINING STRENGTH FROM A DEVASTATING EVENT

I list here the most significant findings and lessons. Please refer to www.atyourownrisk.net for additional information.

What were the attendees' greatest concerns should a similar disaster occur? Collectively, they used this list to start the process.

- Economic viability of the island (foreign investors and other key stakeholders may limit their financial and personal exposure by leaving the island permanently).
- Inability to retain the workforce (fear that the expatriate workforce will lose confidence and not want to be on the island).
- Threat to security of personnel (i.e., civil unrest).
- Inability to manage human resource and social issues such as housing and irrational/unproductive behavior caused by post-traumatic stress (e.g., loss of productivity).
- Additional financial loss from theft or intentional destruction of assets (e.g., inventory, office equipment).
- Inability to recover insured losses from regional carriers (i.e. concerned with liquidity and financial viability of insurers).
- Inability to obtain sufficient and affordable insurance.
- Inability to manage a major health crisis.
- Delayed recovery caused by vandalism and aggressive behavior/panic (e.g., people breaking oil pipes at the port to access oil, theft of propane tanks).

What common problems were encountered during/after Hurricane Ivan?

- Projectiles and water surges caused 80% of damages and resulted in 92% of all properties filing a claim
- People became incoherent, irrational, difficult to motivate, isolated, and defensive (i.e., resisted assistance)
- Loss of housing, tools, transportation, water, electricity, and access to fuel were most prevalent and disruptive

- Shortage of labor to rebuild damaged property
- Equipment and inventory disappeared
- Building materials were in short supply
- Containers were backlogged at the ports
- Airport was closed, hampering relief
- Sanitation facilities were inadequate (bathing, toilet, disposal of garbage)
- Medical supplies and trained personnel were limited
- Safe/secure/dry offsite storage facilities for vital records, back-up supplies and equipment were extremely limited
- Hotel space and accommodations for Caymans natives and emergency support staff was minimal
- Cash was initially unavailable
- Public perception was that the government was slow to respond
- Fuel tanks were damaged or removed

What were the lessons learned from Hurricane Ivan?

- Preparing for a Category 3+ hurricane will require earlier declaration/evacuation (e.g., prearranged mass evacuation including chartered transportation and emergency extrication and 72- vs. 24-hour evacuation).
- A Category 3+ will require significant external help to recover the public infrastructure; therefore, those resources needed should be identified now and activation criteria clearly defined (i.e. shipping, transportation, health, housing, safety and security, energy, water).
- Ensuring the safety and security of employees' families is a critical recovery dependency (e.g., predefined personnel accountability system; personal hurricane plans, temporary/longer-term housing such as trailers, tents, and toilets).
- A shortage of material led to increased prices and delays recovering.
- The lack of a predefined communication plan created difficulties in getting things done quickly (e.g., ability of key executives to communicate with each other).
- Tourists and expats were slow to return to the island. A predefined crisis marketing campaign would instill confidence in the financial industry and bring back the tourists.

- Crisis management was not coordinated between the public and private sector.

How have these organizations improved their programs?

- Company moved their generators up to high ground to avoid interruption caused by flooding. Keep their business leaders separate as an ongoing practice. Warehouse food for essential services/businesses.
- Company shipped in material from Mississippi when they could not get them from Florida. Also, distributed emergency supplies to multiple locations.
- Developed new procedures with key overseas customers for communications and emergency back-up processing.
- Organization enlarged their hurricane-proof building for employees and built higher buildings for vehicles.
- Company plans to store heavy equipment strategically around the island, keep key employees/leaders separate, has tests and drills, and recognize how long it takes to prepare everything.
- Organization has technical tests, which prepare buildings by protecting/locking down projectiles and putting up shutters and vehicles, but no people tests.
- Organization-Enhanced Testing Procedures

Note: The group determined that future perparedness activity had to recognize the relationship between duration of the storm, and extent of damage. The hurricane arrived Saturday night, and did not leave until early Monday morning. In their revised plans they have taken this into account and adjusted preparations accordingly.

The detailed case history of the Caymans—not only in response to the immediate problem but also in the post-disaster analysis and planning for the future—is a good example of how tactical risk activities such as disaster planning can jumpstart the development of a risk-conscious culture.

FIVE TENETS OF A RISK-CONSCIOUS CULTURE

As we have just discussed in the previous example, there are several essential foundational elements of a risk-conscious culture. They are:

1. Motivate and engage all stakeholders—leadership, incentives, penalties and measures
2. Engage in all directions, and continuously validate
3. Establish, communicate, and measure a robust strategy, standards and actions
4. Promote information/news flow—fast, proper filters, resolution, accountability
5. Monitor change (all types) early in the change process, continuously monitored and interpreted, in the context of defined stakeholder expectations

1. Motivate all Stakeholders

One of the most difficult challenges in creating and sustaining a risk-conscious culture is convincing the stakeholders that risk efforts represent value. It goes without saying that this begins with leadership. The organization should designate a leader, but in reality all of the senior executives, directors, and line managers need to be risk leaders. It is part of everyone's job description or service agreement, regardless of where they are in the value chain, to formally consider risk as part of their decisions and actions. In my experience, too much time has been and is still being applied to convincing the decision maker that a threat is going to become real. The conversation must focus on the impacts and the cost, service, quality, and social implications of managing the risk, balanced against the social and economic consequences of not effectively managing the risk It must also present achievable and prioritized solutions. Here are a few questions that one should keep in mind when trying to convince stakeholders to take action:

- Is the issue relevant?
- Are there achievable/cost-effective solutions to the problem?
- What are the economics of primary and secondary solutions?

- What incentives or pain point exists if I address the issue?
- What do I gain by doing something?
- What is the penalty if I don't do something?
- Am I being measured by doing something?
- What amount of time, effort, political capital, and/or money do I have to invest if I do something?

In a risk-conscious culture, there is usually little discussion about whether risk needs to be part of the process because it has already been integrated into the business and operations culture as another major element of running the business (e.g., similar to that of a Six Sigma initiative). Unfortunately, the majority of those taking risk mitigation actions or making decisions about downside risk are being motivated by the headlines, auditors, the boss, personal incentives, and/or the regulators (i.e. the enforcement of public policy). I am aware of many exceptions where an organization will excel in creating a risk-conscious culture for an event-specific risk such as product quality or IT security risk.

How can a culture be created that takes risk seriously and views it from a broad value chain—not an isolated perspective? In situations where the connection has not been made, risk management and planning is not going to be possible. For example, it is true in many organizations that management (CEO, CFO, COO, the board) have the isolated perspective focused on keeping the stock price high, as part of the basis for incentive compensation. At the same time, middle management and rank-and-file are given absolutely no incentive for taking any risk-based initiative (especially costly and resource-intensive ones). In fact, in many companies those who even try are often punished for rocking the boat or causing management to "divert attention from more important business issues." Too many executives have adopted an attitude that risk mitigation is complicated, impacts the bottom line, and "I will take the risk that a disaster will not take place on my watch."

What is needed to fix this problem is a truly enlightened leadership containing ethical and farsighted people who are able to look beyond self-interest. Top management should be populated by long-term risk sensitive thinkers rather than by those with a six- to twelve-month horizon on levels of compensation or job position.

This alignment of risk initiatives around business value is at the core of the modern risk management program. Management has to also consider the attitudes and priorities that jeopardize value and even work contrary to its objectives. Short job tenure and self-serving forms of incentive compensation are only the most obvious of these. The traditional hierarchy of organizational management needs to be reviewed in its entirety. The purpose has to be:

- Identify current organizational thinking and structure that jeopardize effective risk anticipation programs.

- Elicit ideas and observations from all rank and file levels, not only the traditional "safe incentive" ideas, but clear-thinking and even revolutionary new approaches to everything from executive compensation to corporate risk transparency.

- Revise the organizational chart so that internal programs as well as cooperative incentives with vendors and operating units are *led* by the value chain rather than merely observing its existence.

- Make the consequences of a risk failure severe enough to force risk sensitivity.

- Fund and treat an active risk management culture as a priority.

INCENTIVES AND PENALTIES

SUCCESSFUL PRACTICE—BUM OF THE MONTH CLUB

The late John Scicutella, COO, and John Esposito, CFO, started a practice at Chase Manhattan Bank in the late 1980s called the "bum of the month" club. Chase's executive management believed that a good program consisted of rewarding good risk behavior and penalizing bad behavior. However, instead of penalizing just the individual they decided to also make the senior level managers accountable. Accountability was achieved by forcing at least one (sometimes up to a half dozen) guilty party/parties to stand in front of the senior operating committee of the bank at a monthly meeting and explain why risk was being mismanaged and what they were going to do about it. You never wanted to be subject to the interrogation or embarrassment of the call. It forced accountability and, as one might expect, the victims (usually senior to middle level) jobs were at risk and if still employed after the event, they would not make that mistake again. As a result, these victims became very proactive in ensuring all others quickly got into line. However, as one might expect some of the more seasoned managers eventually figured out how to conceal their mistakes or negotiate with the bum-of-the month police (internal/external audit, compliance, product production risk management) to avoid being called on the carpet. Of course, if they were caught doing this the consequences were severe, up to and including termination. Overall, the approach was one of multiple positive and negative reinforcement programs deployed around the bank to raise consciousness and ensure the effective management of risk.

The *San Francisco Chronicle* employ a program similar to "Bum of the Month" to highlight unresolved problems, focusing on city, county and regional government issues ranging from potholes to toxic dangers. The program is called *Chronicle Watch*, and each day it breaks down a problem into several categories:

- What's not working?
- A description of the issue
- Who's responsible? (name, title/department, phone, e-mail)
- Day number (on January 15, 2008, one unresolved program was on day 193)
- Who's looking into it? (public officials taking or promising action)

A responsible public official who does not want to be highlighted for not doing his/her job, much less deluged with phone calls or e-mails, has the incentive to take action. That a problem could remain on the unresolved list for 193 days shows that not everyone will respond to this kind of public shame; but that is more likely the exception than the rule. Good work should be acknowledged and highlighted, but so should incompetence.

The previous example represents a clear standard of measurement that can be used to influence behaviors. I truly believe in the age-old paradigm that an organization measures that which is important. Motivating the stakeholders' performance with regard to risk consciousness along a value chain is important with one caveat—measure the outcomes and results, not the activities. More about what to measure in the section on Tenet 3. "Establish, Communicate, and Measure A Robust Strategy, Standards, and Actions."

2. Engage In All Directions, and Continuously Validate

Risk management is a culture, an attitude, and a process, not a product. It is a deeply embedded behavior and mind-set that is an integral part of the way business and people decisions are made and value chains operated. As such, it must be weaved into the day-to-day operations of a company as well as into an individual behavior. Without incentives, penalties and a top-down, bottom-up, inside-out commitment from all stakeholders—risk management is nothing more than a costly, thin veneer around an organizational, and possibly an economic and societal, time bomb.

WHEN RISK PERSPECTIVES COLLIDE

AT THE INTERSECTION OF ORGANIZATION RISK INITIATIVES

One of the greatest challenges organizations face when managing risk is inefficient, overlapping, or misaligned programs. This applies to any organizational activity that is localized (one department) or those activities that span the entire organization and can be performed by multiple parts of the organization. The good news is that there are probably many issue-based (product risk, security, continuity) and corporate risk activities (insurance risk management, captive financing program, enterprise risk management, regulatory compliance) under way in your organization. That is also the bad news, since these activities might be misaligned with your business priorities and, as a result, are consuming valuable risk capital, management attention, time, and/or resources. The root cause of this issue can either be a lower-level manager who has set the risk priority as just that issue (e.g., Internet security) or, worse yet, a senior executive reacting out of fear to a recent negative story (e.g., product recall). In this case, the executive has probably arbitrarily realigned the organization's risk resources against this particular "hot" event at the expense of most other risks.

Exhibit 6.2 illustrates the potential risk collision (and the battle for risk investments) created by an organization's operating in the functional-view paradigm of risk management. In this operating model, the risk requirements can be acted upon by any or all of four groups:

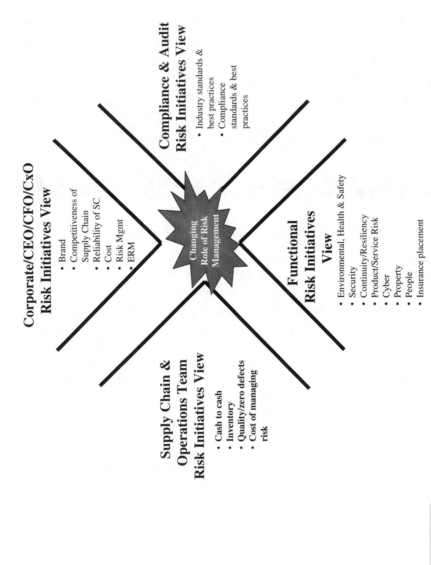

Corporate/CEO/CFO/CxO Risk Initiatives View

- Brand
- Competitiveness of Supply Chain
- Reliability of SC
- Cost
- Risk Mgmt
- ERM

Compliance & Audit Risk Initiatives View

- Industry standards & best practices
- Compliance standards & best practices

Changing Role of Risk Management

Supply Chain & Operations Team Risk Initiatives View

- Cash to cash
- Inventory
- Quality/zero defects
- Cost of managing risk

Functional Risk Initiatives View

- Environmental, Health & Safety
- Security
- Continuity/Resiliency
- Product/Service Risk
- Cyber
- Property
- People
- Insurance placement

EXHIBIT 6.2 Risk Collision

- *Corporate risk initiatives*—what I refer to as the top-down risk initiatives. These are risk initiatives aimed at addressing common risk issues that exist across the organization. The goal of many of these programs is to implement consistent risk programs throughout the organization. Examples include enterprise risk management or the property/casualty insurance management program. However, these programs are usually limited to just the internal management of risk.

- *Functional risk initiatives*—what I refer to as bottom-up risk initiatives. These initiatives are typically created as a response to a specific risk event/issue. Examples include environment, health and safety programs, IT disaster recovery programs, IT security programs, and physical security programs. These programs may be sponsored as top-down corporate initiatives, but over time I have found that the intent, although noble, fails as many organizations decide to implement these programs differently in each of their operating segments or physical locations.

- *Compliance and audit risk initiatives*—these initiatives typically reflect compliance with industry or professional standards such as those dictated by the public accounting profession or International Standards (ISO)/Operational Standards (e.g., OSHA) organizations. These programs usually dictate clear but high-level risk requirements for a variety of risk issues, including quality, security, and safety. These are my least favorite programs, since they seldom take into account investment or execution considerations (i.e., the cost, service, quality, and/or social impacts of weaving these requirements into the day-to-day operational processes along the value chain). However, these programs are necessary, and in almost all instances, compliance is non-negotiable.

- *Supply chain and operational risk initiatives*—these initiatives are most closely aligned with the value chain risk management (VCRM) program described in this book. However, a supply chain risk management program usually is limited to the management of material sourcing and supplier risk. There are, however, a few organizations that can be considered exceptions to this generalization, since they also include the logistics, IT, and public infrastructure in the scope of their risk activities. The most closely aligned risk programs with the supply chain/operational initiatives are quality and productivity programs such as Six Sigma–based programs.

My recommendation is not to abandon these initiatives in favor of a one-size-fits-all. I suggest that the organization plot a path to migrate its risk resources (time, management attention, capital, and resources) to a value-driven approach such as the one—VCRM—suggested in this book. *Note:* Although it's important to focus the risk "energy" internally, external factors could present far greater risk. This was the case on a project I managed last year. I tried to get the management team of a multibillion-dollar blockbuster drug to consider the sourcing risks of the active product ingredients (APIs, source/molecules used to create drugs) in the scope of their activities. Unfortunately, they were unable to expand their line-of-sight and, instead, dedicated their efforts to just the risks to their manufacturing facility (i.e., primarily a hurricane plan). The recent Baxter heparin contamination case mentioned earlier in this book is a good example of why the end-to-end value chain must be considered, especially when the value-based product is generating billions in revenue and its competitive advantage is set to expire (patent expiration) the near future. I believe that the management of risk should be viewed as a paradox, since it is everyone's responsibility, yet it seems that many choose not to act as if this were true.

Key questions that should be asked include: Who are the key players, those individuals who stand to benefit or lose the most? Who are your internal and external "experts"? Who are the stakeholders, and why do they care (from the mailroom clerk, to the dock worker, to the CEO)? Who's responsible and accountable for risk management? Who should be informed? What stakeholders' thresholds and tolerances have been established, that is, what is their tolerance for risk? Do you understand how business operates so that the risk message can be integrated? The project management principle of approaching problems using a RACI (**R**esponsible, **A**cceptable, **C**onsulted, and **I**nformed) chart may be instructive in engaging various stakeholders. Exhibit 6.3 Illustrates a RACI Chart.

Risks need to be discussed as part of all of these conversations and the management team and board must set the tone and culture that risk is

Illustrative

Risk Mitigation Activity	Donald	William	Edward	Karen	Mary	Pamela	Harry	Gene	Brian	Louise	Willie	Giovanni	Margarita	Malcolm
Evaluate the use of risk diagnostic software	R	C	A	A/R			R	R	R	C				
Secure private records from unauthorized viewing	R	C		A							I			
Periodically audit records management vendor controls	C			A			R			C				
Provide annual detailed background checks for those with access to sensitive records		C		A								C	R	
Define email encryption policy and determine standards		C		R							I	R		
Ensure that all design drawings are secured	C	R		A	A							C		

R=Responsible   A=Accountable   C=Consulted   I=Informed

Individual responsible for carrying out task	Executive Role	Typically role can provide valuable insight or advice	Role potentially impacted by task

EXHIBIT 6.3   **RACI Chart for Engaging a Broad Community in Risk Activities**

everyone's job. If every employee understands that their active participation in the risk process may mean having a job/company versus being unemployed, a motivated/empowered workforce *will* surface the issues. Management and the board must assure a seat at the table and funding for the risk experts. Risk management is not a part-time job and, of course, these experts must be thoroughly familiar with the business and external market and have access to critical risk-related information and risk staff throughout the organization. Once the decision is made as to how the business model will change—that is, change driver and change, the risk and operations team can begin to design solutions. The approach must also focus on the relevance of this change, the resources needed to support the value chain, and of course, the potential impact to the processes and resources if the risk is realized. Decision makers need to:

- Ask the right questions.
- Treat risk management as a critical function and contributor to the success of the organization.
- Seek out independent experts to validate

- Develop/gather the information they need to make informed risk decisions.

- Integrate/support risk-conscious mentality for framing their business decisions.

- Think risk, not just the plus side of taking the risk.

> ### KEY LEARNING POINT
>
> Risk management *is* an integral part of everyone's job. It is not separate from what you do, but is a central attribute of how well or how poorly you execute.

The engagement of stakeholders does not always have to originate from the top. I have witnessed many examples where the rank-and-file initiates the action to engage management. In the Cayman Islands example, the rank-and-file surprised management when they showed up for work the next day even though many had suffered severe damage to their homes (some actually lost their homes). Through the facilitated sessions management became more risk sensitive to the needs of the rank-and-file. As a result, they decided to improve communications, do more to provide the basic essentials for the families of these workers, and remain on the island during the crisis to provide leadership and reassurance.

In Chapter 7, I provide a view of risk from various perspectives. By gaining a better understanding, and thus appreciation, of these diverse stakeholder views, one can improve their odds at successfully engaging the stakeholders. However, whether through policy or behavioral practices, stakeholders want to feel that:

- Their point of view is being considered.

- They are engaged, part of the community.

- Their work to date has been taken into consideration, and if they reported a potential risk, someone has looked into it.

- There is clarity regarding stated corporate objectives.

- They have very clear risk incentives and penalties and clearly understand the implications of a risk-related failure.

- They are accountable, and their efforts are measured and acknowledged.

3. Establish, Communicate, and Measure a Robust Strategy, Standards, and Actions

Now, more than ever, an organization must have a risk strategy that defines direction and set expectations, establishes a philosophy, and connects the "what to do" message with the "how do we get it done," process. The strategy must be communicated to all employees and stakeholders and the expectations validated by the board and executive leaders.

I propose a two-pronged risk strategy that I've developed and deployed at numerous organizations over my 30-year career. The overall approach is illustrated in Exhibit 6.4, and discussed at great length in Chapter 8. The approach prioritizes and aligns risk activities with the products and/or services that the organization has identified as greatest value. The first part of the strategy begins with the identification, analysis, and evaluation of risk to determine impact. Next, the potential financing and mitigation solutions are identified, priced, and assessed to determine feasibility of implementation (assessed as to cost, service, quality, and social implications). Finally the financing and mitigation solutions are selected as part of a risk solutions portfolio. The

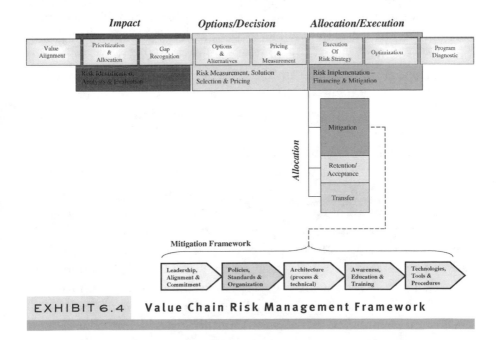

EXHIBIT 6.4   Value Chain Risk Management Framework

second part of the strategy addresses the execution and implementation process of the selected risk solutions. Whether risk mitigation or finance, both most be meticulously implemented to ensure the solution is accepted (with little interference to existing process flows) and sustainable.

One of the most critical initial steps in establishing a risk strategy is to agree on common risk terminology, operating assumptions, and scope of what will be/will not be included. This might appear on the surface to be somewhat trivial but I have personally seen it as one of the primary reasons for failure when risk professionals intersect with business and operating professionals. Following is a brief definition of what is meant by some of the risk terms. Refer to www.atourownrisk.net, for a more exhaustive list. Imagine for a moment a business professional who is able only to speak in Mandarin and a risk professional who can hear only in English trying to communicate about a significant exposure that, if not quickly addressed, could paralyze their business. This is the case when common risk terms such as risk, impacts, vulnerabilities, threats, mitigation, and financing are not clearly defined and agreed to by all parties. For example, the words *threats* and *risks* are often used interchangeably. However, a threat is an event that creates a risk, and if one tries to manage risk based on threats, then they had better have a crystal ball and deep pockets. Being able to predict which threat will happen and when and what the extent of the damage will be is nearly impossible, with the possible exception of a reccurring weather-related event. When I questioned the senior executives of this firm about which threats were their top priorities, they outlined almost 20 different threats. When then asked what programs were in place to guard against these threats, the response was less than three. However, upon further investigation, what all of the managers agreed to was that prioritizing risk activities by impacts was a far better way to define their strategy. In the end, this is what they had meant all along, but somehow their message had been picked up as "manage to threats" and, as a result, the managers of risk went off and followed their orders even though they were not producing the results they expected. All this might sound a bit trite, but I can assure you that successful execution of the risk program is dependent on clear definition and communication of the organizational risk terminology.

TERMINOLOGY

KEY TERMS THAT SHOULD BE DEFINED AND AGREED UPON BY ALL PARTIES

Resiliency—the ability to withstand loss without suffering a devastating outcome or, putting it another way, to absorb a loss without losing competitive and market posture. The risk mitigations programs that are most familiar to us are: business continuity, crisis, emergency, incident, environment life/safety, and product risk management.

Agility—the ability to avoid, move, adjust, and change based on new circumstances. This requires a sound monitoring program, clear business and risk priorities, and executable strategies to avoid the inevitable.

Resource—people, process, technology, and processing, relationships, or the physical environment

Impact—the potential quantitative and qualitative effect that an event has on the organization's value and its ability to sustain consistent ongoing operations. Impact can be expressed in loss of revenue, cash flow, asset value, compliance failure, brand/reputation, and/or strategic value.

Event—threat situation that becomes a reality and has relevance to the organization.

Business continuity planning—the process of developing advance arrangements and procedures that enable an organization to respond to an event (catastrophic) in such a manner that critical business functions continue without essential change. Business continuity planning focuses on critical business processes and functions and the planning necessary to recover and resume after a catastrophic event.

Incident management—the process to provide the capabilities to minimize the immediate impact of an event, achieve stability, provide for life safety, and if necessary, initiate recovery. Detailed incident response procedures are developed to manage all facets of an unexpected incident.

Disaster recovery planning (DRP)—applies to major, usually catastrophic, events that deny access to your facility for an extended period. Frequently, DRP refers to an information technology–

focused recovery plan designed to restore operations for disrupted systems, applications or computer facilities at an alternate facility after a catastrophic event.

Crisis management—primarily focused on the goal of ensuring the survivability of the organization during a potential or actual catastrophic disruption by establishing clear direction (i.e., chain of command) and communications with stakeholders. It encompasses recognition, response, escalation, declaration, and containment.

- Assumptions—discuss and agree on what assumptions will be made by all stakeholder involved. For example, can you assume that a workable recovery plan and back-up system is not only conceived, but in place (and there is no possible contention with others sharing that backup space)? Can you assume that everyone involved knows what they have to do after a loss and they agree on the definition of "loss"? How is vital information conveyed? Who takes the lead in each area? How do we coordinate distribution of information to keep all current and informed?
- Scope—what will be included as part of the particular activity or the task or discussion at hand, even though the overall scope might be much larger.

4. Promote Information/News Flow

In a risk-conscious culture, information about potential threats and vulnerabilities can originate from anyone across the value chain. It is necessary to have the following:

- Unobstructed communication amongst all stakeholders
- An information intelligence process
- Clearly defined path for information to travel
- A person, or people, who can interpret the information, develop a business case, and take action if necessary

In regulated environments the process for managing this information is more formal, such as in the food safety and consumer products industries. For a risk-conscious culture to be successful there needs to be a network of people and a chain of command, simply because one person (such as the CEO or CRO) cannot do it all. However, I have observed that organizations that are best-in-class go beyond the regulations and formal processes.

KEY LEARNING POINT

In these organizations, they have dedicated resources searching for public and private risk indicators, have ingrained effective communications, and set the expectation that it is the job of every stakeholder along the value chain to be risk sensitive. This sensitivity requires everyone to pay attention to indicators, anomalies, or even just a gut feelings.

In a service company, spot awards are given to those who are vigilant. I witnessed the opposite as well, where failure to act has directly impacted the individual's performance review or worse yet, they've been terminated (without the golden handcuffs). These risk-conscious cultures owe part of their success to institutionalizing a culture that emits a sense of pride from watching out for the stakeholder's best interests. I've witnessed this in engineering firms such as Lockheed Martin, DRS Technologies, GE, and BAE Systems; financial companies such as JPMorgan Chase and Goldman Sachs; pharmaceutical companies such as Hoffman LaRoche; and service organizations such as Booz Allen Hamilton, and ADP. The line "It might not be a big deal, but I thought I might give you a heads up anyway" was commonplace in these and other risk-sensitive cultures.

At the risk of dating myself, what follows is one of the best examples I can remember of how a small item can become a major risk event. This story, which later became the best selling book, *The Cuckoos Egg*,[2] and a subsequent discussion with the author, Cliff Stoll, inspired me to become more risk sensitive early in my career. Stoll was an astronomer at Berkeley Labs when he was asked to help run the computer systems. He discovered a discrepancy of 75 cents, an accounting error on a time-sharing system. He decided to find out the reason, and he stumbled on a hacker who had infiltrated the system. But the story didn't end there. As it turned out the hacker (code name Hunter) had gained access to a number of military computers and searched for information on the Strategic Defense Initiative, the Stealth bomber and Strategic Air Command. Stoll did not give up on his probe and tried to convince the CIA, FBI and other government agencies to pay attention. At the time (late 1980s), these agencies would not because of a lack of risk consciousness. Stoll, with the help of the service provider Tymnet, help trapped a spy ring that paid in cash and cocaine, and reported to the KGB. But more importantly, Stoll single-handedly created a greater risk consciousness in both the public and private sector by persevering and eventually publishing a book. Although this was a story about a "lone ranger" dealing with risk, Cliff single-handedly raised awareness and changed the view of IT risk forever.

CASE STUDY	EXECUTION

On May 2, 2007, the *New York Times* published a disturbing report entitled, "66 Workers at Agency Had Records, Inquiry Finds"[3]. The official leading the inquiry stated "the smoke signals were clearly visible; the dots should have been connected." This is a case where the risk information was not available or not being reviewed by the individuals who should have been managing this risk. There was simply a failure to act on warning signs and intelligence. "An investigation into sexual abuse and mismanagement at the Texas Youth Commission has led to the dismissal of 66 employees with records of felony charges or arrests, including one convicted of homicide and another who had pleaded guilty to attempted murder, the state official leading the inquiry reported Wednesday." The employees included guards, case workers, and maintenance staff members. The official leading the inquiry faulted a variety of watchdogs, from the youth commission headquarters itself to a West Texas prosecutor, the governor's staff and legislative officials. Whether information is unavailable, or is not being reviewed, presents two scenarios that should be actioned by corporate management. The first scenario in this case was that the negative information existed but wasn't known. In a risk-conscious culture one rule is to know thy stakeholders, including employees. Background checks are an essential security requirement. The second scenario was that the information was known but not acted upon. Accountability for escalating negative information is a basic rule in the risk-conscious culture.

5. Monitor Change

Although we discussed the need to monitor change in the first and second chapters, it is important to look a bit further. First, we must determine what key internal/external information may be of value understanding and identifying potential risk exposures. The key point is to get engaged early in the process, continuously monitor the external and internal environment for change, and engage the stakeholders to define their risk expectations. Monitoring change requires the collection, filtering, analysis, and interpretation of data/information from multiple sources.

Whether driven by market/demand forces, political/regulatory shifts, personnel/organizational shifts, poor program management, environmental issues, and/or social needs, *CHANGE* will *ALWAYS* be accompanied by increased and broadened risks. Therefore, to manage risk you must begin by understanding the trends and monitoring internal/external events and actions that might change the expected or norm. Listening posts (e.g., pubic/private information sources, lowest-level employee to the executive, internal/external experts, confidential relationships, historical data, industry and professional networks—any source of intelligence) and sensors are just a few examples of how this monitoring might be done. One must consider the numerous implications that the actual or anticipated business change might have. Examples of this include automation, outsourcing, acquisitions, reorganizations, and process/sourcing/logistical changes.

Unfortunately I have found that by the time many executives have decided to factor risk into their business decision, it's too late to change. The reasons for this are many; they are often under competitive or shareholder pressure to react to market conditions; they do not involve qualified risk management talent into the decision making process; they consider only the upside of implementing change.

The typical behavior that accompanies risk preparedness for the unplanned "downside" change is to do just the minimum. Examples of unplanned change include weather, health, environmental safety, new competition, regulation, fading customer interest (demand), political events, and security-related events.

Assessment of risks should be incorporated at the onset of change, that is, when a trend is identified, or the prospective change is in the feasibility stage, and continue all the way through the execution of the change. Here are four questions to ask:

1. **What might change or what has changed elsewhere (e.g., a new competitor that might affect my profitability?** While monitoring the internal and external environment for change, the organization will be constantly assessing business benefits and potential risks of change. In addition to the new opportunities created by change, the potential risks across the value chain will need to be assessed. By understanding the impacts of trends, you can better manage risk. You should also ask—how can you avoid risk by identifying events in the marketplace and checking to see if you have similar exposures? For example, after the 9/11 terrorist attacks, many organizations learned that the concentration of people (Cantor Fitzgerald), technology (American Express), telecommunications (Verizon), and operations (Bank of New York) into a single geographic, high-profile area was a risky strategy.

2. **How might my organization adapt or take advantage of this change? What are my organization's options?** The organization is typically assessing a range of strategic and operational choices that it can deploy to take advantage of the new opportunity. A disciplined, analytical process that evaluates measures and mitigates the risks relevant to each option should be adopted. No shortcuts here—you must make a serious effort to accurately quantify and qualify the potential impacts and the cost of managing risk for each of the new business options.

3. **How will my operating environment change as a result of the selected option?** At this point, the organization will have already decided which change option is best for them. After this decision, a plan to implement the risk solution should have been funded. Remember, it's not just your risk, it's the risk across the entire value chain, whether managed by you, or by others. Implications will need to be assessed and measured, and alternatives for financing or mitigating the risk developed throughout the value chain.

Once the organization has selected its response to change and the appropriate risk strategy, then the strategy should be tested to ensure it achieves the desired results. Consider these additional questions during the unanticipated event postmortem as part of a continuous risk improvement process.

- What are the lessons learned?
- How has the organization improved its risk mitigation and financing activities as a result of this event?
- What problems were encountered?

Here's an example of why you may need to monitor change. As more buildings are being built in areas with loose, saturated soil deposits a significant environmental risk is being introduced to key value chain resources such as the production facility. The environmental concern is a process called liquefaction, the earthquake shaking or other rapid loading forces reduces the strength and stiffness of a soil resulting in the toppling of many large buildings and homes. For example, a 7.5 magnitude earthquake in Niigata, Japan on June, 16, 1964 caused severe damage that was magnified by the liquefaction process causing the collapse of more than 2,000 homes. This earthquake in Japan, as well as another one in Alaska, revealed a significant vulnerability with today's construction. Today's value chains are threatened by liquefaction, because many of the critical facilities, such as large maritime ports, office buildings, and airports, have been built on these loose, saturated soil deposits. The engineers and builders (stakeholders) should (but don't always) reveal this exposure to their tenants, and to the public. First, organizations should have or hire talent that understand these risks and take whatever steps are necessary to mitigate them. Organizations that operate value chains that rely on people, technology, facilities, material, and/or transportation hubs must be aware and monitor the changing environment in which they operate and enhance their resiliency strategy or seek other solutions.

Here is another example of change that occurred in the business processing service industry. Each of these changes presented significant risk.

- Growing volume of content (including sensitive data) adding complexity to locating, accessing, storing, and archiving enterprise information.
- Rapid evolution and obsolescence of business systems and process architectures.
- Rapidly evolving regulatory and contractual requirements and standards compliance requirements transforming the financial services landscape.

- Evolving technology enabling the rapid proliferation and widespread distribution of sensitive information.

- Loss of control created by leveraging third-party providers in the delivery and support of core products and services.

- Growing complexity of information flows and business process connectivity with external entities.

ENDNOTES

1. www.nhc.noaa.gov/2004ivan.shtml.
2. Clifford Stoll, *The Cuckoo's Egg: Tracking a Spy Through the Maze of Computer Espionage.* New York: Pocket Books, 1990.
3. "66 Workers At Agency Had Records, Inquiry Finds." *New York Times,* May 3, 2007, p. A15.

CHAPTER 7

Diverse Stakeholders' Views and Motivations Across the Value Chain

Tell me and I will forget. Show me and I may remember. Involve me and I will understand.

—CHINESE PROVERB

Many executives believe that their stakeholders represent only the individuals under their direct control. Enlightened executives understand that the stakeholders encompass all individuals that directly or indirectly impact the organization's ability to meet its business objectives. Stakeholders range from the lowest-level clerk to the activist worrying about environmental issues. They span the entire value chain—from the source of the raw material in a manufacturing company to the person consuming the product for a food services company. Stakeholders also include public- and private-sector organizations that represent the "infrastructure" that is needed to execute commerce in a safe, secure, and efficient manner. Regulators, investors, and insurers are just a few of the many examples. To discount the importance of understanding the impact and perspective (i.e., motivations and incentives) that each stakeholder could have to successful execution of the business plan is a recipe for failure.

What causes a stakeholder to think about risk and establish a risk *expectation*, and what motivates management to take *action* to meet this expectation? Why do managers frequently take action before the stakeholders are identified, and their expectations defined or communicated? Often, the connection between the expectations and the actions are out of sequence, and as a result, a massive amount of organizational energy and resources are ineffectively unleashed on unaligned risk activities. Instead the initial questions should be, "How does the organization create value? Who are the stakeholders and what are their expectations regarding the protection of that value?"

Stakeholders—management, employees, customers, vendors, business partners, investors, regulators, public policy decision makers, professional service firms—come with a range of specific interests and concerns, and each looks at risk through their own special lens. Their expectations will vary by industry, geography, and point in time. The supply chain manager might view risk through inventory levels, pipeline availability, cash-to-cash movement, margins, and product quality—whereas the risk manager might view it through insurance placement, marketplace events, past experiences, and/or the reporting of risk impact on other, similar companies. The marketing head might look through the market penetration lens, the CFO through a funding lens, and, of course, the CEO would look through a strategy and investor lens. The regulators are looking through a compliance lens, to ensure safety, security, and a level playing field. The rank-and-file would most likely have a very narrow and tactical view of only what affects them. The problem for everyone is that, while none of those points of view are wrong per se, none contain the entire story either. To address risk efficiently and effectively, we have to be able to bring together all of those points of view and construct a comprehensive and all-inclusive view of the risk landscape while addressing the specific issue.

THE RISK EXPECTATION

Establishing the Risk Paradigm

Why is the stakeholder view important when it comes to understanding and managing risk? Because at the end of the day, the stakeholder will determine what risk mitigation does or does not get done based on their personal motivations/interests and incentives/penalties and the impact on their responsibilities under their direct control. The stakeholders will determine how much time, energy, resource, capital, and management focus will be applied. Contrary to popular belief, the CEO or directors of the organization do not always set the risk paradigm. Few set the paradigm, most can influence, set governance standards, enforce the risk policy, and provide a philosophy. However, even with the threat of the heavy hand, even the most senior-ranking individual cannot ensure a sustainable risk solution without other stakeholders' participation and agreement. Unfortunately, the stakeholders' interests are often not aligned with the corporation's highest priorities. To the contrary, if you sit the CEO down with the manager of supply chain or human resources, you are unlikely to find very much agreement regarding the management of risk. Each will most likely believe they individually set the risk paradigm (risk expectations: appetite, thresholds, behaviors, assumptions, and risk mitigation) when in fact the risk paradigm is often being set or influenced by individuals or entities, such as the investors, customers, or regulators. These individuals or entities may not be communicating risk expectations but that does not signify that these critical stakeholders do not know how much and what type of risk they are willing to tolerate.

The value chain risk management (VCRM) program requires an alignment of stakeholder interests, expanded appreciation of different points of view among other stakeholders, and a means for coordinating all of those disparate interests into a single, coordinated strategic approach. Without alignment and standards, it becomes difficult to implement an effective risk program at any level. Additionally, the lack of alignment and prioritization (i.e., implementing the most important activities from a corporate and aggregated perspective) creates tremendous inefficiency. Too often, many overlapping and redundant programs at the functional or organizational level are executed based on what lower-level managers perceive are the greatest risk. Their input should not be discounted, but the priorities should be established only after value has been defined from a top-down, aggregated point of view. Many large conglomerates, organizations with multiple operating segments and regulated companies (e.g., money center banks), have already uncovered the excess costs and sometimes added risk that come from the misalignment of security, environmental, continuity, emergency management, and other individual risk programs.

One thing is for sure—if you know what to expect, that is, if you can understand and anticipate how diverse stakeholders think about risk and how they define their risk expectations, then you can begin to influence or change some of the underlying drivers. This is a major step in the journey to becoming a risk-conscious culture. But first, you must determine who the stakeholders are and their expectations, since this is what is required to set the risk paradigm.

Who Sets the Risk Paradigm?

So far I have used the term *stakeholders* as a generic word to describe anyone who creates, contributes, consumes, and/or maintains value. Stakeholders vary from employees to suppliers, and from investors to public sector organizations that supply the infrastructure (legal, regulatory, health, safety, security, transportation, etc.). Exhibit 7.1 illustrates a view of the many stakeholders. At the foundation of the hierarchy are perhaps the most significant stakeholders with regard to setting expectations. These are the stakeholders that have contributed their own value to create additional value. Of course, they share in the good and bad, but it is their capital that has enabled another organization to exist. In a democratic public-sector environment, the core stakeholders are the general population, investment funds, other corporations, governments etc. However, non-government agencies (e.g. special interest groups), industry groups, and political parties

EXHIBIT 7.1   Private Sector Stakeholder Hierarchy

rank a close second to the above because of their ability to influence public policy, which subsequently influences private policy.

The most significant influencers are those described in the lower four tiers of Exhibit 7.1. They have the ability to:

- Determine the level of risk mitigation spent based on investor tolerance and volatility expectations
- Impact funding decisions
- Determine the breadth and depth of risk financing solutions
- Influence public and local policy (e.g., zoning, private housing, security, and safety)
- Determine what type of talent the organization is willing to invest in (i.e., accomplished via the business/financial model—what can we afford based on an expected return)
- Influence business and product strategy
- Influence the financial model
- Influence the operational model (strategy, skills, operations)

The fundamental stakeholders (lower four tiers) set the expectations to establish the risk paradigm. However, those expectations must:

- Represent all stakeholder views before the overall expectation or risk paradigm is set
- Connect and be aligned with value and value chain
- Be clearly stated and executable
- Change infrequently unless significant events dictate reevaluation
- They must make sense within the context of other expectations even if they are diverse and represent potentially conflicting views (i.e., be rationalized)
- Be communicated
- Be validated and measured

A good starting point to understand existing risk expectations is in the Securities and Exchange Commission 10K public filing, letters, and other reports. The risks are typically spelled out in the Section 1A: "Risk Factors." Although many risks are articulated in these filings, they are there to cover a company if any risk occurs. Many are pertinent to operating a successful and profitable organization. Here's a sample for a service organization and another for a large industrial conglomerate:

Service Organization (ADP Inc.)

- Changes in laws and regulations may decrease our revenues and earnings.
- Security and privacy breaches may hurt our business.
- Our systems may be subject to disruptions that could adversely affect our business and reputation.
- If we fail to adapt our technology to meet customer needs and preferences, the demand for our services may diminish.
- Political and economic factors may adversely affect our business and financial results.
- Change in our credit ratings could adversely impact our operations and lower our profitability.
- We may be unable to attract and retain qualified personnel.

Industrial Conglomerate (General Electric)

- Our global growth is subject to a number of economic and political risks.
- Our credit ratings are important to our cost of capital.
- The success of our business depends on achieving our objectives for strategic acquisitions and dispositions.
- We are subject to a wide variety of laws and regulations.
- Changes in the real estate markets are highly uncertain.

In the disclosure about vulnerabilities to all stakeholders, several important points should be reviewed:

- What action has been taken by the organization to mitigate and/or remove specific risks?
- Has the impact of vulnerabilities has been mitigated through contingency planning, improved disaster recovery plans, security procedures, technology, and diversified value chains?

- These problems are not unique to this organization; every organization in this market faces identical risks—"what are *they* doing about it?"

Although these statements often include everything short of acts of God for legal protection, one can see that these risk factors are general but they provide a starting point to better understand the overall risk priorities of the investors and other stakeholders. A tool used by many multinational organizations, as part of the overall governance process, is the risk register. This tool collects the organizations' regularly monitored major risks. It also contains their risk priorities and expectations resulting from years of actual experiences. I strongly suggest that the risk register be used as a guideline. However, in my experience, I seldom find that the risk mitigation activities that are under way are in sync with the organizational risk programs that are under way. That's not to say that the organizations that I've worked with and for are ignoring what's in their 10K or risk register. What I am saying is that it is my belief that there is a substantial amount of risk mitigation underway that does not align with the business priorities. Many times the lack of alignment occurs because the risk mitigation work—supported by technology, skills, and process—is happening deep within the bowels of the organization without a clear understanding of the most important business issues/concerns and agreement by senior management. Too often, the activities focus on one's perception of the risks and actions applicable to "MY piece of the world" and not the greater organization. Exhibit 7.2 represents what I have personally witnessed in more than 150 organizations (over a 30-year span). Exhibit 7.3 represents the correct business risk model, whereby the expectations are established first and then the actions follow.

One way to identify the organization's highest risk priorities is to analyze the way in which they finance risk. Based on the amount and type of insurance that the stakeholders are purchasing, it is possible to identify their top-of-mind risk expectations. If organizations are purchasing a large amount of a specific type of insurance—let's say political risk or trade disruption insurance—then chances are that the stakeholders are concerned about political uncertainty in a country that is included in their value chain. For example, more than $44 billion in coverage for political risk was written in 2006, up from $37 billion in 2005. Political risk insurance provides coverage from the following perils: violence, government

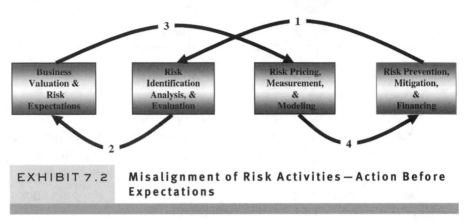

EXHIBIT 7.2   **Misalignment of Risk Activities — Action Before Expectations**

repudiation of contracts, nationalism and expropriation of assets, and inconvertibility (not able to be legally exchanged for another currency).[1] Unfortunately, the purchase of insurance might be misleading since most experts in the industry agree that the insurable risk is far less than that which needs to be mitigated. The purchase of insurance creates other misconceptions: 1) believing that corporate insurance claims are paid promptly and at 100% of the stated value, even though many will experience nonpayment of claims if there is a possibility that management was at fault because there was no viable risk management program in place; 2) stakeholders at all levels have provided input regarding potentially insurable risks they may have.

With the exception of dictated requirements (e.g., government regulation) once a set of broad expectations (all important stakeholders) are gathered, they must be articulated (including the costs and value) and

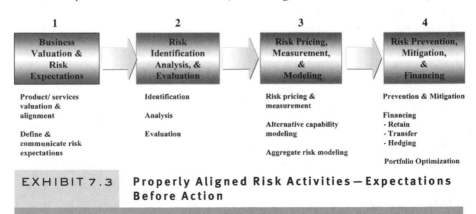

EXHIBIT 7.3   **Properly Aligned Risk Activities — Expectations Before Action**

prioritized based on the greatest value to the organization. Once agreement has been reached, the next step is to transform the expectation into actions. One must have a system to monitor change and continuously verify that the established expectations and committed deliverables are achieved.

An Example of Some Factors that Influence Expectation Setting

As previously mentioned, understanding various stakeholder views is a key ingredient of a risk-conscious culture. One must look both internally and externally to get a true picture of the factors that influence expectation setting. The stakeholders' perspective is also heavily skewed by corporate culture, competing organizations, compensation, motivations, regional/geographic differences, economic viability, competitive pressures, and industry and governmental policies and behaviors.

1. Regional factors—risk expectations will vary significantly by region, primarily influenced by cultural differences, current political, social, economic, and competitive drivers. For example, McKinsey had 201 executives in Latin America; their top risk list concerns were: fluctuations in foreign-exchange rates, regulatory concerns, commodity shortages/price fluctuation, and problems with supply chain infrastructure.[2] However, executives who were interviewed in other parts of the world understandably had a different set of priorities—they listed the following as their key risk issues: general supply chain availability, cost and quality of labor, regulatory concerns, and the reliability of suppliers. Stakeholder expectations in emerging economies have still different concerns: infrastructure, access to transportation, limitations of terrain, weather related limitations, timing, and cost of supply chain.

■ EXAMPLE—REGIONAL INFLUENCES   What is a "jumbo" loan? In the 2007 credit crunch, when markets went through a period of growing mortgage foreclosures, financial-sector volatility, and housing bubbles, the question arose as to whether the secondary market (Fannie Mae, Ginnie Mae), also known collectively as GSEs (government-sponsored enterprises) should raise the limits on loans acceptable within their programs. In 2007, the limit for GSE loans was $417,000, which is fine if you live in the Midwest or South. But if your home is in New York or California, that $417,000 won't buy much. It became evident that setting a single loan limit for every market was unrealistic. The customer requirements varied by specific regions of the country. As a consequence, the risk of not being able to find a loan was far greater in a credit crunch in expensive markets than it was in less expensive markets—regardless of actual market risk levels (defaults and foreclosures). Ironically, default levels in the Midwest were among the highest, even though qualification for the secondary market was the easiest in the country. Somehow, the risk paradigm was turned upside down. ■

2. Industry and regulatory factors—stakeholder expectations will vary by industry. For example, those in regulated industries such as banking, pharmaceutical, and utilities (especially nuclear) are subject to nonnegotiable risk expectations that are set by public policy and regulatory authorities. Noncompliance results in significant fines, censorship and possible shutdown (e.g., Securities and Exchange Commission, Nuclear Energy Regulatory Authority).

One of the most heavily regulated industries is the life sciences industry (pharmaceuticals and medical devices/equipment). In the United States, the Food and Drug Administration is responsible for oversight and auditing compliance with standards. The penalty for noncompliance is substantial, as was recently discovered by General Electric's OEC Medical Systems Inc. unit. In January 2007, a consent decree was filed in the U.S. District Court for the District of Utah (subject to court approval). The consent decree "prohibits the manufacturing and distribution of specified GEC OEC Medical Systems x-ray surgical imaging systems at facilities in Salt Lake City and Lawrence, Massachusetts" until the devices are shown to be in compliance. In another recent case, Baxter's heparin, a blood-thinning drug, was recalled because of suspected contamination. In this case, the question of whether laws have actually been broken has been brought into question, although an FDA policy appears to have been in place for almost 20 years. There does not appear to be any law to require preshipment inspections, although one is being considered now. Either way, whether regulatory, industry, or market pressure, it is essential that the organization monitor the external environment to determine diverse stakeholders' views. These examples should serve as notice to others in the industry that an expectation exists and must be considered.

Industry groups such as the National Association of Manufacturers (NAM) will also heavily influence risk prioritization and stakeholder expectations. In a recent conversation with several senior representatives from NAM they had shared the industry's top risks: energy policy, tort reform, tax issues, trade issues, regulatory issues, legal reform, workforce development (healthcare under pharmaceutical industry), and the newly introduced transportation infrastructure as major projects with significant risk issues. These risks can be used to help establish the risk paradigm.

Another industry group, the Risk and Insurance Management Society, was surveyed by Marsh to rank the industries by risk confidence and current state of risk program (see Exhibit 7.4). The 866 members rated the agriculture, general manufacturing and educational industries lowest in terms of comfort level and current state of risk program. One theory for

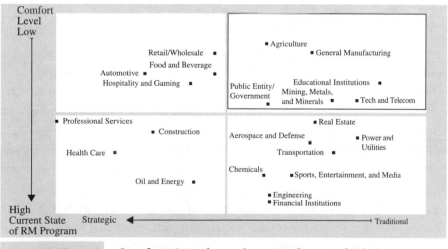

EXHIBIT 7.4   Comfort Level vs. Current State of Risk
Management by Industry

the lower confidence might be because the expectations set by the stake-holders is lower in these industries.

3. Governmental/public policy factors—Another group that varies by country and significantly influences the risk expectations is the public sector agencies such as transportation (DOT, MOT). Public policy and the management of key risks by public-sector agencies have a spillover effect on the private sector in areas such as commerce, transportation, health, and security. This trend will continue as the public sector in developed nations takes on a greater role in providing a financial backstop for catastrophic risk such as terrorism and natural disasters. For example, in the United States the Homeland Security Council in partnership with the Department of Homeland Security, the federal interagency, and state and local homeland agencies established the risk expectations via 15 all-hazards planning scenarios. These scenarios are designed to be the foundation for the development of national preparedness standards from which homeland security capabilities can be measured. They are: nuclear detonation, biological attack, biological disease outbreak, chemical attack, natural disaster, radiological attack, explosives attack, and cyber attack. These standards have and will continue to influence private-sector preparedness.

One final thought about other factors that influence the risk paradigm. Since many organizations are typically driven by headlines and events, the impact that the recognized experts have on influencing the setting of expectations in many cases is significant. For example, the 2007 World Economic Forum Global Risk Report stated, "Mechanisms in place to manage and mitigate risk at the level of business, governments, and global governance are inadequate." This report was presented at the World Economic Forum in Davos, Switzerland, which is heavily attended by public- and private-sector leaders. Key risk issues such as pandemic preparedness, water and resource shortages, and energy price shocks were discussed by the group. This dialogue will typically get replayed back in the board and executive conference rooms and will initiate questions that the organization will have to address. Additionally the local and national media pick up on industry reports like these, and quickly communicate the results as if they were a de facto industry benchmark or standard.

These examples above are excellent sources that can be used to set the risk paradigm. A business-focused view is required by accountants, engineers, and the rank-and-file. This is a critical component of the risk-conscious culture. By looking at the expectations from a top-down, bottom-up and outside/inside perspective provides a full view of what is truly needed to set the risk paradigm. However, investors, employees and executive management must always question whether the expectations that are being established and communicated are enough. Here is a case where just doing what the industry expects is not enough. Although the court recently reversed the ruling, many lives could have been saved if the industry standard was exceeded.

CASE STUDY

THE DANGER OF NOT CHALLENGING RISK EXPECTATIONS: IS THE BAR SET CORRECTLY?

2001 GMC Suburban's Side-Torso Airbag Failed to Deploy in Collision

Facts and Allegations

In 2003, plaintiff Stacey Burry, 40, was a passenger in a 2001 GMC Suburban that was hit on the passenger side by a tractor-trailer. She was wearing a seat belt. The side-torso airbag did not deploy and she was severely injured. The other occupants of the Suburban were not seriously injured. Burry, her husband, and their three minor children sued General Motors Corporation for *products liability* (design and marketing defects) involving the airbag sensor. Specifically, the plaintiffs claimed that after tests showed that the airbags deployed when the doors were slammed, GM decreased the sensor's sensitivity. The plaintiffs argued that the problem could have been fixed by adding a second sensor, at a cost of $10 per vehicle, but that GM rejected the solution. GM argued that the Suburban met or exceeded all government standards; that the airbag system functioned properly in this accident; that Burry was injured when her head hit the head of the driver, not when it hit the Suburban's side structure; and that design features of the Suburban should be credited with saving the lives of the other occupants. Burry suffered severe head injuries and was in a coma for several months after the crash. She was diagnosed with irreversible brain damage and requires constant care and attention.

Result

The jury found design defect by GM. It found GM 49% at fault. The damages were assessed at $38,230,000. (Case: *Chris Burry, Stacey Burry, and Chris Burry, as Next Friend for Rachel Burry, Sarah Burry, and Meghan Burry, Minors v. General Motors Corporation v. Carol Reid,* No. 03-050383, Wise County District Court, 271st, Texas, 2/18/05).

COMMENTARY

Product liability risk is a hot topic, especially in the food services, pharmaceutical, and consumer product industries (e.g., toy). Besides the regulatory guidelines that are required by public organizations such as the U.S. Consumer Product Safety Commission, and the Food and Drug Administration, the organization must gather a 360° view of the expectations of all stakeholders including the best and worst case risk examples for that particular industry. Exhibit 7.5 illustrates this 360° view. Any organization that is a participant in a value chain that creates, manufactures, and distributes products that could have adverse effects on the public, must go the extra mile to identify and mitigate potential risks regardless of whether regulators have established stringent standards.

A PRACTICAL VIEW OF ESTABLISHING STAKEHOLDER EXPECTATIONS

Establishing stakeholder expectations might appear to be a daunting task. However, many organizations that I have worked with have simplified the process by establishing an initial requirement that can be progressively improved upon. This approach is sometimes referred to as a maturity model. Of course, some work is needed to translate these expectations into business priorities and executable actions. What typically happens is that

360° View

EXHIBIT 7.5   A 360° View of Stakeholder Expectations

internal and external experts in each of the stakeholder categories brainstorm to identify what they would consider to be "acceptable standards" for their piece of the pie. The results are then aggregated and used to set priorities, determine feasibility, assess implementation costs, and develop action plans. Unfortunately, too often these plans never surface beyond an individual origin or geography. The drawback of this approach is that by delegating priority and expectation setting to lower levels, someone other than the primary stakeholder artificially sets the bar to that which only the organization can achieve. Money is often wasted solving problems that are small in comparison to the real risk exposures. These localized expectations are seldom communicated in layman's terms back to the original stakeholders to determine their importance in relation to broader issues. Not all organizations can comprehensively attack the risk problem due to such reasons as, a lack of expertise, market pressure, conflicting internal priorities; those less equipped to execute a comprehensive program must start by analyzing each operating entity, stakeholder requirement, and risk posture.

How do you categorize the way risk is managed by the decision makers in your organization? Frankly, many risk management programs (beyond insurance placement) are dismal in that they receive little funding with a great deal of responsibility, no risk management training (looking beyond the obvious) for the masses, few resources are devoted to even defining the scope of the problem (often low-level employees that don't rock the boat), or once known, how little interest there is in tackling the problem.

You can look by function or by behaviors when developing risk program management. If you look at a program by behavior, today's executives can be categorized in to several levels of risk-sensitivity. These include three broad types of risk managers: enlightened/informed, risk taker/gambler, and brain dead.

The *enlightened/informed* risk manager is risk-sensitive; fully aware of the nature and scope of risk, and at the very least, understands that there may be severe risks not even identified. This executive/manager wants to fix the problem rather than ignore it. They are able to prioritize risk solutions and make decisions regarding trade-offs/value of proposed initiatives. They adequately fund a comprehensive risk management program, acquire talent, support the ongoing effort, and motivate risk managers. The enlightened actively encourage and seek the participation of all in the value chain, and want risk disclosed, regardless of the potential exposure, so that appropriate risk-related trade-offs and decisions can be made.

The attitude of the *risk taker/gambler* is that of keeping the bottom line strong, which requires accepting risks and playing the odds that a risk will not become an adverse event on their watch. They resource the risk function at minimal levels and spend just enough to make sure the risk checklists are checked and the auditors are happy. They don't want the boat rocked, do not encourage participation at all levels of the organization, and spend nights praying that nothing will happen. Incidentally, investors might not be so happy (if the investors are risk sensitive) with executive management adopting the gambler's point of view, realizing that it is their capital at stake and not necessarily the gambler's.

To term the final category *brain dead/ignorant* may seem harsh but, in the real world, a significant percentage of key decision makers and risk managers are unaware of risks and want to remain that way, or refuse to fund any resources to the risk management function or acknowledge the vulnerability. Unlike the risk taker/gambler praying that something does not go wrong is not even a thought—they sleep well. The brain-dead executives/managers are *dangerous* and discourage the surfacing of risk-related issues. If encountered, they must be enlightened or *removed*.

Active stakeholder involvement in risk management is not a static matter, either. Risk is as dynamic as expanding markets, introducing new products or acquiring a new company.. For example, new business partners often are created through acquisition of competitors, sensible joint ventures with existing competitors, or other arrangements of mutual convenience. Because the partnership benefits both sides, joint risk management also makes sense. And because any change in the relationship between organizations brings up new risks, a fresh look at existing programs and their relationships/interactions new partners is required. Unfortunately some think that it makes no sense to simply try and expand a current risk management program to a newly expanded venue. The attitude that "My risk management programs are excellent and that new entities/partners must be placing the same importance on their risk programs" is a fatal flaw in thinking and will result in increased risk and unplanned consequences

Any organization that does not perform a full risk analysis (playing the odds) places it and its new partners at risk. By the nature of the partnership itself, the organization has the same responsibility to the partner and its stakeholders as it has to its primary stakeholders.

ACTION AND EXECUTION

Organizations can begin to take action once the expectations have been collected and aggregated, value priced, and prioritized. One caution, since the transition to a risk-conscious culture will take extreme management attention and funding, and several months to years to achieve and sustain: it will be necessary to continue or manage and respond to event-driven risks as they occur. In other words, if those who set the risk paradigm convey the need to address a specific risk issue—and the clock is ticking—then without exception the tactical and immediate need must be addressed. If you are in the toy industry and your investors or the general public is raising product quality as an issue, then it goes without saying that the organization must respond. The risk is relevant, immediate, and must be treated as a priority, often regardless of the costs involved.

One of the measures of a successful product recall process is the ability to have the information and systems needed to track the logistics process to establish traceability back to the source. Collection and mapping of key data, key processes, and the resources for a given product/service is a fundamental requirement of the VCRM approach. Using a common approach, such as value chain process and resource mapping, that can be leveraged across all types of risk categories will increase efficiencies and ensure consistency (e.g., product risk traceability, and continuity risk requirement).

THE NEED TO TAKE IMMEDIATE ACTION

It was my first day on the job in New York City. As I was being introduced to my new co-workers, the director of audit interrupted and asked me to join him in his office. I was a bit nervous, but I suspected this was just a formality and he wanted to welcome me to the group. Instead, he blurted out a request to go across the street to the newsstand and retrieve one copy of each of the day's local papers. Needless to say, this bothered me but I didn't say a word. Here it was, 1980—I'm making $15,000 a year and I'm being asked to be an errand boy (at the time I considered $15,000 an enormous salary).

I reluctantly left the skyscraper on 40th and 3rd and began my hunt for one copy of every newspaper. I picked up the papers and brought them back to the director's office. He then proceeded to tell me that I needed to search the papers for a particular individual's name. I decided not to share the name in this book but I will say that this name is forever burned into my memory. It also served my first dose of the reality of risk.

I returned to my cubicle and began the search. It wasn't long before I discovered the first instance of the infamous name. It was a horrible story that described how this named person had been accused of murdering a number of women who were suspected of being prostitutes. All this was interesting, but I thought, "What the heck did that have to do with my job?" I continued to search the other papers, cut out the articles, and then forwarded the information to the director.

As I handed him the articles, I asked him, "Why do you want this information?" He didn't answer my question but instead led me across the hall and into another office. He opened the door and there stacked floor to ceiling were at least a dozen, 10-foot-high piles of fan-folded green and white computer paper. The paper printouts contained SMF audit records (now I am dating myself, SMF or Systems Management Facility audit records were produced by the IBM MVS operating system and represented the activity logs or "smoking gun").

He looked me straight in the eye and said, "Gary, the accused is the night shift manager in our data center." He had access to everything: millions of sensitive health and financial client records, all of the applications and operating systems that ran our mainframe computers, and thousands of tapes containing the financial and other critical records of the firm. Then the director said "Gary, we need to find out what else this guy might have done." In the coming months we discovered very little about this individual, primarily because at the time the records were too general and the amount of manual review was overwhelming.

Did we have the right information, and did we know what to do with it?

WHICH LENS ARE WE LOOKING THROUGH?

One of the most difficult tasks when viewing risk is to get the right perspective and acknowledge that the organization does not have the resources to support and respond to every identified risk. If it were just one view that had to be considered, the task would be simple. However, many diverse stakeholders' views contribute to the success or failure of the risk solution. For example, the risk manager may want to implement mitigation technologies such as virus protection for all employees' laptops. The CFO is conscious of the numbers, and sees expenditures that, over three years, add up to over a million dollars for something that *might* happen. The CIO might view the issue as a necessary security precaution, but is concerned with how it might interfere with his technical support's ability to maintain high levels of service. When implementing the risk paradigm it is necessary to have an appreciation of the different stakeholder views and how they might impact successful deployment or support of the risk mitigation solution. Here are the perspectives based on a few key roles, and their area of risk responsibility. One word of caution here—each risk organization is different, so roles and perspectives may change.

The key to a successful risk strategy is to appoint a high-level respected individual capable of traversing the organization and all external stakeholder environments. This individual will be assigned the responsibility of influencing risk policies and encouraging executives to champion and implement effective risk management programs. Organizations have begun to place this position (sometimes representing a risk committee) reporting to the board to ensure independence and objectivity. Each company must develop an organizational structure that properly aligns with this function in a way that promotes an aggressively executed risk management program.

- **Chief executive officer, business unit head, operating group head or product manager**—typically responsible for the portfolio mix, growth initiatives, concentration risk, mergers and acquisitions/integration, geographic dispersion, consumer preference changes, and geopolitical changes. Functions primarily as coordinator, and has the primary task of ensuring that those others within the organization have, in fact, addressed the scope of risk activities.
  - **Primary risk responsibilities:** political, economic, and reputation/brand risk.

- **Chief operating officer**—typical responsibilities include product development, supply chain, pricing, marketing/sales, vendor integrity, alliances/outsourcing, joint ventures/partnerships, project management, construction management, change control, customer satisfaction, quality control, capacity, BCM/DR, crisis management. Works with CEO to ensure execution of the risk management, and follows up with subordinates to (a) review the scope of risk management activities, (b) assess effectiveness, and (c) propose alternatives or action steps where needed.
  - **Primary risk responsibilities:** reputation, economic, financial, social, environmental, labor, and operational risk.

- **Chief financial officer**—consolidates and protects financial assets, with keen awareness of current vulnerabilities; devises and presents a plan for protecting these assets in coordination with external auditing consultants; and presents a detailed procedural summary for all to follow, with additional emphasis on action plans as well as changes in current procedures. Typically responsible for capital structure, policy and risk (credit, currency, interest rate risk, commodity), investment, derivatives, liquidity, tax strategy, revenue recognition, financial disclosure, investor relations, collateral, insurance, contingent liabilities, fraud.
  - **Primary risk responsibilities:** financial and operational risk.

- **Chief information officer**—goal is to support needs of business by identifying cost-effective technology to give us a leg up on competitors. Also responsible for growing a community of skills and talents and supplying, maintaining and protecting IT infrastructure. Ensure effective and efficient IT operation that allows free flow of information and secure high-performance environment.
  - **Primary risk responsibilities:** informational, technological, operational and natural/weather hazards that can impact networking and processing risk.

- **Human resource executive**—supports aquisition and retention of labor, development of skills, deployment of succession plans, establishment of benefits and compensation plans.
  - **Primary risk responsibilities:** health, labor, social, weather, psychopathic, criminal, and terrorist risk.

- **Risk manager**—imbedded in all organizations, Corporate Risk head coordinates all risk activities. Risk head may be housed is any organization that takes the responsibility. Primarily responsible for setting the risk financing and mitigation execution strategy. Primary responsibility to ensure effective and prudent risk financing options is in place to smooth earnings volatility.
  - **Primary risk responsibilities:** all risks.

- **Chief safety officer**—physical, personnel, ergonomics, OSHA, technology, C-TPAT, document retention, foods safety programs, product recall, espionage, container security, FAST (Fast and Secure Trade).

  ○ **Primary risk responsibilities:** psychopathic, criminal, and terrorist, weather, informational, and labor risk.

- **General Counsel**—supports regulatory compliance (varies by industry and region such as F.D.A, U.S.D.A), international trade agreements, Homeland Security Act, statutory filing, Sarbanes-Oxley compliance, sustainability index issues, community affairs, communications strategy, lobbying, ethics, and governance rules.

  ○ **Primary risk responsibilities:** legal, regulatory, and compliance.

- **Auditors:**—audit, compliance and operational risk management personnel typically have responsibility for reviewing and highlighting risk and should be included in all of the above categories of risks.

  ○ **Primary risk responsibilities:** oversight, risk validation.

TURNING EXPECTATIONS INTO ACTIONABLE REQUIREMENTS

Setting expectations is important, but without a clear path to actionable, executable standards, creating a risk-conscious culture is impossible. A process that I've used at many times different organizations is to establish listening posts. A listening post is a method of gathering intelligence about risk requirements and tolerances (market, regulators, competitors, industry, risk standard), then converting that information into specific requirements and actions.

Exhibit 7.6 represents a sample of a legal and regulatory listening post for the pharmaceutical industry, and the expectations that have to be met according to requirements.

In a risk-conscious culture expectations must be clearly defined, actions must be aligned with expectations, and the actions must be followed up with organizational commitment, policies and standards, education, awareness and architecture, and technology tools and procedures.

Legal & Regulatory	FDA 21 CFR Part 11 (cont)		
	Signature/Record Linking		
	■ Electronic signatures and handwritten signatures applied to electronic records shall be linked to their respective electronic records to ensure that the signatures cannot be removed, copied, or transferred to falsify an electronic record.		
	General Requirements		
	■ Each electronic signature will be unique to an individual and should not be reused by, or assigned to, another individual.		
	■ Before an organization establishes, assigns or certifies an individual's electronic signatures, the organization shall verify the identity of the individual.		
	■ Persons using electronic signatures shall certify to the FDA that they are using electronic signatures intended to be the legally binding equivalent of a traditional handwritten signature, and may be required to provide additional certification that a given electronic signature is the equivalent of the signer's handwritten signature.		
	Electronic Signature Components and Controls		
	■ Electronic signatures not based upon biometrics should employ two distinct identification components such as an identification code and password.		
	■ When executing a series of signings during a continuous period, the first signing should be executed using all signature components and subsequent signings at least one signature component.		
	■ Electronic signatures shall be used by their genuine owners, and be administered so that attempted use of an individual signature by anyone other than its genuine owner requires collaboration of two or more individuals.		
	Control for Identification Codes/Passwords		
	■ Persons who use electronic signatures based upon ID codes and passwords should employ controls to ensure their security and integrity and include:		
	Maintain uniqueness of each combined ID code and password to avoid duplication of		

EXHIBIT 7.6   **Legal and Regulatory Listening Post**

CASE STUDY   A STORY OF NOT PROPERLY
EXECUTING YOUR
EXPECTATIONS

Why El Paso cares—health and safety of individuals and community higher cost of mitigation after the fact: In July 2007, El Paso Corporation (NYSE: EP) reached a settlement that involved the U.S. Departments of Justice and Transportation from the explosion of 30" natural gas pipeline (gas transmission line no. 1103) that occurred at 5:26 a.m. on August 19, 2000, in Carlsbad, New Mexico. Twelve people were killed and service was disrupted from the loss of transmission line no. 1103 and the precautionary shutdown of lines 1100 and 1110. As a result of this settlement El Paso Natural Gas will spend $86 million to repair its entire 10,000 miles of pipeline and pay $15.5 million in civil penalties.

The complaint filed by the Department of Justice alleged EPNG did not employ personnel who were qualified in corrosion control methods; failed to investigate and mitigate internal corrosion in two of its pipelines transporting natural corrosive gas; and failed to correctly monitor those pipelines to determine if the steps they had taken were working properly.

ENDNOTES

1. "Of Coups and Coverage." *The Economist*, April 17, 2007.
2. The McKinsey Quarterly, May 2007.

CHAPTER 8

Executing the Plan

No amount of experimentation can ever prove me right; a single experiment can prove me wrong.

—ALBERT EINSTEIN

Investors select their market risks through specific analytical tools, risk management tactics, discipline, trial, analysis, and execution. Our plan for addressing value chain risk and building a risk-conscious culture thus far has focused on all of these elements with one exception—execution. Perhaps the most critical of all elements, execution represents meshing the plan with reality, aligning resources with goals, and achieving the results promised.[1] Key words from this definition that drive successful execution: reality, alignment, resources, and results. Throughout the book, I have attempted to present a real, and sometimes not so pretty, picture of today's operating and behavioral risk environment as seen through the collective experience of many stakeholders. What we discovered is that the discipline of value-driven prudent risk management is an iterative and evolving process, one that requires trial, execution, prioritization, validation, continuous adaptation, and improvement. Business realities must constantly be checked to ensure that the approach is achievable. There is no silver bullet—text book or practitioner/consultant—with the answer. But all those responsible for creating value share a common thread, the urgent need to manage risk. Uncovering the business value provides the organization the context that is a critical prerequisite to execution. Now let's look at what it takes to link reality with alignment and results, effectively manage identified risks, allocate resources to the risks that will have the greatest impact to value, and protect that value.

PUTTING IT ALL TOGETHER

Value Chain Risk Management

Six Steps to Successful Execution

1. Value Alignment—identify value and prioritize
2. Risk Identification, Analysis, and Evaluation—determine impact
3. Risk Measurement, Solution Selection and Pricing
4. Risk Implementation, Financing and Mitigation—prepare the roadmap for execution, optimize the portfolio allocations
5. Risk Solutions Execution—deploy solutions
6. Program Monitoring, Measurement and Continuous Improvement—validate and refine

STEP 1: VALUE ALIGNMENT

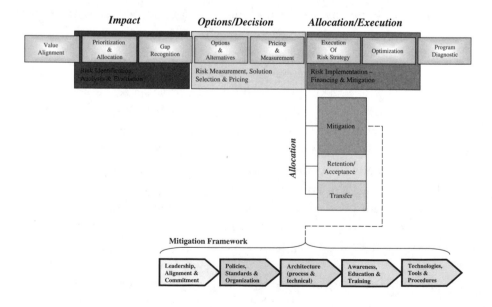

Goal: Identify product(s)/service(s) that represent the greatest "value" to the organization so that the VCRM approach can be efficiently and effectively executed.

Our earlier discussion about Risconomics asserted that the organization simply did not have unlimited time, resources, management attention (i.e., competing priorities), and capital to address all of the organizations risks. Therefore the goal of prudent risk management is to efficiently and effectively allocate scarce risk resources to the product(s)/services(s) of greatest value. This is also where the VCRM process begins. As a first step in that process the organization must seek input from all key stakeholders (refer to Chapter 7) to determine their views of value. Each area of the organization will have its own view which may not represent what is most important value to the organization as a whole. Once the organization has determined which of these product(s)/service(s) possess the greatest present and future value to the firm, then it can begin to prioritize the products/services, and set-up listening posts to monitor change. The intent should be to eventually integrate the VCRM process into every single product(s)/service(s) value chain when operating realities permit.

Therefore, our process begins with the question: "What are our most important products and services?" The answer to this question should serve to establish the organization's product(s)/service(s) *value* at risk and the focus of risk activities. In my experience the client often defines value by revenue alone. In many instances that is a good place to start; however, the client must consider other definitions of *value* as part of the overall prioritization process to include products and services that will:

- Represent little current value but enormous potential future or *strategic* value
- Reflect the *brand*, reputation, or image of value
- Require *compliance* with a regulation, contract, and/or statutory obligation—without which, value would could not be created
- Create value by generating large *cash flow* (liquidity)
- Represent large capital investments or an enormous *asset* base that is used to generate value

These factors, when considered in the aggregate, represent the total "value" concept. This is important when one considers internal/external point-in-time influences, such as increased regulation, liquidity pressure (e.g., like those experienced by financial institutions during the subprime lending crisis), and risk events such as a product recall.

Let's look at some of these "value" factors in greater detail.

A product/service line with *strategic value* might far exceed any product/service that is currently generating revenue. An example of a product with tremendous strategic value at a large capital-intensive organization such as Airbus or Boeing, might be the next generation airliner (Airbus A380 or Boeing 787 Dreamliner) usually product lines that require large future capital investments or ones that shift the focus of the organization (such as a major rebranding) qualify as having *strategic* value. For a vendor in the defense industry it might be the next generation warship (e.g., DDX) or fighter jet (JSF—Joint Strike Fighter).

Another qualitative value category, a product with significant *brand/reputational* value that could be a product line that has held true for many years—the household name product such as Tide, Kleenex, or Q-Tip that does not necessarily represent the top revenue producer but instead is seen as the icon of that organization. A recognized brand represents trust, customer confidence, and competitive advantage. Harm to a valued corporate or product name can come from an individual such as an executive. For example, more people know the name Ken Lay than the names of most other CEOs, based on the infamous Enron scandal. If the general public associates a company name with a disaster, such as the years-long association between Exxon and the 1989 Exxon *Valdez* oil spill disaster, it creates a huge brand name problem. Harm can come to the brand through many sources, such as:

- Bad behavior/integrity issues with senior management
- Bad behavior/integrity issues with the communities it serves
- Overall behavior toward something that put a large part of the population at risk (or where the organization was not risk-sensitive and conscious)

An equally damaging loss with potentially more permanent negative impact is *embarrassment*, growing from damage to brand and reputation due to losses and trust. Most people today still remember the disaster in December 1984 in Bhopal, India, when 8,000 or more deaths resulted from a 40-ton toxic spill at the Union Carbide (now part of Dow Chemical) subsidiary plant. To this day, the name of Union Carbide is still associated with that loss. In fact, the disaster involved yet another form of financial loss, that of *community impact*. Not only were many families tragically affected by the loss; the perception continues that Union Carbide abandoned the community after the spill occurred, and controversy over this continues to the present day. On the personal side, impacts are also varied. As the Bhopal incident revealed, *people die* from many kinds of risks. Losses from mining, oil drilling and refining, and other industrial activities are significant around the world, and these continuing dangers require risk mitigation and reflect the lack of effective measures. For example, the coal industry experiences numerous mine cave-ins and loss of life caused by known violations of mine safety standards. These problems still need fixing decades after they became apparent.

The third, and final category, is *regulatory/statutory* and/or contractual. This is a product that might need to be considered a top priority because it is currently being investigated by a national/federal public sector agency (e.g., Securities and Exchange Commission) or is facing remediation action. An example in the regulated financial sector is that of options, and the investigation into backdating that they prompted. The many companies that spend much time, management attention, capital, and resources to remediate the risk and reduce the direct *fiduciary exposure* of those executives who, through action, inaction, or negligence, failed to anticipate this risk. Today's litigious society causes this specific fiduciary exposure, which the corporate shell and insurance may not protect. Few people have forgotten the outcome of the Enron scandal of a few years ago. The company was dissolved and its key executives sent to prison, and its auditor, Arthur Andersen was forced out of business. That company, once known as the bastion of auditing ethics, suffered irreparable damage as a result of its implication in the Enron accounting fraud. More subtle, perhaps, is the *strategic loss* resulting from the failure to realize some risks. For example, Eastman Kodak was late to acknowledge the digital camera revolution. As the traditional film production company for the world, Kodak missed an opportunity to lead the new, non-film camera world and as a result, has seen a decline in its financial strength and stock price. This was a blind spot in a strategic area from which Kodak is still attempting to recover.

Aggregating Value

Determining the products and services that represent the greatest value is especially complicated in organizations that have large product/service portfolios.

To illustrate the aggregation process, let's take a look at a sample life sciences/pharmaceutical company that produces more than one hundred products. One of these products has recently received Food and Drug Administration (FDA) approval and is considered to be a "blockbuster" drug. Expected third-year-sales are forecasted at $5 billion. However, at the present time this drug does not generate any revenue. This is the future cash generator for the company and, as such, qualifies as a top priority because of the tremendous *strategic value*. It should be one of the first products that the VCRM process is applied to. In another example, we find that currently, 60% of the cash flow is being generated by another drug whose patents will expire in 18 months. At that time it will be subject to intense generic competition. This drug would probably be considered as one of the first products that we apply the VCRM process to because of its *cash flow value*. As a final example, the organization is also engaged in the capital intensive business of producing medical devices and equipment. Upon further examination (pardon the pun), the organization determines that 42% of the total asset base is tied up in production of one particular medical imaging device. From the *asset* standpoint, this medical product might qualify as one of the products that represent the greatest value to the firm.

In these examples we can quickly see that the organization would need to align the VCRM process with at least two, possibly three major product lines. This contrasts the more obvious and usual decision to focus risk activities (time, resources, capital, and management attention) either: 1) broadly, an at a general or corporate level; 2) narrowly, and at a functional (security) or resource level (a piece of equipment, software or contract); 3) inappropriately, at a value creation level that only considers only the best selling product or services that may not align with the critical business priorities at that point in time; or 4) individual managers protecting the revenue source that gives them the greatest compensation/incentives. *Note*: It must be recognized that this is a continuous process. It evolves as the organization, products, and services value changes.

Other Industry Examples Where Value has been Prioritized:

- At one of the large beverage companies the key product was its bottled water product rather than the popular brand soda product

- For a large utility company, the value was the power generation service line versus exploration, storage, trading. Power generation was further narrowed to fossil fuel generation because it represented eighty percent of power generation revenue. However, the utility also had to select nuclear power generation because of regulatory compliance requirements.

- A large consumer products company identified a set of stock keeping units (SKUs) as their top priority because it represented the firm's most profitable product line.

- A mortgage company identified the servicing operations, rather than mortgages origination, as having greatest value.

- A money center bank identified its wholesale operations as the priority and global payments/settlements as the key to creating the organization's value; here regulatory considerations weighed heavily

To assist with this process, I have provided a simple spreadsheet (Exhibit 8.1) that can be used to apply the approach. The column on the far left represents all of the product(s)/service(s) offerings. A weight may be assigned to each category to act as a "timing" factor (i.e., reflects the changing market priorities, previously discussed in this chapter). For example, if a particular drug is under investigation by an external agency, then the weight for compliance impact would probably be higher. The results of this process should not be used a precise measurement, but rather the results should be stratified to product and group priorities.

Who should be responsible for prioritizing which product(s)/services(s) create value? The senior leaders of the organization; executive management at the operating group/division and corporate level. The stakeholders, including the board, should be made aware and should validate the

	Quantitative Impacts						Qualitative Impacts						Overall
	Revenue Value	Wt.	Asset Value	Wt.	Cash Flow Value	Wt.	Brand	Wt.	Compliance	Wt.	Strategy	Wt.	Score
Product 1													
Product 2													
.													
Product X													

EXHIBIT 8.1   **The Value Matrix**

aggregated results of the analysis. The senior leaders should communicate the results to all stakeholders of the value chain in a clear and consistent way. As a result, the emphasis of the risk program resources will be on these value-producing products/services but will not be at the expense of all other products and services.

There is an exception to this process, anticipated or impending threat (e.g., civil unrest, hurricane/typhoon). If the organization is aware of a threat that appears "relevant" to a particular resource in the value chain then the organization must alter its priorities and pro-actively manage that risk. This is the business reality check that must be performed continuously.

Identify and Communicate Stakeholder Expectations

As discussed in the prior chapter, setting stakeholder expectations is a critical process that must be executed once *value* has been defined. Setting these expectations helps to identify who sets the risk paradigm. The stakeholders must then communicate their expectations to all these stakeholders along the value chain.

STEP 2: RISK IDENTIFICATION, ANALYSIS, AND EVALUATION

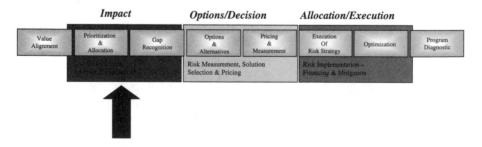

Goal: Determine the impact of a risk being realized across the value chain (*Note*: risk solutions are assessed, modeled, priced, and selected in the next steps).

In Step 1, we identified the organization's product(s)/service(s) that create value and defined stakeholder expectations. Next, the risks are identified, analyzed and evaluated, and impacts measured. Step 2 consists of several tasks. They are:

- Value chain process and resource mapping (establishing the line of sight)
- Impact analysis and modeling
- Relevance and threat analysis (where applicable data exists)
- Current-state gap evaluation

Value Chain Process Prioritization and Allocation

Once *value* has been identified then the the organization will need to determine what is needed operationally to create and maintain value. This is accomplished by associating or mapping the major processes and resources across the entire value chain.

First the processes are mapped, then the resources, Exhibit 8.2 illustrates a simple process flow map. The resources are critical because risk is typically realized in the context of a resource (e.g., failure of product, fire at a plant, or theft of intellectual property). Processes sometimes become victim to risk as well such as the mismanagement of a critical program or project—referred to a program/project management risk. After 30 years and 300 ways to define and categorize resources, I settled on the following four groups of resources (see Exhibit 8.3). I strongly suggest that the resources be grouped to more effectively and efficiently manage the execution of this process. It is up to you and your organization to determine the correct categories of resources. Here are the four:

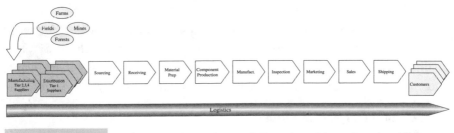

EXHIBIT 8.2   **Illustrative View of *Process* Flow Across The Value Chain**

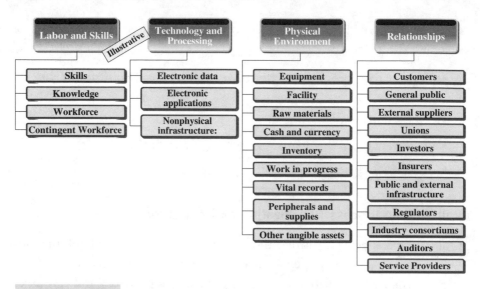

EXHIBIT 8.3   Illustration of the Universe of Resources

1. People

2. Information and technology processing

3. Physical assets/environment

4. Relationships and interdependencies

Note: Processes might be considered a fifth category, although processes better describe how the resources are used.

To complete the mapping, the resources now must be connected to process flow along the value chain (Exhibit 8.4). By doing this one can begin to see why the task of managing risk in the value chain becomes so complex. Risk can be realized anywhere in the value chain—at the process or resource level. An important note—the process and resources that we identified thus far represent the value chain for one product/service or one set of products/services. Organizations will typically rely on hundreds of value chains (both internal and external) therefore, the need to prioritize value and apply the VCRM to that which creates and maintains the greatest value.

Impact Analysis and Modeling

An impact-based approach is used to maximize risk investment activities. For an impact-based approach, it is assumed that the risk has been realized

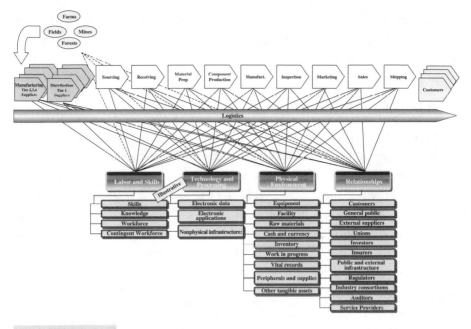

EXHIBIT 8.4   Value Chain for a Specific Product

(e.g., for continuity risk, a critical facility has become unavailable for an extended period or, worst case, the resource has been destroyed). To determine the impact, the organization must analyze risks by resource categories and then model the quantitative and qualitative impacts if the risk were realized. This step is performed for each category of resource. A long list of resources and their impact will be created during this step. Upon completion of the analysis, the aggregated list of impacts is evaluated and prioritized. The resources and associated risks, if realized, that represent the greatest impact to the value chain are then further analyzed in the next step (risk measurement, solution selection, and pricing) to determine risk mitigation and financing options.

Relevance and Threat Analysis

As part of the analysis, if accurate industry-recognized data is available (e.g., actuarial data for property-related hazard events), then the relevance and probability of a particular threat's being realized can be incorporated into the model. Other factors that are useful when determining relevance include timing of threat, probability of occurrence (historical/actuarial data), motivation, opportunity (ease or simplicity—how the threat can be realized), newness of technology or resource, type of change, and frequency of change.

Current-State Gap Evaluation

Based on the information gathered during the business process and resource-mapping step, the risks considered to have the greatest impact are further analyzed to determine the effectiveness of the current risk strategies. Interviews are conducted with those responsible for supporting/providing the resource and managing the risk to determine if existing risk strategies would significantly alter the impact evaluation. The results of this task should be incorporated into the model, impacts recalculated/assessed, and the results aggregated and prioritized.

The Value of an Impact-Based Risk Approach

As we discussed earlier, there are significant benefits of an impact-versus threat-based risk approach. If you perform an impact-based approach, then you typically do not have to try and determine what caused the risk to be realized. However, if the data is available to calculate the probability that a threat will be realized, it should be used. Threat-based risk management requires the definition of a threat and a scenario. I call this *situational risk management* because it assesses and manages the consequences of a risk being realized—but only as it applies to a particular scenario. For example, if I am managing the threat of a hurricane/typhoon to a manufacturing plant then the threat-based planning will take into account certain predefined assumptions such as: the time of day and day/week of year the event will occur (is it high or low tide), how specifically their facility will be impacted, how specifically the "known" infrastructure will be impacted, how people will behave (not a predefined assumption, but still assumed). As you can see, these are assumptions which management may not get right. It is nearly impossible to imagine, or address, all the possible scenarios. I am not suggesting that all of the mitigation and preparation for hurricanes is unnecessary. Quite the contrary—functional risk preparedness is essential—emergency evacuation plans, generators, and the like, are all required. Functional preparedness is necessary to address life safety and emergency issues. In other words, the organization should be addressing known risk and those risks that can be managed as part of a comprehensive functional planning. However, threat-based risk management as the primary risk approach is much too subjective and complex to apply to the organization's value chain(s). Instead, an impact-based approach is recommended (as described throughout this chapter). The impact approach is not based on the *unknown* event, but rather assumes that the risk will be realized, and the impacts can be measured, quantitatively or qualitatively. Threat scenario planning still has a significant role in the process, but it is at the end—that is, testing and validation.

■ **EXAMPLE**   I had an opportunity to interview all of the senior executives of a large manufacturing organization while working on an assignment. At the time, the organization had many "functionally based" or situational risk programs underway. They included business continuity, IT security, disaster management, emergency management, physical security, environmental/health and safety, product liability, product quality, and succession management. The overall cost to deploy, manage and provide ongoing support to these programs was estimated in the millions (one executive believed it was in excess of $100 million). As part of the assignment, I asked the management team to highlight which risks, from a list of fifty, they were most concerned about. They consistently acknowledged a dozen or so that were of greatest concern. Next I asked, "Of the dozen risks that they care about most, how many of these risks do you feel are being adequately managed and mitigated?" Their response—three. I also asked "Is the risk management and mitigation program in place consistently implemented across the organization?" Their response—only for one program. The final question I asked, "How many of the risk solutions that are part of your overall risk management program are regularly validated, via testing?" The response—they don't know. As startling as that finding was, what was more startling was the time, effort, management attention, and funding that was being allocated to these programs. What made matters worse was that the organization was assessing the possibility to allocate more funding to threat-based risk mitigation programs for all of the remaining risks. More functional programs and more functional silos without alignment with value—*a recipe for disaster.* ■

Impact-Based Continuity Risk

As previously mentioned, the impact-based approach does not ignore threat-based planning at all, and in fact should incorporate it in terms of its usefulness and applicability later in the process for testing and further justifying risk investments. Consider seven action steps in the action-based plan:

1. Begin with the assumption that a resource is destroyed or unavailable.

2. Define impacts (quantitative and qualitative) to set priorities and boundaries.

3. Identify weak links or gaps between the best-case desired recovery time and worst-case actual recovery time.

4. Identify how effectively and to what degree your proposed response supports financial recovery (effective coverages via insurance coverage, for example, as well as the ways in which your strategy protects assets, revenues, cash flow, and market share).

5. Identify the highest impact and highest cost threats and match these to show qualitative considerations for a short list of priorities.

6. Define how specific recovery strategies have been matched with the organization's ability to meet recovery objectives within the constraints of financial and resource limitations.

7. Document the plan completely.

FINAL NOTE

Procrastination, the most popular *modus operandi* of risk management, creates even more problems in the future. In the value chain, where anticipation leads to alternate process routing and contingency alternatives, the importance of recognizing the economy in risk planning is glaringly evident. A better approach than procrastination, avoidance, and *total denial* is development and implementation of an impact-based risk plan. Either address the issue and fix, thereby making a conscious decision, or change the operating model, to avoid the risk. Another option is to publicly acknowledge that the risk does not pose a material impact and therefore, management is willing to accept the risk.

STEP 3: RISK MEASUREMENT, SOLUTION SELECTION, AND PRICING

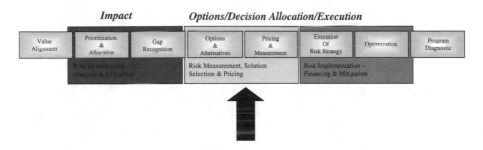

Culture, attitude, and process are just a few of the many characteristics of a strong risk management program—one that creates a risk consciousness, stakeholder participation, and social responsibility. But as we mentioned in the earlier chapters, the program does not and cannot stop there because the world is moving faster, universally connected, much more empowered, and constantly changing. Fortunately the available options for treating risk have improved over the past decade. They include: risk financing (e.g., transfer/insurance), alternate financing (e.g., catastrophe bonds), advance mitigation solutions, avoidance, and of course, acceptance. We can look at developing the business case to support investment decision now that we know what could hurt us and what the impact will be.

Following the risk identification step, the next step is to price, prioritize, measure, and model the risk. This is where the process of risk alignment/commitment with "value" begins and the business case/justification is built.

The objective of the risk measurement process is to price the risk in terms of the potential cost/impact of the exposure versus the cost to fund, hedge and/or mitigate the risk. This is where the business case is defined. Pricing includes an evaluation of current state coverage, mitigation, and retention. To do this you must evaluate insurance coverage (scope, additional overages, limits/sublimits, retention, and use of nontraditional risk vehicles such as captives, catastrophe bonds, and other hedging options/hedges) and alternative mitigation strategies.

The first step makes us aware of the potential impacts that a variety of risks can have on our product(s)/service(s) of value. The next step is to research and assess methods and technologies to finance, mitigate, accept, and/or avoid this risk (see Exhibit 8.5). We previously discussed how

Risk Financing & Mitigation Portfolio

Labor and Skills	Financing and Alternative Financing Directors and Officers Liability insurance Disability/Workers Comp insurance Kidnap and Ransom insurance Professional Liability (D&O, E&O) insurance Expatriate insurance Travel insurance Health Insurance	Mitigating Emergency, evacuation and life safety planning Overseas employee safety and security planning Kidnap and ransom planning Physical security/civil disturbance/terrorism planning Privacy policy/background screening
Technology and Processing	Cyber-insurance	Disaster recovery planning Restart/recovery planning IT access control/firewalls/biometrics Incident management planning
Physical	Property insurance Marine and Cargo insurance Motor/fleet insurance Environmental liability insurance Product liability insurance Business interruption insurance Terrorism insurance Captives Catastrophe Bonds	Emergency, evacuation and life safety planning Physical security/civil disturbance/terrorism planning Fire safety planning Product tampering/quality planning Product recall emergency planning Environmental management planning Vital records recovery, restoration and security management
Relationships		Contractor emergency planning Business partner/joint venture crisis planning
Other	Political risk insurance Trade disruption insurance Captives	Directors and Officers Liability Disability/Workers Comp Kidnap and Ransom Professional Liability (D&O, E&O) Expatriate

organizations typically avoid the tough risk activities—those activities that require a significant investment in time, management attention, resources and/or capital (Chapter 4, Exhibit 4.3). It is during this step that we decon-struct the resource impacts and effort needed to address risk. There are two primary tasks: (1) identifying and assessing risk solutions, and, (2) pricing the solution and measuring its effectiveness.

Options and Alternatives

For many years, I've heard risk and resiliency terms such as *recovery time objective, mean time between failure, maximum tolerable downtime, maximum quality, acceptable security,* and *volatility thresholds.* So, like many others, I packed these terms up in my trusty risk bag and set off to work with busi-ness management in an attempt to improve their risk management practi-ces and overall level of preparedness. Everything was moving along well with the business managers, we followed the process together and they produced the recovery time objectives for several key business operations. Simply stated, this is how much downtime or exposure they were willing to tolerate as a result of an outage or risk related incident. We then ex-plored alternative solutions to try and resolve the gap between what they desired and what they claimed their organization already provides. Then came the meeting with the executive—you know, the one where you beg for investment money to protect their interests. Here it comes—the critical and deal-breaking line of questions:

- How much is this going to cost me?
- How long will it take to implement?
- How much time will be needed by my people and will this interfere with the day-to-day—you know we are working on a very tight pro-duction schedule?
- What will change if I make the investment?
- Will changes make us less productive—hurt the bottom line ?.
- Will this impact my product delivery schedule?
- What are the business reasons this should be done?

Good questions but difficult to provide a clear answer. Why? Because most lacked process, analytics, or commitment of time to think through the exposure and the business case. That is why it is necessary to not only look at the options but also to assess the integration impact/consequences. For example, what are the ramifications of stakeholders up-and down-stream in my supply chain? Does this solution create a redundant process? Other examples include: cost of additional maintenance, possible impact to service, social acceptance, quality implications, and impact on committed schedules. Beware of upstream or downstream ramifications and always assess interdependency implications.

EXAMPLE   While at the Gartner Group, I developed a retro-spective view (i.e., models) with two large banks to better understand the cost of managing electronic data and systems security risk. We analyzed the cost of acquiring, deploying, and maintaining PC and server-based security software such as antiviral, PC security, and in-trusion detection packages. At the time, we used the acquisition cost as the baseline for calculating the deployment and maintenance/sup-port costs. We used real capital and labor costs. Our analysis focused on deployments of this software on an environment of 10,000 or more units. The result of our analysis revealed that consistently the deployment cost of the risk solution was 4 to 6 times the defined ac-quisition cost and that the maintenance/support cost was 10 to 15 times greater than the acquisition cost. It's no wonder that the great solution that was being recommended was seldom sustainable. As a result of our analysis we directed additional management attention at the platform vendors (e.g., Microsoft, IBM) to include risk controls as part of their standard offerings.

Pricing and Measurement

The second part of the risk measurement step is to price the prioritized risk options, validate feasibility, and create the business case and the decision model that can be used to support risk decisions at time of the event.

Pricing the risk options is fairly straightforward. However, as mentioned in the prior section, the total cost of the risk option must be considered assuming that the impact to stakeholders has been considered. All these costs must be considered to complete the business case. They include:

- Internal/external labor costs (including any premium pricing such as demand for very specialized service or seasonal price differential)

- Capital/expense costs to alter existing process flows or physical environments

- Testing/validating the risk mitigation solution

- Additional cost of any downtime/service disruption while the mitigation solution is being installed or maintained

- Impact on productivity (internal and external stakeholders)

- Ongoing future costs to sustain the program and assure it is adequately monitored

There are many possible analytical approaches to measuring and pricing risk. Loss distribution is an attempt to: 1) use probability graphing to define the potential loss resulting from a risk, and, 2) define how loss vulnerabilities can be economically spread, or diversified, away from a single or central point. Through economic modeling, the potential losses and exposure can be defined, and from that an expectation of loss can also be modeled. This is useful to risk managers in determining risk priorities as well as a method for explaining the real exposure to managers who are likely to resist spending money in this area.

Measuring risk is also effective through the use of scenario analysis, a method of thinking ahead and demonstrating: 1) how unexpected losses result from existing vulnerabilities, 2) a scope of most likely losses arising from the current conditions, and, 3) how steps, often low-cost or simple, reduce or eliminate those losses. When risk mitigation is explained as a form of self-insurance (spending a relatively small amount of money today to prevent potentially large costs later), the program is more convincing, even to managers who do not want to spend money anticipating losses.

Employing a proven system-wide quality-based approach will assure consistency when communicating the process to all stakeholders throughout the value chain. This approach is especially effective when delegated to employee teams, even across departmental lines. For example, many Fortune 500 companies have Six Sigma programs in place within their organizations. A quality-based approach to risk management is a good fit for the already-trained Six Sigma employees.

Finally, when valid information is available (e.g., statistical and actuarial information) its use makes risk, and the degree of exposure more realistic (i.e., fact-based versus conjecture/subjective influences). From a probability analysis, your organization will be able to derive a "risk factor" which incorporates probability of occurrence, potential dollar value of the loss, and the cost of mitigation based on past experience.[2]

STEP 4: RISK IMPLEMENTATION, FINANCING, AND MITIGATION

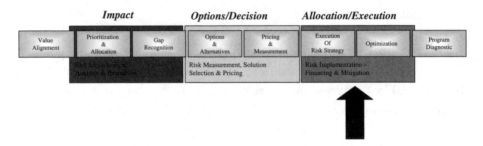

The next step is to deploy the selected risk solutions and optimize the overall risk solution portfolio. One point worth driving home is that prevention and mitigation are not only effective, but are well worth the investment required. Prevention and mitigation save the money that otherwise would have been spent recovering from a loss or saving the brand.

Exposure Avoidance

Under *prevention and mitigation*, the first step is basic: exposure avoidance. By identifying and removing hazardous conditions, improving internal security, and protecting assets as well as employees, companies escape the vulnerability itself.

The key to risk avoidance is implementing an all-inclusive (all stakeholders across the extended value chain) system that promotes the reporting, gathering, and analysis of risk-related intelligence. Creating and sustaining a risk-sensitive culture (all understand their responsibilities and the penalties for risk failures) will help assure that the concerns of stakeholders (lowest-level clerk to final delivery) are surfaced. Another critical approach to risk avoidance is to have risk managers plugged into the external risk management world. This includes involvement with industry risk management groups and law enforcement agencies. One must develop both public and private channels that supply information regarding the experiences of other risk managers. Identifying and mitigating (before it hits) exposures already experienced by others could save the day. The development of "confidential and trusted" information channels among other risk managers, critical vendors, and law enforcement is especially critical to risk avoidance. I emphasize the words *trust* and *confidential*—an environment where potentially embarrassing experiences are shared with others with the conviction that an unreported experienced risk is not a competitive advantage.

Prevention and Mitigation Based on Value

The level of resources and attention devoted to prevention will vary based on many factors.

For example, if a particular type of loss has been occurring on a high volume, preventive measures need to be put in place. If your company is losing from employee theft in a warehouse, improved security is a sound investment. If employees have been misusing automated systems, improved monitoring will cut down on the idle time and system misuse. If unauthorized outsiders have been able to enter the organization's property, improved security needs to be put in place. In all of these examples, the cost of improved prevention will be lower than the cost of the continuing losses.

The question of loss severity has to come into play. For example, it makes no sense to spend a large amount of money to prevent relatively small losses. In many instances, low-cost measures can be incorporated to cut down on petty losses; but large-scale internal systems should be reserved for truly severe losses. Once specific vulnerabilities are identified, losses can be prevented through segregation. For example, in the accounting arena, losses from embezzlement can be reduced through improved internal security and approval systems, and steps such as increased and enforced authorization, spot audits, and prosecution of offenders all help prevent future losses by segregating risk. Another example is improved security in warehouses and other areas where valuable assets are stored, to avoid losses resulting from a lax oversight system. If the company determines that the exposure is too expensive to devote its resources to improve security, it can choose to outsource this function. For example, many organizations with remote inventory employ private security companies because using full-time employees in low-volume sites is not cost effective.

Actual *financing* will include two kinds of risk management: retaining or transferring the risk. On a practical level, your organization will be wise to make a distinction between these two, because many relatively small vulnerabilities are best managed by retaining them. This does not mean potential losses shouldn't be prevented or mitigated, but it does mean that there is no justification for increasing budgets. In addition, in many instances, higher budgets will not reduce losses dramatically.

If your company retains a risk, it may simply decide to expense it. For example, periodic theft of office supplies may be fixed with a stringent internal requisitioning system, two-party approval, and storage security monitoring; but the cost of these measures is likely to exceed the value of stolen items. The company may be better off to make minor changes (i.e., centralized office supply purchasing and storage, which may reduce the overall cost by itself) and simply accept the relatively small losses.

An additional retention method is to set up reserves. Organizations already do this for their accounts receivable, as a means for anticipating and expensing bad debt. The bad debts reserve is a reduction of the current assets on the balance sheet. The same approach can be employed to establish reserves for stolen or damaged inventory, weather damage, or mechanical costs of repairing machinery, to name a few.

When losses are not otherwise mitigated, the actual loss can be fixed with borrowed funds. This approach makes sense when an organization's working capital is marginal and it cannot afford to simply replace unexpected losses. Borrowing spreads cash outlays out over many months rather than requiring absorption within a single month or quarter.

A loss is also retained when it is treated as a defined captive. A captive loss is a more formalized kind of reserve system, but may serve as an alternative when potential losses may be high or insurance is not available through normal channels. When organizations want to self-insure, they may form a separate insurance system for themselves or spread risks by assigning relatively small portions of the overall loss to operating segments, a form of reinsurance within a self-insured strategy. When actual losses are lower than the captive loss reserves, the difference is returned to the parent company as a form of miscellaneous profit.

Financing also involves transfer of loss, which is the best-recognized form of risk management. Commercial insurance (casualty and liability, lost revenues, etc.) is not only essential but widely used to cover assets and profits as well as mitigation for legal liability and other contingencies. A contractual transfer also may be effective, in which a business partner, operating unit, or insurance company agrees to absorb the cost of a loss. Items like continuity insurance are typical. Finally, transfers occur whenever companies hedge against potential losses. In an investment portfolio, long stock positions can be protected by buying put options. Noninvestment versions of the same strategy apply to inventory management (i.e., increasing inventory levels to hedge against delays further down in the supply chain, or maintaining inventory levels in different locations to hedge against catastrophic weather-related losses) and supply chain vulnerabilities (contracting with a secondary supplier, for example).

When your organization has put effort into identifying its weak links, the places where the greatest protection will be needed will become quite obvious. Your organization should coordinate the three-part study (identification/prioritization, measurement, financing) with the prioritization derived from weak link analysis. This kind of multifaceted study is a perfect project for the quality control team.

APPLYING THE PREVENTION AND MITIGATION PROCESS TO MANAGING CONTINUITY RISK

Step 1: Optimize the risk program. Establish a risk appetite based on how much continuity risk the organization is willing to take as a dollar amount or percentage of something (e.g., percentage of share price, operating budget). Establish the optimal balance between continuity risk and what makes sense. Mitigate volatility by effectively and efficiently distributing continuity risk across the financing and retention (including mitigation activities).

Step 2: Provide adjustments based on the level of confidence the organization has with management's ability to manage the risk. Consider the following: 1) does a risk program exist, 2) is the program effective, and 3) is the program implemented consistently across the organization?

Step 3: Formalize responsibilities. Identify specific individuals for home and field office emergency, crisis, and recovery management teams and roll out formal continuity initiatives throughout the organization. Form tactical subteams to gather information required to evaluate the current and proposed strategies.

Step 4: Validate strategy. Examine the cost, service, quality, and social impact of implementing the current and proposed alternate strategies on people, processes, and technology. Determine the true amount of capacity needed internally, as well as the amount and cost of external emergency capacity also needed.

Step 5: Create follow-up teams. Create operational teams to execute, implement, and document the emergency, crisis, and recovery plans. Distribute and review emergency, crisis, and recovery procedures at the operational level.

Step 6: Requisition infrastructure. Estimate the amount of excess equipment, facilities, and software needed, and plan to requisition them or create a plan for emergency requisition.

Step 7: Develop detailed procedures. Develop detailed responses at the functional and operational level. Document, distribute, and review procedures with front-line personnel.

Step 8: Rollout. Develop an emergency, crisis, and business continuity awareness and training campaign for employees throughout the program, creating a sense of urgency and broad-based education program.

Step 9: Tabletop test. Conduct a thorough test of the developed procedures. Evaluate test results and recommend changes to procedures.

Step 10: Update procedures. Refine procedures and conduct another test until the final iteration meets the organization standards.

STEP 5: RISK SOLUTIONS— EXECUTING MITIGATION

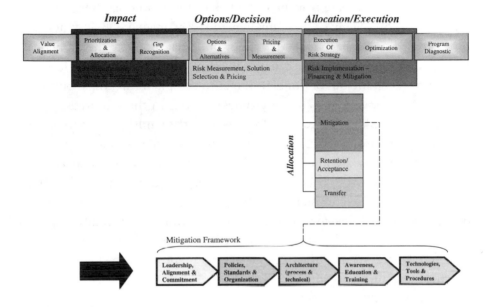

That the risk plan will have to be deployed into an economic environment that is uniquely different, for each industry, geography, and set of customers. To begin the process, one must be realistic and seek short-term wins, and then adjust to a more formal process that begins with value definition, impact assessment, and risk priorities. This approach would take into account both internal and external stakeholder sensitivity needs. The short-term development strategy should assume that you would be integrating the program into an existing value chain, rather than when the value chain is first defined.

Before we can manage risk, the stakeholders must first identify the products and services that they recognized as significant "value." This starting point focuses on the "why" and "what" questions long before the "how" question. It has been my experience that a great deal of risk activity is actually under way at most organizations, especially financial institutions, but unfortunately most of this ac2tivity is happening in the "trenches" and disconnected from the broader and more critical business priorities. Dr. Stephen Covey, a renowned self-improvement professional, uses the example of someone's climbing the ladder as quickly as possible only to find, when he gets to top, that his ladder is leaning against the wrong building. We must be sure that we are managing the risk of those products/services that matter the most. Many of these misaligned risk management activities can be attributed to localized incentive plans, ones that motivate the individual to respond to the personal scorecard to complete a risk mitigation task for "my area" (keep me out of trouble). I refer to this phenomenon as bottom-up risk management, which many times number in the hundreds, if not thousands, of risk activities (usually assessments or mitigation activities). Having lived through many of these bottom-up/partitioned activities, I can say that they are neither a productive nor a rewarding experience. Because these activities begin at different times, by different people, often with different motivations and in different parts of the organization they become a political free-for-all. Whatever fiefdom is in power at that point in time gets all the risk-management attention and budget. This behavior creates a dangerous situation because management might believe that risk is actually being managed well. Even if there were true, the management of risk is probably inefficient, as was the case at many of the financial institutions with which I have worked. Further, with bottom-up risk-management, critical risk investment decisions become delayed because of a lack of alignment with business priorities. The decision makers simply cannot make the commitment because they struggle to understand the relevance of something considered of "value" to the organization. The end result: politics, procrastination, poor prioritization, and pitiful risk management.

A Strategy for Executing Risk Mitigation

Value Chain Risk Management and Assessment Methodology   Until this point I have presented a great deal of information on the value identification, as well as the risk identification, evaluation, measurement and financing/mitigation process. I have developed a methodology that captures the multiple dimensions of what is needed to actually execute and sustain risk mitigation solutions. The full process, if you're interested, is on my website, www.atyourownrisk.net. There is not enough space here to provide a detailed description or show you how to implement the complete approach from the expectation through the actual mitigation settings.

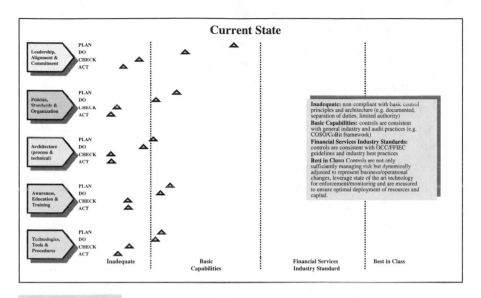

Current State

Inadequate: non-compliant with basic control principles and architecture (e.g. documented, separation of duties, limited authority)

Basic Capabilities: controls are consistent with general industry and audit practices (e.g. COSO/CoBit framework)

Financial Services Industry Standards: controls are consistent with OCC/FFIEC guidelines and industry best practices

Best in Class Controls are not only sufficiently managing risk but dynamically adjusted to represent business/operational changes, leverage state of the art technology for enforcement/monitoring and are measured to ensure optimal deployment of resources and capital.

EXHIBIT 8.6   TRA Diagnostic

However, I think it useful to at least provide an overview of this process tool I call the TRA Diagnostic® (TRA was a start-up that a few close friends and I started during the Internet era). Here's what it looks like (see Exhibit 8.6) and a brief description of how it works.

Critical VCRM Program Elements   The five critical component elements that are required for the successful implementation and support of a risk mitigation solution are:

1. Leadership, alignment, and commitment
   - Clearly driven strategy, business driven and value oriented, proactive leadership, and measurements
   - Culture, routing reporting, expansive communications (both good and bad—no surprises)
2. Policies, standards, and organization
   - Clearly defined policy, roles and responsibilities, operational processes, baseline standards, and risk-driven standards
   - Central policy-making driven by business positions, distributed responsibilities
   - Staffing, skills/knowledge/experience requirements

3. Architecture
   - Comprehensive technical and process architecture (intrusion detection, logging, user authentication, separation of duties, network security, etc.)
4. Awareness, education, and training
   - Clearly defined and executed general awareness programs (id theft, fraud), education programs aligned with security roles & responsibilities, and training programs for individuals with hands-on security operations responsibilities
5. Technologies, tools, and procedures
   - Selection and deployment of security products and support procedures (aligned with standards) as well as use of security features and functions in supporting platforms (e.g., hardware, firmware, applications, systems and network management facilities)

These program elements are assessed against the four execution phases: plan, do, check, and act.

Execution: Plan, Do, Check, Act

1. Plan
   - Effectiveness and efficiency of design including alignment with business culture and objectives
   - Planning, including design of processes, selection of measures and technology, and deployment of requirements
2. Do
   - Execution and support of the defined plan
3. Check
   - Validation and monitoring of the stated plan against execution
   - Assess progress, taking into account internal and external results
4. Act
   - Response to defects, commitment to correction and continuous improvement
   - Revise plans based on assessments, findings, learning, new inputs, changes, and new requirements

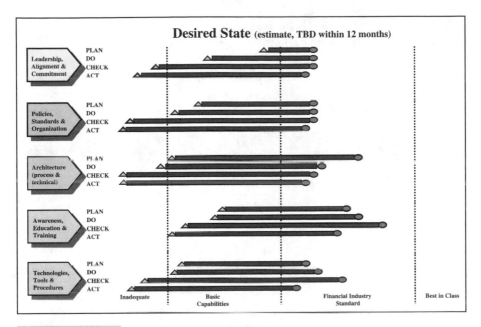

EXHIBIT 8.7   Gap Analysis of the Actual State (△) Versus
Desired State (●)

- Audit to detect changes and assure procedures are still being followed

The process begins by setting an expectation (sound familiar?) prior to conducting the assessment (or following the program element flow as part of a broader program management plan). First, the critical stakeholders, those who set the risk paradigm, are polled to understand their approximate risk expectation. This gets tuned later, but for now we will use the following categories: basic capabilities, industry standard, best in class (world class can also be used if the organization truly wants to exemplify global leadership). This expectation is critical since the assessment will measure their current state against their desired state. Exhibit 8.7 illustrates the measurement process.

Step 6: Program Monitoring, Measurement, and Continuous Improvement

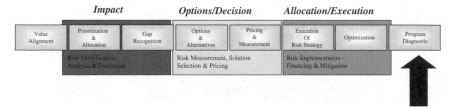

As we discussed in previous chapters, it is essential that the organization anticipate, monitor and respond to change. A static business model, value chain with predictable events would be simple to manage. However, the reality is that the external environment (and related threats) and the value chain are constantly changing. For example, often without your knowledge, a primary supplier outsources part of its production to others. Value alignment requires that the organization monitor these changes through proactive auditing, sensors, and listening posts, an intelligence network, impact and decision modeling, a process that encourages information to move quickly throughout the value chain, and a management team that supports a risk-conscious culture.

The enactment of both the procedural and cultural changes required for addressing losses from risks and, more to the point, for preparing for them effectively, can be achieved through a Six Sigma quality control program. Some recurrent problems found in most systems, notably those aimed at risk reduction, include: 1) noncompliance with new procedures as employees create shortcuts or walk-arounds; 2) well-meaning but ineffective changes, oftentimes replacing older risks with new ones; and 3) impractical and overly complex "improvements" that do nothing to reduce risk. Six Sigma is one of many approaches that overcomes these common problems. Although the concept began as a quality control procedure employing the team approach across departmental lines, it can be effectively employed in risk management as well.

APPLYING THE SIX SIGMA APPROACH: CRITICAL PROCESSES

One concept at the core of Six Sigma is *voice of the customer*. This idea tells us that in all quality-based programs, the customer's interests, concerns, and desires have to dominate the decision process. This applies to risk as well, with one adjustment: Everyone has a customer, even internally. Thus, the accounting department cutting payroll checks has every employee as a customer, and the mail room has a universal internal customer. Once a process is assigned the voice of the customer (whether external or internal), the Six Sigma concept applies universally to quality as well as to risk programs.

Six Sigma creates a specific project to address a problem. The methodology for identifying and resolving problems is called DMAIC (define, measure, analyze, improve, and control). Compare this to the traditional audit-driven and budget-driven procedures within the organization, which usually involve a two-part process: define and control. Thus, an opportunity is identified for cost cutting, and that is incorporated into the budget. It is simple, direct, and—unfortunately—ineffective, especially when the "problem" is more complex than overuse of telephones or photocopy machines. Internal cost cutting is not only ineffective for risk mitigation; it often creates greater risks in the long term.

Under the DMAIC method used in Six Sigma, the process is more comprehensive and thoughtful. It involves development of visual representations of the process, development of standards, checking for quality and compliance, changing systems and procedures, and developing permanent procedures that solve the known problems. Six Sigma is perfect for developing a value chain–driven risk management program because of its methodical approach. The steps are:

1. Define
   - Identify the specific business problems and project goals
   - Charter the project (determine resources, risks, and timing)
   - Develop a high-level process map, or SIPOC (suppliers, inputs, process, outputs, and customers, the elements required to proceed with solutions To the problem)
   - Kick off the project

2. Measure
   - Document the customer needs and requirements
   - Identify the process metrics (visual of the value chain)
   - Translate metrics into performance standards
   - Measure performance within existing standards

3. Analyze
   - Analyze the collected data
   - Identify potential sources of process variations (diversify)
   - Prioritize sources of variation

4. Improve
   - Identify improvement opportunities
   - Determine the most effective improvements
   - Pilot and budget improvements
   - Compare results to objectives
   - Implement improvements

5. Control
   - Document the new process
   - Measure the process regularly to ensure that gains are maintained
   - Report results regularly to key stakeholders
   - Seek out future improvement opportunities

When you consider that DMAIC is not a routine but a dynamic process of risk management, it becomes evident that the value chain can be managed and controlled, and that potential losses can be mitigated through identification of the weak links in any process (specifically where responsibility is passed from one person or department to another, which is the most likely point for vulnerabilities to exist).

Six Sigma is an effective avenue for changing the organizational culture with its traditional reliance on audit checklists and budgets as guiding decision-making tools, *and* for putting a value chain–driven program into place. By realistically assessing the impact of risks by keying in on vulnerable points in the value chain, Six Sigma enables you to turn passive policy and procedure into *critical process* management, which in turn may become a guiding force in the overall risk management approach (and change within the organizational culture itself).

CONCLUDING SUMMARY

The Major Case for an Enlightened Risk Management Initiative

The major case can be summarized in 10 key points:

1. Change is escalating and causes risk to escalate. The traditional approach is to deny that risk exists, ignore the threat, or procrastinate. The longer we wait to fix the problem, the greater the disastrous result.

2. The greater the IT efficiency, the greater the IT-generated risk. In many respects, computers have taken over and we now face the problem that IT may become our worst enemy. If we become so dependent on electronic versions of everything, a simple electrical failure could literally shut down commerce around the world.

3. The risk paradigm is expanding on all fronts. (For example, easier and more affordable travel may translate to rapid spread of a pandemic, whereas in the past travel was restricted; in 1900, for example, before auto and air travel, most people in the Unite States lived on farms and *never* traveled more than 20 miles from their birthplace.)

4. Looking at the problem through the stakeholder's lens enables us to develop multiple points of view and to begin viewing risk as a manageable team effort.

5. A revolutionary change is required in organizational culture. Audit-driven, checklist-style, budget-oriented management has to go the way of the precomputer age. The entire philosophy of twentieth-century management is obsolete.

6. Organizations lacking resiliency and agility are vulnerable. The equation is quantifiable. The greater the lack of resiliency and agility, the greater that vulnerability. Thus, $<R => V$ and $<a => V$. Combined, this is deadly: $<R + VA + V^2$.

7. The value chain is a concept that enables effective risk management. This chain, an expansion of the well-known supply chain, applies to every process. By identifying weak links in that chain, we are able to identify points where vulnerabilities exist and where losses can be reduced or avoided.

8. The Six Sigma team approach to risk management is a key to addressing these massive problems and overcoming them. By applying the quality cultural concept to the overall organizational culture, the change may occur rapidly and over the entire organizational framework (management, rank-and-file, and stakeholders).

9. The entire risk management process should also be evaluated from the investor's point of view. Not only are stockholders unaware of the tangible and serious risks their companies face; the point of view further helps management to function outside of the traditional "perception bubble" that is the common organizational theme preventing progressive risk management from taking hold.

10. The problem is, indeed, the organizational challenge of the twenty-first-century, and it is an exciting but perilous time. When you consider where the world was 100 years ago, organizations were struggling with many new ideas. These included assembly line production (Henry Ford's innovation), making labor less essential; the complete lack of any retirement or pension systems and, in fact, no *concept* of retirement; air travel; application of these innovations to warfare, leading to massive casualties in World War I as well as 20 million deaths from the flu after the war; expansion of telephone service to a majority of homes; improved innovation in the investment world; and unparalleled inventions and developments in engineering, electronics, transportation, communication, medicine, and elsewhere. The social and cultural turmoil we face in the twenty-first-century is, in fact, very similar to that of the early twentieth century, but at a more rapid, global, and expanding pace.

CHECKLIST OF SUCCESSFUL PRACTICES

Least Successful	Most Successful
☐ Checklist/reactive approach	☐ Business value-driven (priorities)
☐ Scope—entire organization	☐ Scope—extended supply chain
☐ Threat analyses and scenarios driven	☐ Impact driven
☐ Just the assessment of risk	☐ Full life cycle of risk
☐ Qualitatively measured	☐ Quantitatively and qualitatively measured
☐ Undefined level of risk volatility	☐ Defined acceptable volatility thresholds
☐ Does not leverage common risk process and tools	☐ Leverages common processes and tools—specifically for risk mapping and assessment

Building a risk-conscious culture is achievable but it is hard work. The effort requires an ongoing investment in money, time, learning, knowledge sharing, technology, and management focus. It also requires leadership, continuous monitoring, and testing. It is not a science but an art, not a one-time effort but an ingrained culture—trial, error, learning, and continuous improvement are all key ingredients of successful execution. Organizations must be more aware of the external environment and the stakeholders they depend on—their risk attitude and aptitude, up and down the value chain. But it can be accomplished; it just requires focus, the involvement of others, strong leadership, and common business objectives. The culture is everyone's responsibility and incentives must be created and penalties established, with a top-down, bottom-up, inside-out commitment from all stakeholders.

ENDNOTES

1. Larry Bossidy and Ram Charan, *Execution: The Discipline of Getting Things Done*; New York: Crown Business, 2002.
2. Doug Hoffman, "Managing Operationsal Risk: 20 Firmwide Best Practice Strategies." Hoboken: Wiley, 2002.

Index